ORPHANS: REAL AND IMAGINARY

Also by Eileen Simpson

THE MAZE
REVERSALS
POETS IN THEIR YOUTH

ORPHANS
Real and Imaginary

EILEEN SIMPSON

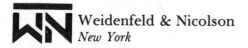 Weidenfeld & Nicolson
New York

Published by Weidenfeld & Nicolson, New York
A Division of Wheatland Corporation
10 East 53rd Street
New York, NY 10022

The author gratefully acknowledges permission to reprint from the following:

First Love and Other Shorts by Samuel Beckett. Copyright © 1974 by Samuel
Beckett. Reprinted by permission of Grove Press, Inc.

The Autobiography of Bertrand Russell by Bertrand Russell. Copyright © 1967
by Bertrand Russell. Reprinted by permission of Allen & Unwin Publishers Ltd.

Collected Poems of Stevie Smith by Stevie Smith. Copyright © 1972 by Stevie
Smith. Reprinted by permission of New Directions Publishing Corporation.

Library of Congress Cataloging-in-Publication Data
Simpson, Eileen B.
Orphans : real and imaginary.
Bibliography: p.
1. Simpson, Eileen B. 2. Orphans—United States—
Biography. 3. Orphans in literature. I. Title.
HV983.S55   1987   362.7'9 [B]   86-28921
ISBN 1-55584-077-9

Manufactured in the United States of America

Designed by Irving Perkins Associates

First Edition

10 9 8 7 6 5 4 3 2 1

FOR MARIE, MY COMPANION
IN THE WILDERNESS.

Contents

It is, or it is not, according to the nature of men, an advantage to be orphaned at an early age.

—DE QUINCEY

PART I

CHAPTER 1

The Crisis

THROUGHOUT MY ADULT life, when people asked about my childhood, and I said I was an orphan, their surprised looks made me quickly add, "A lucky one." From the long gray early years, I had emerged unscathed. Hospitable to happiness, tenacious in adversity (of neither had I been cheated), I appeared to myself, as to others, cheerful and well balanced. Even the physical weaknesses traceable to my early medical history were masked by high coloring that made me appear healthier than I was. As people said, I didn't *look* like an orphan.

Nor did I feel like one. It is true that in the past I had. Following my mother's death from tuberculosis when I was eleven months and my sister twenty-one months old, we were separated from our father except during school vacations. Shortly before I turned seven, he became ill at a dinner, was rushed to the hospital, and in three days was dead from ptomaine poisoning. It was after his death that I learned what it meant to be an orphan. But in recent years, while I thought about my childhood as frequently as others do (and even wrote about one aspect of it), I had long since ceased to think about my orphanhood.* It had ended, I thought, when the law said it did: when I came of age. So strong was my need to believe that as an adult I was affected little by my early losses, that I was unprepared for the recent, shattering crisis that had been lying in wait for the right constellation of events. It hurtled me back through the years of my growing up to the opaline days of infancy, and forced me to reexamine the past.

The first sign I had of it (although I didn't realize it at the time) came when we learned from a routine medical examination that my husband had cancer and, after surgery, that it was inoperable. During the months Bob underwent treatment, what kept me going was my inability to believe that a youthful-looking fifty-six-year-old man, who had recently been so vigorous, could have only a year to live.

During a period of uneasy calm and false hope after he survived the year, and went back to his office, I returned to a writing project I had been working on before his operation. For a book about orphans (what kind of book was not yet clear), I was reading through the card-catalog listings in the Forty-second Street library. Now, taking it up again, I found that I was increasingly dispirited by accounts of the lives of children raised in institutions. Something had happened to make oppressive the descriptions of their drab surroundings, ill-fitting clothing, and inadequate diets. I seemed to have lost the distance I had felt between myself and my material that had allowed me to read objectively as, say, a sociologist would. Bob, who ordinarily would have urged me on, dissuaded me from continuing with what he

---

*And my sister and I had given up comparing notes about it. Nor did we talk about it while I was at work on this book. Although I will sometimes say "we," I have written from a single point of view, my own, based on my memories and emotions.

called my "sad subject." Perhaps, given the grave preoccupation that was never far from my mind, no subject would
have been able to hold my interest. I put my notes away.

I was turning away, I see now, as I had turned away from
the Hopewell Orphanage, which I used to pass during the
years I practiced as a psychotherapist in Princeton. There
was no missing this large red brick building. It stood naked
in a field, with neither trees nor shrubs to soften its bulky
outline. Although by the mid-fifties the number of orphans
had diminished so sharply in the United States that asylums
were beginning to close down, this one still had inmates.
Whenever I passed it, I said to myself that the next time I
must go in and volunteer my professional services. There
was surely something I could do for the children. But each
time I made an excuse.

Dickens chided readers of his newspaper articles for not
visiting almshouses and orphanages to see how the inmates
were being treated. In a country where until the early part
of the nineteenth century the gentry had regarded a visit to
Bedlam to see the insane as a Sunday's entertainment, it
was self-protectiveness that kept them from responding to
Dickens's prodding. Orphans provide no entertainment.*
They don't cry, scream, shout, or behave bizarrely. Instead
they observe visitors in searching silence. It was an unwill-
ingness to look into these eyes, and to read their message,
that kept people away. It was fear of being pulled by invisi-
ble strings into a web of sadness that made me accelerate
rather than slow down on the Hopewell road. For me, the
children's eyes would have unspoken messages: You were
more fortunate than we are, they would say. Or, more dis-
tressingly: Take us with you.

How favored I had been I felt acutely on a visit to Nashville to see my sister. While earning her Ph.D. in clinical
psychology, Marie was working at the Tennessee Industrial

---

*Although in eighteenth-century Italy they had. Orphanage choirs in Naples
and Rome were well known, and one in Venice attracted all music-loving travelers, Goethe and Rousseau among them.

School, administering intelligence tests to orphaned boys who were to be given manual training according to their ability. There was such a backlog of cases when she took up the job that I offered to do some of the testing with her. Although by this time I had seen a wide range of children in clinics, these malnourished, undersized boys with pale, wizened faces seemed to be from Dickens's day. Tidied up for their appointment, made superficially clean by the swipe of a cloth, they showed that even the attention given to their routine care was light-years away from the care given to the clinic children that I saw at home (however poor they were). Their closely cropped heads and masklike faces made them all look related.

They knew their names. About their date of birth they were uncertain. (They had no memory of their birthdays ever having been celebrated.) They guessed they were seven, or ten, or twelve. Each carried, or rather clutched, a small wooden matchbox which he let go of reluctantly, and only on the promise that it would stay where he had put it on the testing table in front of him. What was in the box? "Things," they said. One of them, a recent arrival at the school and younger than the others, allowed me to look into his. It contained a canceled stamp, a bit of twine, a paper clip, a single jack, a marble: his possessions. The only way he and the others could be sure of not having their things stolen was to carry them around with them. For a long time after I left Nashville, these boys' faces stayed with me. What, I wondered, would become of them?

With my attention riveted on what could be done to keep Bob alive, the two years of his illness, and even the final months of his ordeal, did little to prepare me for his death. After the funeral, I went through the motions of living, telling myself that there was no cure for grief but time (time that had raced by during the twenty years of our marriage, and was now standing still). My friends reminded me that I was luckier than many widows: I had my work. And it was true. It wasn't long before the well-learned discipline of my profession allowed me to see patients again. Writing, that fair-weather friend, deserted me completely. Each morning (normally my writing time), I pushed myself through my ordinary routine—made a pass at breakfast, put the apartment in order, watered the plants, did my back exercises, dressed, went to the typewriter—and fell apart. I had not realized to what degree I had written to interest and entertain Bob, how much I had depended on him for encouragement and criticism. In losing my husband, I had also lost my audience. Now I would have to imagine him in the role of first reader, imagine what he would question, what disagree with, what suggest.

After six months of daily failures, words began to come again. By the end of a year, the book he had many times urged me to write, about a group of poets I had known, was taking shape. It became my companion in a sometimes agreeable, sometimes turbulent relationship, filling the silent evenings as well as my usual writing hours.

My mourning was long but I don't think it differed greatly, except in detail, from the mourning of other widows. After the funeral, there was a brief period of numbness during which I did whatever needed to be done mechanically, like an automaton. One evening, coming home after dinner with a friend (who said she found me in remarkably good form. "You're strong," she'd reassured me in parting. "In six months you'll be your old self"), as I was letting myself into the empty apartment, grief sprang out of the dark hall and clubbed me. I collapsed in tears, and for weeks wept uncontrollably. Then for months I stared vacantly at the sky. I lost weight and was beset by ailments. I played the Mozart *Requiem* until the records wore out, trying to feel the triumph of the resurrected dead promised in the music, and repeating the "*. . . et lux perpetua . . .*" the prayer I'd said for my father after he died. Other music I couldn't listen to. Nor could I read for pleasure.

It was after I was out of mourning, and thought I had

recovered, that the crisis began. I found I was suffering in a new way. What I told myself at first was that nothing had any resonance. Then that I disliked the new role I was asked to play: widow. Then that I was experiencing the letdown that comes to writers after they finish a book; I felt bereft at losing my constant companion.

But the time for those feelings to pass had gone by, and the dissatisfaction that was troubling me gave way to discomfort, discomfort to anxiety. A shrill alarm awakened me in the dead of night. When this happened after Bob died, and I was again able to focus my attention on the printed page, the right book, cautiously selected (art history seemed the safest subject), helped me through the hours until it was time to get up. Now between my eyes and the book's page I saw a moonscape, pitted, rocky, limitless. The figure wandering on its surface was me. Alone.

The black ink of anxiety spilled and spread, saturating the fabric of my life. The anguish I felt was greater than any I had known in mourning. Looking back to that period, I realized that Bob had been such a constant preoccupation that he had seemed almost palpable. Once, in a taxi driving through Central Park, the feeling that he was sitting beside me was so strong that, though I knew it was absurd, I couldn't resist putting my hand out to his reassuring presence. At other times, I thought I caught glimpses of him— the tall man in the camel's hair coat turning the corner; the jogger in the park with his longer-legged gait. I wept with frustration that it was not he, but for a moment it had seemed possible. When I traveled restlessly during those two years, without realizing it I had been searching for him. In Paris, I visited the apartment where we had lived, had coffee at our café, retraced his daily route from our house on the rue de l'Université to his office in the place Vendôme. In Egypt, where I thought I had gone to see the monuments, I had been looking for traces of the life he'd led there before I knew him.

The dialogue we continued, one side becoming increasingly muted, had now come to an end. I no longer imagined I heard him call my name as he came in the door in the evening. The distance that separated us had grown so vast that while not a day passed without my thinking of him countless times, I could not remember distinctly the timbre of his voice. As it had taken six months for me to understand the events of the day my father had been buried, so it had taken more than two years for me to feel the full impact of Bob's death. He was no longer here. Nor was he out there somewhere. He was gone. I was alone.

For the first time in my life, I felt profoundly orphaned. What that word meant I had learned over many years and in uneven stages. To be what Mother Superior had called "a poor little orphan" meant not to have a father to take one home from the Convent at Christmastime. Later it had meant to have fantasies that he was alive. Later still, when I accepted that he was not, it meant to look for substitutes for him. After Marie married, it meant to stand shakily on my own and to crave sisterly closeness with friends. Always it meant to be excessively affected by separations from those I loved. When Marie left home, I felt it so acutely it was like a sickness. Ever afterward, when we embraced, and I boarded the train or plane that would take me away from her, a heavy, prickly blanket woven with mixed stripes of apprehension and gloom enveloped me. For hours, I would remain pinned under it. "Such is man," as Isaac Singer said, "that if he has the name for something, it ceases to be a riddle." After I learned, during my analysis, that this wretched feeling was called "separation anxiety," I found it easier to cope with. Activity was the cure. Sometimes furious activity, as I had discovered after Bob and I married and his work frequently took him on longish business trips to Europe and Africa. In preparation for his absence, I arranged a crowded schedule of work, seeing friends, and putting the house in order.

The day we sailed for France, where we were to live for four years, the blast on the ship's horn, and the emptying of our crowded stateroom as those who had come to see us off hurried ashore, brought on an attack that rivaled in severity and unpleasantness the seasickness other passengers suffered during the crossing.

Trying to understand my second orphanhood, I was coming to see that I had not been as completely free of the first as I had thought. There had been nebulous yearnings and flare-ups of awareness of what I had missed, and was missing, in not having had parents or grandparents, especially during the years when I lived in France. In Paris, I became conscious of family life in a way that I had not been before. While my American contemporaries had fought free of their ties to home in their efforts to fashion independent lives, and envied my lack of them, Parisians I was meeting lived near their parents by choice, telephoned them daily, dined together once a week, and in conversation referred often not only to them but also to brothers, sisters, grandparents, aunts, uncles, nieces, nephews, godparents, and an equal number of in-laws and their relations. They took their obligations to one another seriously, and filled their engagement books with dates for birthdays, weddings, baptisms, confirmations, hospital visits, and funerals. At Christmas and Easter, they went off to country houses where they crowded together (often in surprising discomfort) and returned looking well satisfied. This was a style of life my grandmother had described and that I had seen in the photographs that lined the walls of her apartment. I had imagined it had vanished with her generation.

Reeling from the blow of having had a miscarriage, with the gradual acceptance that I might not have a child and found a family of my own; separated from my sister, from friends and colleagues; away from the close-knit society of a university town (and the capacious cloak of Alma Mater that envelops its residents) such as I'd known in Princeton; very much at loose ends because it was illegal for me as a foreigner to practice my profession, I found myself romanticizing the French family and wishing I belonged to it.

These feelings were magnified by the curiosity stirred in our new acquaintances on learning (in answer to their questions) that Bob, having lost his parents in his twenties, was the last of his line, and that I had only a sister. They felt a kind of patronizing sympathy for us which was tinged with the suspicion that we must somehow be at least a little to blame for our poverty of connections (echoing Lady Bracknell in *The Importance of Being Earnest,* who says, "To lose one parent may be regarded as a misfortune. To lose both looks like carelessness"). Certainly we had made an unwise alliance since neither of us could bring to the other the riches of family life. As a French psychoanalyst (whom I was interviewing on another subject) put it to me, "It's not convenient to be an orphan in France. Too much depends on family ties. The French don't have the mania for pushing their children toward independence you Americans have. They like to keep them close. When a young couple marry, their parents set them up. When they begin a career, they seek the patronage of relatives. Throughout their lives they know that in adversity they will have the family behind them."

Paris was so rich in distractions that after I reorganized my life with work, new friends, and travel, this yearning to belong subsided, erupting again at moments that took me by surprise. On solitary walks in Turin, Madrid, or Lisbon, where, with my new and not altogether comfortable freedom from employment, I explored the city on my own while Bob was busy, I became aware that after the siesta the streets filled with women doing errands. What struck me was the number of mothers and grown daughters walking arm in arm. Unhurriedly, yet purposefully, they made their way up the avenues, stopping to admire a display of leather goods in a shop window, picking up a package at a silversmith's, greeting another mother-and-daughter couple coming in the opposite direction, dropping into their favorite café for pastry and coffee, the whole time talking animatedly. This intimacy of mothers and daughters was also new to me. I thought I was observing them with a professional eye (as, in Paris parks, I observed children at play for an article I was writing), but as I turned down a quiet side street, I wondered at the constriction in my throat. Could a grown woman wish for a mother she had not known? Especially when she had previously claimed never to have felt the lack of maternal attention? If my mother were alive, would she and I be compatible in the way these women were? What would her voice sound like? How would she look? The reverie always broke off here because when I tried to imagine us together she was still twenty-six and I was her senior by twelve years.

When Bob was dying, it was the companionship of *his* mother I longed for. She had died before I met Bob, but I felt I had learned some things about her he could not have told me from the carton of letters and papers he had found among her possessions, had put in storage, and was about to throw out as we tried to consolidate our possessions after we married. Here, vividly, was a mother in the role of historian and keeper of documents. Beginning with the opening comment in the baby book—"Robert, [age: ten days] seemed to enjoy the autumn foliage as we drove through Central Park on the way home from the hospital" —each stage of his development, first smile, tooth, step, word, was observed and recorded. Preserved also were his first attempt to write his name, his school compositions, ribbons, medals, and diplomas, a copy of his Princeton thesis, and newspaper clippings about his exploits as a diplomat. To Bob's astonishment, his mother had kept to this job until shortly before her death.

The woman I imagined from this collection might have shared my vigils during the weeks when I was on terms of such intimacy with death I felt it taunting me. Later, she would have understood and shared my insatiable need to talk about Bob (thwarted by well-meaning friends who, seeing it as a sign that I was holding onto grief, directed our conversations toward more cheerful subjects). Together we would have shared what was closest to our hearts, and in so doing would have shortened rather than lengthened mourning for both of us.

But by the time of the crisis I had finished with mourning and had thought that I was ready to make a new life. Why then, night after night, was I jolted out of sleep in terror? This time it was not a moonscape, but a dark wood. "In the forest, in to the very thick of it . . .": fairy tale language. Children were taken into a dark wood by their parents, or by a wicked stepmother, and abandoned. Though it used to comfort me to be reminded by these stories how much better off was the full orphan than the one whose remaining parent remarried, it didn't give me sufficient courage to continue reading. The excuse I made was that fairy tales were "too hard." Hard, yes, but also scary. Perhaps if they had been read to me, I would have listened long enough to learn that it all turned out well in the end. On my own, I never got beyond the first paragraph; caution made me back away. Of course there was no way to avoid fairy tales completely. Other children repeated them. They were acted out in school plays. The genre was epitomized for me not by "Cinderella" or "Hansel and Gretel," but by a very brief one I heard (where? I wonder) and never forgot, called "The Death of the Hen":

> So the cock was left all alone with the dead hen, and he digged a grave and laid her in it, and he raised a mound about her, and sat himself down and lamented so sore that at last he died. And so they were all dead together.

In *The Uses of Enchantment,* Bruno Bettelheim says that fairy tales carry important messages to the preconscious and unconscious minds of children from which they can learn the correct solutions to their predicaments. For children with parents and Oedipal conflicts, this is probably so. For me, they carried only threats of separation and death. What I learned from "Hansel and Gretel" was how fortunate these children were to have each other. My greatest piece of luck was to have had Marie as older sister and companion. But while I tended to think that we had never been separated, my illnesses had kept us apart for weeks and months at a time during our boarding school years. With each bout of pneumonia, I was moved to the infirmary and didn't see her until I was well enough to sit up. And there were the months at Columbus Hospital after my mastoidectomy before she was brought down for a visit. Of these periods I remember little but a generalized fear of death that the administration of the last sacraments told me was imminent.

During my recent crisis, when I awakened in anguish at being alone, reason told me that this was absurd. I had only to pick up the telephone. Marie was in Boston. Friends lived close by. Through the distorted lenses I was wearing, Boston looked to be at a greater distance than Mars, friends even farther away. As the vise of anxiety tightened, I imagined that should I overcome my paralysis and dial a number, there would be no one to hear the ring. And if one of them did answer, what would I say? Quote Auden, "as unattached as tumbleweed," to describe my sense of being unconnected to others. Or say more candidly, and more exactly, that I felt as if I'd been sewn into a skin too small for my body. Or that it was as if I'd been trapped and isolated in a cage—no, it was a crib!—as impotent and dependent on others as a baby who cries bitter tears of frustration at being unseen, unheard, untouched.

Say, also, that in coming to terms with the newly dead, I seem to have agitated the spirits of the long dead. They were stirring uneasily in their graves, demanding to be mourned as I had not mourned them when they were buried. I was plunged into retroactive grief for my father, and could no longer deny, though I still tried, the loss I'd suffered at the death of my mother.

For one who had prided herself on being reasonable,

independent, and resourceful when alone, these things would have been difficult to say.

Was this not self-pity? I might be asked.

Perhaps, but wasn't self-pity more comfortable and less morbid?

Was it possible, they would wonder, that one could mourn over losses that had occurred more than half a century earlier?

It seemed unlikely. Nevertheless, as Augustine of Hippo felt he knew with what greed he had demanded the breast in infancy, so I felt I now knew what it was like for an infant to cry out for reassurance that it was not alone, and to hear only the opaque, tomblike silence that now, in the middle of the night, isolated me from the living.

Since work had always been the remedy that cured whatever psychic distress I'd suffered from, I prodded myself to begin writing again. After having reviewed my notes on orphans, and found they interested me again, I went back to the library. Most of the reading was so absorbing I felt grateful to have an excuse to do it, but as I'd shied away from the Brothers Grimm in childhood, so I now shied away from the work of an English psychoanalyst, John Bowlby. For his trilogy I would have to wait for a block of free time, I told myself. When I had the time, I realized that his titles, *Attachment, Separation,* and *Loss,* and the jacket photographs of the last two—one a boy gazing forlornly out a window, the other a depressed child, sitting alone in a dark room—had been putting me off as effectively as had the opening paragraphs of fairy tales.

Two years of reading about death, bereavement, and orphanhood were beginning to take their toll. However, blinded by what Thomas Mann called the writer's "apparatus of self-deception," I refused to admit that the book I was working on was exacerbating the crisis. So I pushed on.

In my hypersensitive state I found Bowlby hard going. I

complained to myself that he was long-winded (1,231 pages!), repetitious, and that often the quotations with which he headed a chapter said in one sentence what he then belabored for thirty pages. My irritability and scrappiness were partly disguised resistance and uneasiness. As I made my way through the volumes, I felt that he, like Uncle Sam in the World War I recruiting poster, was pointing an aggressive index finger at me, and saying, *"You. You're an orphan like the others."*

In rebuttal, I would try to think of all the ways in which I had been treated differently from his subjects. Our relatives, unlike those he wrote about, were enlightened enough to see that Marie and I attended our father's funeral. Perhaps if we had remained with them in the days that followed, they would even have talked to us about his death. Probably not, however. They were too stunned by the loss of a brother so young to talk about him, and also could hardly bear to look at us when they thought what full orphanhood would mean in our lives. And in theirs. Even later, when I asked questions about either parent's death, they answered them shyly, reluctantly, as if to say, You really don't want to be reminded of those unhappy events, do you? What I now know (by no means all I'd like to know), I learned piecemeal, a bit from this aunt, a bit from that uncle:

"Ptomaine poisoning."

"Yes, but from what?"

"Shellfish."

"What kind?"

"So many questions! Clams. Beware of clams."

Another said, "Oysters. One shouldn't eat oysters in the summer." (It was a long time before I dared eat either, in any season.)

Had we been taken out of our accustomed routine, and gone to live with one relative or another, the move would have forced us to recognize the radical change that had taken place in our lives. Or had I been older, Marie and I might have talked about the events of the July day on which he was buried and tried to understand them. What we did instead was pray for the repose of our father's soul.

About my mother's death I, of course, remember nothing. Until I was in college, I was told that she had died of influenza. Before that, I began to realize that one didn't go to the Trudeau Sanitarium for flu, and slips about "the family disease" made it clear that it was the dreaded tuberculosis that had killed my mother, her father, and her sister, and had kept one brother in the hospital for twenty-five years, until his death.

How I was looked after during my first year I don't know. (Orphans lose the historian of their early years, and frequently the documentation as well.) A photograph celebrating four generations of women showed my great-grandmother and grandmother, with my mother holding baby Marie. By the time I was born, the picture-taking had stopped. Soon after my birth, my mother became bedridden. In a household with two seriously ill adults, and a fourteen-month-old baby, my needs were undoubtedly taken care of by the nurse, or the maid, but not as they would have been by a healthy mother.

Hard as I resisted Bowlby, he was forcing me to question my view of the past. Had I felt abandoned, as he says bereaved children do, by first one parent and then another? Had I felt rage? When Bob died and people said that I must be angry at him for having deserted me, the closest I could come to such a feeling was to rage at my old enemy: Fate.

The child who had been taught the Ten Commandments before she was able to read and write had learned so well the lesson that one must honor one's parents, especially dead parents, that she would have found it more comfortable to blame herself for her losses. Where my mother was concerned, that was easy for me to do. Countless times while I was growing up I heard that she should not have had a second child so soon after the first. It was her pregnancy with me that had enfeebled her, lowering her resistance. My birth had hastened her death.

Suppressed memories floated up to the surface to remind me that I hadn't taken all the blame. More than I cared to admit to myself as a child, I had been ashamed of being an orphan. Later, as my college friends expressed envy at my freedom from constricting parental ties, I had rejoiced at my difference from them. But as a nine-year-old, I hadn't wanted to be different. Or look different. The clothes I was made to wear proclaimed that I was an orphan, a poor little orphan. Who was to blame for putting me in the position of being pitied and patronized? It was the living relatives I blamed. But each time I heard the story, and I heard it often as a cautionary tale, about my mother wearing "thin silk dancing slippers" and catching the cold that led to her fatal illness, and my father's having been "run down" from the rackety bachelor life he lived after my mother died, which weakened him in the fight against ptomaine, I wondered (as I was meant to wonder) if their carelessness had shortened their lives and taken them from us prematurely. I had banished these thoughts so quickly that what I'd remembered through the years was having used both instances to enhance the picture of my parents as fun-loving, and ill-fated.

What the crisis did was to blast through the powerful defense I'd built up of the lucky orphan. I had had to believe that my losses had not been devastating. The middle-of-the-night panics at being alone in the world, the intense anxiety and depression I suffered in the recent period of profound orphanhood, had not to do with the present. They were holdovers from the past.

Had I been as uninhibited about expressing my previously denied longings, I might have echoed Tolstoy's belated orphan cry:

Yes, yes my Maman, whom I was never able to call that because I did not know how to talk when she died. She is my

highest image of love—not cold, divine love, but warm,
earthly love, maternal . . . Maman, hold me, baby me! . . .
All this is madness, but it is true.

(So wrote the bearded patriarch in his journal—age
eighty!)

Instead, I timidly struggled to come to terms with my
new knowledge about myself. I was forced to recognize that
behind my cheerful façade there had always been a broad
vein of sadness, and that my emotional balance had seemed
equilibrated because it had never been tested at its most
vulnerable point. If I was not an unlucky orphan, neither
was I as lucky as I had believed. I bear some of the scars
the former inmates of the Hopewell Orphanage, the
Tennessee Industrial School, and the Hebrew Jewish Orphanage (which as a girl I used to pass on my way to school)
bear. And there is a way in which they make me closer kin
to these orphans than to my cousins who had parents. It is
this newly found kinship I wish to explore.

CHAPTER 2

The Convent

GREEN-AND-WHITE-STRIPED awnings shaded the windows
from the July sun. Against the heat they were powerless.
The air was so heavy with the odor of flowers it felt as if one
of the blossoms had got trapped high in my nose.

My sister and I sat side by side on folding chairs rented
for the occasion, white-gloved hands clasped in our laps.
To distract my attention from the queasy feeling in my
stomach, I started to swing my foot in its new shoe. Thinking better of it, I turned my attention instead to the smock-
ing on my white dress, bought in haste, like everything else
I was wearing, the previous day.

The room was filled with grown-ups, strangers mostly.
They were all in black but for the white handkerchiefs they
used to pat their faces as they whispered to one another
about the heat, the humidity. From time to time, they stole
glances at Marie and me. The men looked away, as if they

were embarrassed. The women put their handkerchiefs to their eyes.

When there was the signal to go, one of the women led me over to where the flowers were banked. She held me up and said, "Kiss him good-bye." I leaned over to do as I was told. When my lips touched the skin, cold and hard as stone, I retracted them in horror. I would not kiss this man, another stranger.

After a long, slow ride out of the city, we stood in a circle while a priest intoned prayers. A light breeze stirred the odor of freshly turned sod, forcing the stuck blossom farther up my nose. The ribbons hanging down the back of my leghorn hat floated in front of my eyes. They looked like swimming fish. Blue grosgrain fish.

At the sound of pebbles hitting wood, a woman cried out. Someone whispered disapprovingly, "Laura!" Laura crumpled to the ground and was carried away.

When the others started for the limousines, Auntie, who held Marie and me by the hand, took us to the next grave to say a prayer. "Now they are together again," she said. It was frightening to see grown-ups cry.

On the drive up to Dobbs Ferry, Marie and I were alone in the backseat of the old Packard. We were silent. So was Milton, the driver. At last there was the sound of gravel under the tires, and the statue of the Sacred Heart in the little glass house on the lawn. Milton rang the bell. When the door opened, he kissed us and gave us a little shove toward the nun. The dark entrance hall smelled familiarly of wax—sharp and clean, not sickly sweet like the odor of the flowers in that room.

Mother Superior came gliding toward us, her habit billowing out behind like the wings of a giant bat. Enfolding us in the wings, she cried, *"Povere orfanelle."* Behind her glasses, her eyes looked like black olives that had been rolled in oil. She led us to the chapel and told us, as we knelt, to pray that perpetual light would shine on our papa. Perpetual light sounded nice, like a sunny day at the beach.

Mother Serafina, the dormitory nun, took us to our room. She helped us change into our uniforms and straightened the kerchiefs on our middy blouses. I felt sad at having to give up my new dress so soon. After three days in the outside world, we were convent girls again.

The Convent, an Italianate villa with a crescent driveway and a handsome porte cochere, stood on a bluff overlooking the Hudson River. It was not its site, which was splendid, nor any other quality of excellence that had attracted my father to it as a school for us. He had been desperate. Following our mother's death, he kept us with one grandmother, then the other. We did not flourish. The doctor advised that with our family history, we should be sent away from New York (which had the highest incidence of tuberculosis of any city in the United States). So that we would have country air, we were boarded with a series of families in Staten Island and New Jersey. Each, before long, talked about separating us for the sake of convenience; or, equally distressing to my father, hinted at adoption. He decided it would be better to give us to the nuns. The Ursulines, at Tarrytown, who had educated his sisters, agreed to keep us temporarily in a cottage near the gatekeeper's house in the care of a baby nurse whom they supervised. It was they who suggested that Daddy look for a more permanent arrangement with the Italian nuns at Dobbs Ferry.

At the Villa Maria (so we were later told), a nun who spoke no English took the card Daddy offered her and showed him into the parlor. It was an elegantly proportioned room with floor-to-ceiling windows giving on a veranda. Furniture and draperies in rich brown velvet made the room dark, with here and there a touch of light from the antimacassars of ecru lace. Everything not velvet (even the giant rubber plants) looked and smelled as if it had been freshly waxed. On one wall hung a large wooden crucifix. On another, photographs of Pope Pius XI, and the foundress of the order, Mother Cabrini.

The rhythmic tapping of metal on wood, keys hitting against rosary beads, announced the approach of Mother Superior. She came in holding the card Daddy had handed in at the door. She was dressed like the others of her order in unrelieved black, with no touch of coquettish white around the wimple such as the Ursulines wore. She invited him to sit down and, in heavily accented English (mimicked to perfection by our aunts in the many retellings we begged for when we were growing up), asked about his trip up from the city. Her shrewd black eyes took him in at a glance: tall, boyishly slim, a straw boater in his hand.

How young he was to be a widower! she said. He was . . . ?

Twenty-seven . . .

How had he lost his wife?

She had survived the flu epidemic, but after the birth of the second child had had a relapse. He did not mention (one did not in those days) the time she had spent at the Trudeau Sanitarium at Saranac.

Mother Superior murmured something about the mysterious ways in which God works. How old were the children? He had not said over the telephone.

He had not said because he had been afraid of being rejected out of hand. The older was four, the younger three. Or almost.

Very young for boarding school. Were there no relatives?

None ideally suited to take in two little girls. And then there was the doctor's advice.

The children were not in good health then?

They were somewhat fragile.

Mother Superior clacked her tongue, whether in sympathy with his problems or at those he was posing her was not clear. She studied his card still held in her hand. His given name was Raphael. With his coloring and profile, he could be taken for an Italian. Did the children have any Italian blood? Too bad. That would have made things easier.

Mother Cabrini, foundress of the Missionary Sisters of the
Sacred Heart, had been sent by Holy Father to do missionary work among Italian immigrants. They were living in
deplorable conditions on the Lower East Side. There were
many homeless children, waifs. Every bed in the dormitories was taken.

Were there no private rooms? He could pay.

It would not be easy.

If she could take the children for just a year, give him
time to make other arrangements . . .

Mother Superior patted his hand familiarly, as if he were
a child. It was up to the Board of Directors, but she would
see what she could do. In the meantime, would he like to
be shown around a little before it was time for his train?

He followed her down the broad central hall, which was
lined with sepia photographs of the Colosseum, St. Peter's,
the Leaning Tower of Pisa, to the kindergarten (which had
been a gymnasium in the days when the Villa had been an
exclusive boys' school), to the chapel (formerly a swimming
pool). She led him out onto the veranda, and through the
grape arbor to the garden. They stood together on the
parapet taking in the view. A Hudson River Day Line boat,
its decks festooned with colored pennants, steamed by.
The captain gave a blast on his comical horn, a salute to the
Convent children who ran to the fence to wave, some vigor-
ously, others with listless envy, at the families out for a day
of pleasure. From below the parapet came the sound of the
New York Central train as it flew along the tracks.

On feverish nights, a wakeful child could hear the band
as the riverboat passed again on its way back to the city, and
could imagine the couples dancing under swaying paper
lanterns. Later still, the sound of a milk train's plaintive
whistle would become incorporated in a nightmare.

There was no lack of subjects for nightmares, but the
theme most favored was separations. There had been so
many of them that the day Daddy left us in the Convent
parlor may not have been more painful than the others—

only the usual clutching at his neck as he held us in a simultaneous embrace, the usual promise of frequent visits, the usual wrenching apart, and, after he had gone, the tears and holding on tight to one another.

Saint Roch would look after us, Mother Superior had said the day we arrived, pointing to the statue in the niche over the door of the room to which we had been assigned. It was a sunny room with two brass beds covered with white cotton spreads and embroidered pillow shams. At 6:00 A.M., when the first bell awakened us, we got down on our knees for morning prayers. Half an hour later, dressed in our uniforms, the room in order, we filed, two by two, index finger on our lips to remind us to be silent, down to the chapel for morning mass. After the spartan dormitory, the dark, warm chapel, fragrant with incense and candle wax, had a womblike coziness. In the flickering candlelight, pastel angels, painted on the ceiling overhead, floated through a pale blue sky. On the altar the priest, weighted down with gorgeous vestments embroidered by the nuns—in green, white, rose, black, or purple, depending on the ecclesiastical season—moved in slow motion, while we in the congregation, nuns and students, knelt, stood, sat, and thumped our breasts as we made the proper responses. And I, at least in the early years, snoozed, to be roused from time to time by the tinkle of the altar bells, the sprinkling of holy water, or the waving of the thurible, whose burning embers enveloped me in soft gray blankets of incense.

For the fasting child, there was a secret pleasure to be had in chewing the celluloid cover of a missal. It was sweet and crisp and more satisfying in a way than anything there would be to eat later in the day. Breakfast, which we younger children ate at trestle tables in the downstairs dining room, was unquestionably inferior. Standing behind my chair as we said grace, I watched with apprehension, then resignation, as a skin inexorably formed on top of the cocoa cooling in my cup.

There was little that came from the Convent kitchen to

tempt a sickly child's appetite. What should have been liquid was solid, what should have been smooth was lumpy; what crisp, soggy; what tender, tough; what hot, tepid; what warm, cold. Only the Sunday meal of pasta was prepared by the uprooted Sicilian peasants who did the cooking with something like care. It was not a question of measuring this food against home cooking, as most boarding school children do. We applied no such yardstick. But a child needs no standard to know when food *feels* wrong.

What gastronomical pleasures there were came from outside the kitchen and away from the table. Discarded vigil candle wax could be molded into a savory chewing gum. Communion wafers that were imperfectly shaped, and therefore not consecrated, made a Nabisco-like wafer. In fine weather, there was sorrel growing wild on the river bank, which we washed down with the icy water bubbling out of a nearby spring.

On feast days, of which there were many, though never enough to suit us, we could count on the dazzling array of sweets brought up from New York's Little Italy by visiting parents and benefactors. There were pink and green candy-coated almonds, panettones, panfortes, macaroons in twisted pastel papers, the Infant Jesus in almond paste (Christmas), breads baked in the shape of a lamb, or a ring, and studded with purple, green, and orange hard-boiled eggs (Easter), Sicilian confections of spun sugar—dolls, houses, baroque churches—made in flamboyant colors and almost too good to eat. Still, one cannot live on communion wafers, sorrel, and sugar dolls, so great skill was needed to lift the skin from the tepid cocoa, and to palpate the bowl of cereal for undercooked lumps.

It was at breakfast that punishments were meted out. Whisperers, pinchers, gigglers, players-with-string, who had been yanked out of the pew by a policing nun at mass, stood with their faces to the wall: no breakfast for them. Chronic nail-biters had hung from their necks a loaf of bread, threaded with twine, which they wore through the

day like grotesque necklaces. Bed-wetters, most shameful
of all, stood on a platform with sheets over their heads.
These ghostly apparitions, which I tried not to look at,
added terrifyingly to the strangeness of convent life in the
early days.

During the first two years, before I reached school age,
when Marie and the other children were in class, I tagged
around after Mother Rita, who was in charge of the chapel,
helping her with her chores. She and I made the communion host. She let me stir the batter and press down the lid
of the iron on which the hosts were made. She and I
changed the altar linen, poured holy water into the fonts,
replaced the burned-out vigil lights with new ones. Since I
helped dust their plaster wings, I was on terms of great
intimacy with the baroque angels that knelt at either side
of the altar, and I knew every fold in the Blessed Virgin's
robe. The Infant of Prague, whose statue stood just inside
the altar rail, I thought of as a doll too big and precious to
play with.

In spring and fall, I joined the other children at the end
of the long European school day to play outdoors on the
swings and slides before supper. With the onset of the cold
weather, we were confined indoors, as sealed in against the
winter air, which the nuns considered unhealthy, as Russians in an isba. In the basement, under a sulfurous yellow
light, we played hand-clapping games like "Ibitibibiti-
sibitisab," while the older girls clustered in groups whispering unimaginable secrets.

At bedtime, we formed a circle in the dormitory hall for
night prayers and examination of conscience. This was an
awkward time for me, for while I was willing to accuse
myself in a general way, and pounded my breast like the
others, I could think of nothing specific to confess. When
we were alone in our room, Marie and I undressed in the
dark, kissed each other good-night, and, once in our beds,
began our private prayers. There was the ever-growing
litany of our dead. Our mother, her sister Aunt Eleanor (as

close in age to her as I was to Marie), their father. We had been taught it was not enough to say words of the prayers. One had to visualize what one was saying. When I tried to picture my mother, my mind was like a blank screen. In the end, I settled on a double-exposure image of my mother as she looked in a photograph Daddy had on his dresser at home and of our Blessed Mother, whose statue I dusted every day and knew far better.

The living relatives we prayed for were only somewhat easier to imagine, for we saw them infrequently. Once a year, during Christmas vacation, we were taken to call on our maternal grandmother and great-grandmother. A smooth-faced, white-haired woman, dressed in black silk with a bertha of Irish lace, Great-grandmother was as serene and carefully arranged in her high-backed chair for our visits as a Frans Hals. Since we had been told by Mother Superior, when one of the Convent children died, that the good die young, I wondered as I looked at this ancient woman what terrible thing she had done to have been kept alive for so long. Prayers for her required special fervency.

Our paternal grandmother had died soon after we'd gone to live at the Convent, but her husband, a favorite of mine, was very much alive. Grandpa, a wiry, energetic man, is my tie to history. At fifteen, he had joined the Union Army (and later posed for a statue to his regiment that, in our high school days, we were taken to see at Gettysburg). Grandpa was a temperance man, a vegetarian, a daily churchgoer, a Democrat, and an amateur boxer. During the draft riots of 1863, he single-handedly boxed off an angry mob that attacked a group of Negro women, according to a contemporary newspaper clipping I have. My special affection for him came, I later learned, from his having spoiled me—that is to say, when I cried, as I seem to have done without letup after my mother's death, he made clandestine visits to the nursery, his pockets bulging with graham crackers and unscheduled bottles of milk because he was convinced that food would comfort me.

In our night prayers, Marie and I prayed that the living would stay alive, and that on Sunday, visiting day, they would come to see us.

At the announcement that there was someone in the parlor for us, we raced to the dormitory to wash our hands, brush our hair, and have the silk kerchiefs on our dress uniforms rearranged by Mother Serafina. How difficult it was to stand still! The real pleasure was in these moments of anticipation, when one enjoyed the thrill of having been summoned and did not yet have to make awkward conversation. For awkward it was, especially with our maternal grandmother. We curtsied and stepped forward to receive her cool kiss. A tall, fair-haired woman with the carriage of a diva, she came dressed in mauve (still in half mourning for her husband and daughters), wearing pearl earrings, a veil tied under her chin, and a fur scarf over her arm. Since all the other grandmothers were short, plump, swarthy, wrinkled, and as enveloped in black as the nuns, her arrival always caused a stir. She brought us carefully chosen, identical, little-girl presents: tortoiseshell combs in cases, sandalwood fans, handkerchiefs of Irish linen trimmed with lace, change purses of Moroccan leather. After we'd opened our gifts and expressed our thanks for them, we could think of nothing further to say. She asked us questions. We answered. Before long, she gave up trying to make conversation with us and addressed herself instead to Mother Superior, or asked to see Mother Serafina to interrogate her about our well-being. Then, and later when I saw her on the opposite side of a courtroom, I found it difficult to believe she was *my* grandmother. Had she not lived to a good age, I might still remember her as aloof and intimidating.

The Convent did not provide the healthy environment the family doctor had prescribed. Three winters in a row the old priest was summoned to give me extreme unction. As the runny nose and cough endemic among the children turned, in my case, into pneumonia, it became harder and harder for me to lace my high shoes in the morning. At breakfast, the odor of scorched cocoa turned my stomach. Instead of playing clapping games with the others at recess, I lay on a bench curled up in a ball, the index finger of my left hand pressed against the roof of my mouth for comfort.

When chills shook me, fever burned me, and pain raked my side, I was put to bed. The pinwheel of colored disks of which I became the center turned faster, faster, faster, spun higher, higher, higher. If it slowed down for a moment, I saw a blurry ring of nuns around the crib I'd been put in and heard, as if from a great distance, the rumble of their prayers. Or, more startlingly, there was the sound of male voices. My father had arrived and was talking to the doctor. A bitter powder was put on my tongue, a mustard plaster was stuck to the pain, my drenched nightdress was changed, and the pinwheel spun again, this time carrying me down. The bed split under me. I was being sucked *down*. A scream (my own) woke me. The nuns now held candles. The priest's face as he leaned over to anoint me grew so elongated it seemed in danger of dripping, like melted wax. Disembodied hands packed me in ice. Zeppelin-shaped figures floated toward me and bounced me off their rubbery surfaces as if I were a ball.

After the crisis, I found myself in another room. My sister was not there. Nor was there the sound of other children. Mother Giovanna, a tall, large-boned woman who seemed to be of a different race from the others (a Lombardian), nursed me through weeks of convalescence. Awakening from a feverish dream, I would find her sitting by the side of my bed, one elbow resting on a massive knee, her chin in her hand, her eyes closed. (Years later, I found her image again among the massive, brooding, genderless figures in the spandrels of the Sistine ceiling.)

During the listless hours of the afternoon, as time stood still and my unstable temperature rose, she read to me from *The Lives of the Saints*. As girls who are read fairy tales daydream about becoming princesses, we who were read the lives of the saints daydreamed of becoming saints. The atmosphere in which we lived was dense with celestial spirits who existed, depending upon one's intimacy with them, from just above the right shoulder, where one's guardian angel hovered (busy, in my case, trying to keep my temperature down), all the way up to heaven. It was true that, so far, there were no American saints, but we all knew that it was only a question of time before Mother Cabrini, a naturalized American, would be canonized.

It was during one of these illnesses that I committed my first sin. Except for paroxysms of coughing, I suffered no pain during my convalescence, only terrible fatigue, and an insatiable thirst that the brandy-flavored water Mother Giovanna doled out to me in small drafts left unquenched. It was tap water (for some mysterious reason forbidden me) that I craved. One night, after a struggle with my budding conscience, I could restrain myself no longer. As Mother Giovanna sat dozing in the chair, I climbed over the crib's railing, found my way through a series of storage rooms and corridors to the dormitory, and ran down its length to the bathroom with its familiar row of sinks. Shinnying up on one of them, I diverted the water from the faucet into my mouth and drank greedily. Mother Giovanna was still asleep when I got back. I lay under my covers, panting from the effort, the forbidden water rolling heavily in my stomach. Thirst was replaced by a new and more disagreeable sensation: guilt. I had committed the sin of disobedience, and had disobeyed the nun for whom I felt the most affection. When next I was well enough to join the other children for the nightly examination of conscience, I said the *mea culpas* in earnest, and knew at last what to accuse myself of.

On afternoons when I was able to sit up, Marie was allowed to come to the door of the sickroom so that we (especially I) would be reassured the other was not far away. My father, who had felt that our security lay in our being together, had had his intuition verified the winter I had a mastoidectomy. I awakened in the middle of the night to find myself in a crib-filled ward. The light in the high-ceilinged room was the color of an ether dream, nacreous blue, the blue of a milk of magnesia bottle. It made the world look cold and indescribably sad. When I cried out, as much at the color as at the pain in my head, nuns dressed in the familiar habit, but with unfamiliar blue-white faces, said they couldn't make the color go away. In the morning, when the blue paper covers were removed from the overhead lights, the world of unfamiliar nuns, white-coated doctors, and bandaged children took on a less nightmarish aspect.

It was some time before I understood where I was. My father must have told me more than once that I had been operated on for the pain in my ear, and was in a New York hospital staffed by the same order of nuns I knew from the Convent. In a photograph of me taken at Columbus Hospital, I was shown, turban-headed, holding the teddy bear almost my size Daddy had given me for company. I loved this animal and trailed it with me to the small operating room for the changes of dressing (that were even more painful that the old earaches), to the chapel for mass, to the roof where I was taken to get the air. The teddy bear was a comfort, but it could not replace my sister. I asked for her repeatedly. When, week after week, she didn't appear, I took it that she had died.

As weeks grew into months and there was little forward movement in my convalescence, it became clear something was wrong. What explained my listlessness, tearfulness, lack of appetite? The doctor, looking for somatic causes, prescribed various tonics, to no avail. My frantic father, who had been wondering if it was the separation from my sister that was to blame, convinced the doctors, and Mother Superior, to allow Marie to come to the hospital for an extended visit. From my response to her seeming resurrection, and the spurt my convalescence took, there could be little doubt that he had been right.

Mother Superior and Daddy were so often in disagreement about our care that he was little better pleased to leave us at the Convent than he had been to board us with families. But because he could find no more satisfactory arrangement, we stayed at Dobbs Ferry not one year but five. From the time of his first visit, to see how we were settling in, until shortly before the telephone call three years later summoning us to his bedside, he and the nuns kept up a tug of war over us of which we gradually became aware. At Christmas, and in June, when he picked us up for vacation, he took us directly to Best and Company. With the resources of a Fifth Avenue department store that specialized in children's clothing, he transformed us as quickly as he could from the institutional children we had become to the daughters he had given the nuns. Pastel dresses of crepe de chine and patent-leather slippers replaced blue serge uniforms and high shoes. The store's barber was directed to cut and brush our hair the way Daddy liked it worn, parted on the side. To document that this was the way we really looked, the store's photographer recorded the metamorphosis.

Vacation over, the nuns combed our hair *their* way, removed the dresses, and put us back in uniform. So successful were they in making us over that in the black-and-white school photographs in which our fair complexions and hair don't show, we are so like our Italo-American classmates that, though we've studied the pictures long and hard, we have never made out for certain which two figures, identical in every detail as a row of paper dolls, we are.

The toys my father sent for us to play with, the food to enrich the institutional diet and help us gain weight, were expropriated for general use. We didn't know enough to complain, but our blankness when questioned—What dolls? What Ovaltine?—led to explosions of temper at home, and at the Convent, which taught us our first lessons in equivocation. Even after we caught on, we occasionally made an accidental break. For the gravest of these, I was responsible. At Christmas, Daddy's oldest sister, Auntie, who helped look after us during our vacation, decided to supervise my bath. Resisting like a frightened puppy, I ran from her and hid in a closet. When caught, I resisted being undressed. The water in the tub was rising. So was Auntie's temper. If I wouldn't take off my clothes, she would remove them for me. Ordinarily timid and lacking in spirit, I fought her off. My father was called. Between hysterical sobs, I blurted out that I could not take a bath with-out-my-bath-ing-gar-ment. It was a sin, as until this moment I thought everyone knew, to bathe naked.

My sister, who had followed our usual holiday procedure (a modest washing at the sink), was interrogated. What came out was that at the Convent bathing was a serious activity, controlled by ritual. On Saturday nights, we lined up outside the room with the row of sinks, the row of toilets, and the pair of tubs as massive and ancient-looking as sarcophagi. Mother Serafina handed us bricks of yellow soap to rub on the outside of our bathing garments, which were made of unbleached muslin. It was into the tub, scrub, out. No time for playing with the soap, or lolling about in the warm water, as we would have liked to do, to put off the moment of extreme discomfort that awaited us when we stepped out onto the bath mat and felt the air hit the water-logged muslin.

These conflicts between Daddy and the nuns provided the subjects for my earliest speculations on morality. Though I only imperfectly understood the reason for his indignation where toys and food were concerned, I was on his side. Private property didn't exist at the Convent, but it was agreeable to believe that the beautiful fire engine that all the children played with was in some remote and un-claimable way mine. On the issue of modesty, I was squarely on the side of the nuns. I submitted to the humi-

liating experience of being bathed at home, suffering not
only from my shameful nudity, but even more painfully
from my first crisis of loyalty. Nakedness was sinful. Yet
here was Daddy agreeing with Auntie that the wearing of
a bathing garment was medieval and unhealthful, and that
it was undoubtedly to blame for my having had pneumonia
every winter.

The brief vacations, two weeks at Christmas, two months
in the summer, during which I was under my family's influence were no match for the endless months of uninterrupted conventual life. Holidays on Long Island in the
summer, and at my paternal grandparents' brownstone in
Chelsea in the winter, were brief and dreamlike. At the
Hedges, a Victorian seaside hotel, Marie and I passed our
days on the beach, sun-bonneted, in matching gingham
dresses, pail and shovel in hand, playing in the water, col-
lecting shells on the sandbar, building sand castles with our
cousins.

The highlight of any vacation was a visit to Daddy's bachelor flat in Greenwich Village. Milton, a down-on-his-luck
chauffeur who drove for my father on an erratic and informal basis, picked us up in the Packard touring car. Through
the isinglass windows, we saw the pillars of the El speed by
as we careened down Sixth Avenue. Indoors, the two men,
who had little experience entertaining children, improvised
games more suitable for boys than for girls. A seesaw,
which they fashioned out of an ironing board, bounced us
perilously high in the air. There were sliding races down
the highly polished hall floor to the French doors of the
dining room (from the handle of which I sustained a promi-
nent bump on my forehead that stayed with me for years).
When we tired of these rowdy games, Milton made lemon-
ade for us, Orange Blossoms for them, and tended the
phonograph, while Daddy, an expert dancer, taught us the
one-step, the foxtrot, and the waltz.

Did he tell us, or did we learn later, that courting as they
did during the later days of Vernon and Irene Castle, he

and our mother passed their time at the tea dances then fashionable at New York hotels? Among our relatives, there were those who were scandalized that my parents continued dancing during their three years of marriage, and my mother's pregnancies. In the photographs of them that I scrutinized when I was old enough to wonder what they had been like, they look static, enigmatic, sad, as if they had a premonition of what lay ahead. It is through the pictures of the Castles, and especially of Astaire and Rogers impersonating them, that my parents came alive for me. There they are together, smiling, in motion, Mother in a flowing white dress, Daddy whirling her around. It is always three o'clock in the morning and they, with the limitless energy of the young and healthy, have danced the whole night through.

What else Daddy tried to teach us in the short time he had with us I don't know, but our passion for dancing undoubtedly comes from the spins, dips, pivots, twirls, whirls, leaps, taps, feints, slides, and glides he and my mother executed when we were *in utero,* and from those holiday afternoon lessons in the Village. Today, when I hear the syncopated rhythms of ragtime, or the plaintive wail of a saxophone, I smell again the Turkish tobacco of Daddy's Murads, and feel the beaded frost of his silver cocktail shaker that, after a particularly energetic number, I rested against my burning cheek. At such moments, infrequent and evanescent, he comes to life for me again.

CHAPTER 3

The Convent—Continued

THE SUMMER MY father died, we did not go to the Hedges. The day after the funeral, we settled into the Convent routine as if nothing had happened. No mention was made of our loss. Our new state made us more, rather than less, like the others. Saint Roch, many of the nuns, and most of the children had been orphaned early. We said our prayers, went to mass, and, school being closed for the summer, played outdoors with the others, the homeless, who never left the Villa. The only change was that in our private prayers the litany of our dead had been increased by one.

For the first time, I was at the Convent for my birthday, my seventh, and, more important, for the Feast of the Assumption, Ferragosto. There was to be a procession. For weeks, we were drilled in how to walk backwards, two by two, slowly, solemnly, facing the priest who would be carrying the monstrance.

In the dormitory, Mother Serafina unlocked the clothes presses and took out our First Communion dresses. She and an assistant worked in a fever of activity, taking a stitch here, dropping a hem there, washing, starching, ironing. The parlor, the chapel, the dormitory, and private rooms were turned upside down with waxing and polishing. On the eve of the feast, we fasted and were silent (harder, far, than going without lumpy pudding). In the late afternoon, we gathered up the dahlias, roses, peonies, and zinnias in the flower garden and, carefully pulling them apart, petal by petal, laid them in wicker baskets decorated with blue satin ribbons, the blue that was Mary's special color.

No alarm was needed to rouse us next morning. Up and down the dormitory white-gowned figures popped out of bed and ran barefoot to the window to check the weather: clear, with the promise of heat. Mother Serafina, who had been up half the night making wreaths of smilax for our hair, supervised our dressing. Although vanity was a sin, a little preening was allowed the day of the procession. Waiting for the dignitaries to assemble in the parlor, we checked each other to be sure our petticoats were not showing, fidgeted with our white gloves, pulling them off and on, and suffered, willingly, the tickle of green leaves on our brows.

Mass was late and high. Every seat in the chapel was taken. The priest was resplendent in white vestments, the altar buried in flowers. At the moment when four nuns came forward with the baldachino to hold over the celebrant's head, we children, straw baskets over our arms, led the way—backing out of the chapel, under the grape arbor, through the vegetable and flower garden, strewing the path with petals. As the bishop, monsignors, visiting priests, lay dignitaries, and patronesses followed, the air became filled with the odor of incense, the perfume of crushed flowers, and the sound of unaccompanied female voices singing, *"Lauda, Zion, Salvatorem."*

At the grotto of the Virgin, which was banked with ferns and deliciously cool from the water dripping down its rocks, we crowded around the statue for the climax of the ceremonies. The honor student in the graduating class climbed a ladder that had been set up behind Our Lady and placed a crown of roses on her head. A little more to the right, the nun in charge of the procession signaled. Now to the left. There. A sigh of satisfaction rose from the spectators when the wreath was perfectly in place. Then the priest swung the thurible and made the sign of the cross. Verse upon verse of *"Ave, Ave, Ave Maria,"* and more petal-strewing, took us back to the chapel.

During benediction, the concluding service, we said the Litany of the Blessed Virgin. "Mystical rose," chanted the priest. To which we responded, "Pray for us."

So he chanted, "Tower of Ivory," "House of Gold," "Ark of the Covenant," "Gate of Heaven," "Morning Star," and each time we responded, "Pray for us." I didn't understand what the words meant, but I loved the rhythmic dialogue, at once exotic and soothingly monotonous.

The chanting, the heat, the flickering candles, the overpowering odor of wax, incense, and perfume, the hours of excitement on an empty stomach kept one just this side of fainting. Not a moment too soon, the celebrant gave the final blessing and left the altar. We filed out of the pews, genuflected two by two, and marched out to a triumphal recessional.

Sometime that autumn one of the nuns in a sister convent up the Hudson died. After a funeral mass in our chapel, her coffin was set up in the playground and we children, and our nuns, walked slowly around it, reciting the rosary. At first I resisted looking inside it, but the prayers went on for so long that before they were over, I stole a glance at the dead nun's face. Bordered by the black cap and veil, it was chalk white. A plug of cotton in one of her nostrils startled and frightened me. I tried hard to concentrate on the Hail Marys and not look back at the cotton, which I was on the edge of connecting with the hot day in the room shaded by green awnings, the words "perpetual light," the stone-cold lips, and the finality of death.

From that day on, I was troubled by a malaise that was like the onset of an illness (and yet was not like it). It gave me a lump in my throat and made me wish I could cry. It came over me strongly on visiting days as one long Sunday after the other went by without a call to the parlor. At the beginning of the Christmas season, when there was no sign that the usual preparations were being made for us to go home for vacation, the feeling became acute.

The previous year, after the school play, Marie and I had been dressed in our Sunday uniforms, leggings, and coats, and had sat in the parlor with the few others who were going home for vacation. We listened to the crunch of chains on snow and watched the arc made by headlights as each car came into the driveway. Whose parent was it? All of us sat up a little straighter at the sound of the doorbell. There was a moment of suspense, an agonizing delay, before Mother Superior came in to beckon the lucky child. One after the other they were called.

Marie and I were old enough to have learned that promptness was not one of Daddy's virtues. We sat in the parlor until well after bedtime, our ears strained for the sound of chains. It was very late when Mother Superior came to tell us that something must have happened: our papa would not come tonight. Perhaps tomorrow. We must take off our coats and leggings. Bursting into tears, we pleaded to be allowed to wait a little longer. We waited.

Snow had buried the world in silence. Even the highway was quiet now. All traffic had stopped for the night. Mother Superior snapped off the light in the porte cochere. She was leading us up to bed when the bell rang. We raced down the stairs, and as Daddy was apologizing to Mother Superior—". . . a late start from the city . . . the snow . . . a flat tire . . ."—we threw ourselves into his arms. What did it matter what had delayed him. He was *there*.

When Mother Superior told us that this year we would

not be going home, the events of the previous July—the hot room, the stranger in the casket, the weeping relatives at the cemetery—took on meaning for me. I understood for the first time that Daddy would never be late again.

The weeping relatives—where were they? I wondered when month after month went by and they didn't come to see us. If, as happened on an occasional Sunday, we were called to the parlor, it was to see a woman the nuns said was our Italian godmother. Later, when we asked about her at home, no one seemed to know who she was. I think now that she was one of the patronesses who came up from New York on feast days with cannoli and sugar dolls. Sensing what it was like for children who had no visitors (had she, too, been orphaned?), she came Sunday after Sunday and saw in rotation those of us without parents. Conversation with her was easier than with Grandmother. She was in closer touch with our routine. How well she knew institutional life was shown by the present she brought out of her reticule. It was a block of chocolate, shaped like a frying pan and attached, lollipop fashion, to a wooden stick. Tortoiseshell combs and sandalwood fans went the mysterious way of all private property, but chocolate, eaten in the gift-giver's presence, was safely tucked in our stomachs.

Of course she wanted to know how we were getting along. I suppose we said everything was fine. Certainly it wouldn't have occurred to either of us to say that since our father's death things had been going badly. Had he been alive, he would have been outraged to hear that a new nun, Mother Gaetana, had punished Marie severely, and for dancing. As if dancing could be a sin!

The Dixie Inn, a roadhouse on the property next to the Convent, was close enough for us to hear its band on evenings when it was warm enough for the windows to be open. At the sound of drums rolling and trombones moaning, the older girls would come for Marie and take her to the bathroom, the perfect place for lessons in the Charleston. One night, as the dancers were gyrating over the marble floor, Mother Gaetana snapped on the overhead light. The older girls fled, leaving Marie to take the full brunt of her wrath. When she could think of no more sins to accuse Marie of, she grabbed her by the arm and dragged her, kicking and screaming, to a broom closet, and locked her in for the night. Marie's screams, as she pounded on the door to be let out, could be heard up and down the dormitory until, at last, overcome by fatigue, she fell asleep, surrounded by the menacing silhouettes of mops and brooms. In the morning, she came out of the closet with rage in her heart. Rage nourished rebelliousness.

A favorite subject of the whispered conversations among the older girls was running away. They, and now my sister, were less interested in a destination than in escaping. The New York Central whistle was a constant reminder that the railway station was close by. One could get to New York, and then . . . The risks were great. Escapees, if caught, were sent to the House of the Good Shepherd, a correctional institution for wayward girls.

The night of the broom closet incident I had cried myself to sleep, yet I lacked the courage to cooperate in the runaway plan. How would we pay for our tickets on the train? Where would we go after we arrived in Grand Central? Trying to formulate my own plan of escape, I wondered about the Gypsies. Families of them camped along the Hudson and came to the Convent to beg. One of the kitchen nuns gave them food and shooed them away, warning us never, never, never to speak to them: Gypsies *stole* children. Would it be so bad to be stolen? Gypsy children wore earrings and long colorful skirts, and didn't go to school. From the tambourine I saw one of them carrying, I imagined that they passed their time dancing instead of learning to read and write. What if Marie and I stationed ourselves outside the kitchen door? Might we not get stolen? But what if—I terrified myself thinking of it—they stole Marie and, deciding that I was too young, left me behind?

Sometime in the spring, a group of us were taken to Brooklyn to sing the funeral mass for the Convent's chief benefactress. Her pretty married daughter, who wore a rope of pearls down to her waist and perfume that smelled like crushed flower petals, took me out of line and had me sit next to her during the banquet that followed the mass. She urged more and more food on me, insisted I fill my pockets with *amaretti* and candy-coated almonds and, putting me on her lap, stroked my hair and asked the others at the table to admire its color. So shy and giddy did this attention make me that I almost missed the seriousness of her question: How would I like to be adopted, to come to live with her and be her little girl? If I had thought for a moment that this would be an alternative to running away, I changed my mind as soon as I realized that she didn't know I had a sister and meant she would adopt me alone. Becoming apprehensive, I slid down from her lap and went looking for Marie.

On the ride back to Dobbs Ferry, we were asked to donate the crisp, new one dollar bills each of us had been given for singing to purchase a new statue. The older girls parted with their money resentfully. It would have bought a train ticket to New York. I blocked my ears against their whispering, but I knew that when the moment came, I would join the runaways. To be separated from my sister was unthinkable, worse far than being incarcerated together, as we surely would be, at the Good Shepherd.

The year dragged by. A forlorn Christmas; the long somber weeks of Lent, followed by the greatest feast of the year, Easter, on which few were not called to the parlor; Pentecost; Corpus Christi, with another flower-strewing procession; the Feast of the Sacred Heart, for which we gathered around the statue in the glass house on the lawn and sang hymns to our patron; the lethargic and interminable months of summer (which seemed an altogether less agreeable season away from the beach, the ocean breezes, and the cool verandas of the Hedges); Ferragosto; Advent and, once again, preparations for the Christmas play.

While we were putting on our costumes—Marie's a long white gown and a cardboard halo of gold for her part as Christ at the age of twelve, teaching in the temple; mine a pair of unstable crepe-paper wings pinned to my back for an angel in the tableau—the nun in charge of the play told us we had a visitor who had just arrived and was in the audience.

When Marie appeared on the stage, her hectic flush made her look to Auntie uncannily like our mother in the months before she died. As the play continued, and Marie's hacky cough interfered with the delivery of her lines, Auntie became convinced that Marie was seriously ill. At the end of the performance, she asked Mother Superior to get us ready to leave for New York immediately. Two days later, a decision was made that transformed our lives.

Dr. Hess, a specialist in lung diseases, took our family history. He weighed us, auscultated us, X-rayed us. How had we been allowed to get into such a state? We were suffering from malnutrition, were pretubercular, and in my case what looked to Auntie like poor posture was to the professional's eye a curvature of the spine that would give me trouble later. With a history such as ours, no time should be lost in moving us to a preventorium. He was on the board of one in New Jersey that took children our age. If the family agreed, he would arrange for our admission.

A hastily arranged family council was held in the parlor of the Chelsea brownstone. The nagging question of who would raise us had been troubling our relatives since the hot July day when the sight of Marie and me had made the men at the funeral avert their eyes and the women weep. At the time when my father had asked Mother Superior to take us for a year, he was being urged on all sides to find a new wife, one who would help him look after us. (The woman he was considering marrying was Laura, the disembodied voice at the graveside. About her, the only thing I later learned was that she resembled my mother.)

In his will, he had named his only unmarried brother, Vincent, as guardian, but as often happens with confirmed bachelors, Vincent had married and, between the making of the will and Daddy's death, had had a child. Neither Vincent nor anyone else in the family was in a position to take in two rather unhealthy little girls. Dr. Hess's recommendation, which allowed for another postponement of the vexing question, was unanimously accepted.

At the end of vacation, we returned to Dobbs Ferry, but the nuns knew that we would stay only until the move could be arranged. The day we left, there was one suitcase to pack, Daddy's old Gladstone. In five years, we had accumulated nothing but the dresses he had bought us, which we had long since outgrown, our rosary beads, and prayer books. When we were ready to go, and were waiting for the taxi, Mother Giovanna took me to the sickroom where she and I had spent so much time together. She had great hopes that I had a vocation, she said. Would I always remember that I was a convent girl? Ah, what did a child know of the temptations of the world? There were atheists everywhere, and especially where I was going to live. How could she protect me? I was wearing scapulars (a pair of felt holy pictures that hung down the chest and back from a cord around the neck). They were insufficient protection for what lay ahead. From a table, she took a picture of her favorite saint, the Little Flower (Saint Thérèse of Lisieux), and pinned it, still in its Florentine leather frame, to the bodice under my middy. She placed my index finger against my lips: not a word of this to anyone.

In New York, when Auntie was getting us ready for bed, Mother Giovanna's shield against the infidels was exposed. No, I hadn't stolen it, I insisted, astonished that she could think me capable of such a sin. My sister, who was not bound by silence, came to my defense. Nothing further was said after her explanation, but that night as the two of us lay in bed, wakeful with excitement, we heard the grown-ups laughing about Mother Giovanna and the picture. What was there to laugh at? I wanted to ask in defense of my nurse. With her warning about the world of unbelievers we were going to live in whirling in my head, I finally fell asleep, holding tight to the companion who would accompany me into the wilderness.

CHAPTER 4

The Preventorium

THE JITNEY BUS that met the train at Farmingdale, a whistle-stop on the New Jersey branch of the Pennsylvania Railroad, bounced us through a wilderness of scrub oak and pine. Each turn of the wheel took us closer to our new home. It would be very different from the Convent, we had been told. We would be looked after by nurses (dressed in white) instead of nuns (dressed in black). There would be boys as well as girls. The nutritious food we ate would help us put on weight, and the out-of-door life we lived would fill our lungs with the salubrious air for which the region was famous.

The Preventorium for Tuberculosis, as it was ingenuously called, was built on property donated to the state by the newspaper tycoon Arthur Brisbane as part of a national drive to wipe out the "Great White Plague." At Farmingdale, and similar institutions throughout the country, chil-

47

dren followed the regimen in fashion in sanitaria. It was
hoped that sequestration in a climate thought to be health-
ful, an enriched diet heavy in milk, eggs, and starches,
frequent rest periods throughout the day, and sleep on
porches at night would allow them to develop a resistance
to the tubercle bacilli and protect them, as they reached the
dangerous period of adolescence and young adulthood,
from succumbing to the disease.*

At the administration building, a staff doctor studied the
X rays we had brought from New York. He thumped our
chests, asked us to breathe, cough, and stick out our
tongues. He peered into our ears, noses, throats, pulled
down our lower eyelids, examined our scalps, and pronounced us ready to go to the Lower House, a rustic cabin
down in the valley, where we were to spend two weeks in
quarantine, to insure that we were not incubating measles,
mumps, chicken pox, or other contagious diseases that
could cause an epidemic.

Quarantine seemed to mean that there were no lessons,
no homework, no bells, no uniforms, no punishments, and
so little supervision that, except when it was time to go to
bed, the ten or so children at the Lower House spent the
day doing more or less what they pleased. The closest thing
to quarantine I had previously experienced was summer
vacations at the Hedges. But if at the Hedges there had
been a current of excitement between the sexes, which
showed itself in giggling and blushing among the girls, and
teasing and bold laughter among the boys, I had been too
young to be aware of it.

The diffuse eroticism pervading the Lower House was
as contagious as measles. Never having lived intimately
with boys before (except, in the summer, with one boy
cousin), I had no immunity to it. Previously I had been

---

*As late as 1930, tuberculosis was the leading cause of death among fifteen-
to forty-year-olds, and remained high on the list until Selman Waksman's discovery of streptomycin, and later of isoniazid. When he was given the Nobel Prize,
it was said of Waksman that he "wrote the requiem for a great killer."

aware of my body only when it hurt—the pain in my ear, the soreness in my throat, the tightness in my chest, the shakiness in my legs. For the first time, I discovered that my body was capable of giving me real, if unlocalized, pleasure. How was I to respond to these new sensations? Discovering the house mother's talcum powder in the bathroom one day, I applied it to my face, dusting it liberally with the big puff. The image the mirror reflected was so pleasing I felt compelled to show myself to Jimmy, the boy who usually sat next to me at the table, and was now playing tag outdoors. Since the powder was dead white, my hair red and my eyes brown, I must have looked clownish, but my first conscious act of coquetry produced the desired effect. On seeing me, Jimmy left the group he was playing with, came over, and tapping me on the shoulder said, "You're it." From then on, it was established that I was Jimmy's girl.

To be boy and girl friend meant, as far as I could make out, that you sat together at mealtime. On walks, you walked together. In games, you played on the same team. If there was nothing much to do, as was the case most of the time, you engaged in a kind of endless tag—the girl running from, being caught up, and tapped on the shoulder by the boy. Not knowing what to do next, you stared at each other until one or the other broke down under the strain and started running again. Only a coughing fit, to which all of us were subject, allowed a temporary respite. It was exhilarating and exhausting.

Cooking and coughing fits kept the housemother busy. If a cough went on too long, she would run to the child taken with the fit, grab its arms, and hold them over its head. In the evening, she checked foreheads, to see if anyone's fever had risen higher than usual. Except for an occasional dose of cough medicine, however, we had no active treatment and, best of all, were never made to stay in bed. I knew Marie had been sick enough to alarm Auntie and Dr. Hess, but, quite exceptionally, despite the low-grade fever

I was running, I felt so well that I wondered if a mistake had not been made in sending me to the Preventorium. Since I was afraid that if this was discovered Marie and I would be separated, I kept my suspicion to myself.

One morning, after we'd been there about a week, we awoke to find the ground blanketed with snow. At the Convent, snow had been an enemy. It kept us indoors. The nuns were convinced that, like the night air, it was dangerous. While it remained on the ground, which it seemed to do interminably, the only pleasure we got from it was looking out the window while it was falling, after which we turned our backs and waited for it to go away. Now (it seemed too good to be true) we were going to be allowed to play in it. After breakfast, dressed in earmuffs, mittens, and mufflers, we hurried after the leader who said he knew the way to the pond. The sun was blindingly bright. In the sharp, clear air, there was the not unpleasant odor of skunk. Deeper and deeper into the woods we trudged, galoshes sinking into the virgin snow, until we came to a clearing. In the valley below was the pond, frozen gray, a waterfall bewhiskered with icicles, and a brook whose rushing water churned around stones dressed with gnomelike caps of snow. As we got closer to the brook, we saw that the bare branches of the trees lining it were filigreed with ice. They formed a cathedral tracery against the cloudless sky. From time to time, there was the sound of chimes as a high branch snapped and fell, striking notes from the branches below.

My experience of nature had been limited to the seaside, to the odors of low tide, the caress of the salt moist air, the heat on one's back as one explored a sandbar looking for shells and, before dinner, the blaze of theatrical sunsets. The beauty of winter was new to me. My playmates were as moved by this magical scene as I was. We stood in silence, taking it in, fearful that it might evaporate before our eyes. Our breaths made clouds of mist before our faces. Another branch fell from the sky, ringing a chime. It sounded against the baseline of the gurgling water in the pond. One of the boys, made uneasy by our silence, broke away and threw a snowball. The spell was broken. The game of tag was on again.

When we got back to the cabin, we changed from our wet clothes into robes and slippers. We made ourselves mounds of cinnamon toast that we washed down with sugary cambric tea. We were content to read or look at picture books quietly, while our wet garments steamed dry before the fire. That night we slept like stones.

The two weeks at the Lower House stand out in my memory as a time of pantheistic bliss. Never before had I known such freedom. Even on vacations at the Hedges, which contrasted strikingly with the rigid routine of convent life, we had followed a prescribed schedule and were closely supervised. There was always an adult close by to say, Do this, do that, don't do the other. But now the French-Canadian housemother was so overburdened with cooking and cleaning that she had no time to keep after us. The only demand she made was that we eat. "Eat! Eat!" she pleaded, as, red-faced from her labors in the kitchen, she put platters of food on the table.

For the rest, we were left on our own, governed loosely, if at all, by the older children who knew how to find a path in the forest, check a hand for chilblains, arrest a cough. It was a period of sweet anarchy. Something told me it was too good to last.

At the end of the incubation period, we boarded the jitney with the others going up the hill. In a brief indoctrination at the administration building, we were told we would be assigned to one of four cottages, two of which were for girls, two for boys. Each consisted of a central or living room, flanked on either side by sleeping porches. Since the porches were unheated, at bedtime we would undress in the heated living room, changing from our daytime to nighttime clothes. In bed, we would wear long woolen underwear, woolen pajamas, knitted caps with earmuffs, booties and mittens.

Our trunks having arrived, we were given our clothing and possessions, assigned a locker for the one, a cubbyhole for the other.

In the living room, as we prepared for bed, the noise and confusion caused by thirty children shouting at the tops of their lungs over the noisy banging of locker doors gave me a splitting headache. There seemed to be so many of them, and they were so *boisterous*. After the quiet of convent life, where the girls glided down corridors, and talked to each other in hushed voices, mimicking nuns, the Preventorium living room sounded like a gymnasium.

Never before having shared a room or undressed in the presence of anyone but Marie, it took me some doing to get out of one set of clothes and into the other without exposing an inch of flesh, eyes averted from the flashing flesh on all sides, as the others stripped openly and athletically (less as though they were disrobing than competing in a rough-and-tumble game). When I was bundled up in my go-to-bed clothes, the matron led me to the sleeping porch. It was a primitive shelter of wood, closed on three sides, the fourth opened to the lawn that led down to the pine woods. Army cots were arranged in three rows, each cot just out of touching distance to the one next to it. Marie and I were placed a row apart.

The first and longest night at Farmingdale I passed in a state of paralyzed alert. My original plan, to spend the night in Marie's bed, had been thwarted by the matron, who, making a bed check and finding us huddled together, led me back to where I belonged. I lay on my cot, crouched under a mound of heavy blankets, every muscle flexed. The cold, starry night stretched out before me when I dared to peek out from under the covers. Mostly I listened for ani-

mal noises. The night was orchestrated with wild cries and
screeches, or so it seemed to me. My sister's bed was too
far away for us to whisper back and forth. I was dressed in
itchy garments, surrounded by sleeping Protestants, exposed to the elements in the dead of winter, to the night
air I had been warned repeatedly was dangerous to the
health. Surely this was a new form of punishment, rather
than a treatment to make us well. I examined my conscience, said the litany of my dead, prayed for my sister, for
Mother Giovanna, Mother Superior, the Convent children.
I prayed also for our misguided relatives, and begged God
to let me survive the night, as Saint Roch had survived
when he, too, had been exposed to the cold.

The first Sunday when we learned there was no church
to go to, we were dumbfounded. How was it possible? The
French-Canadian at the Lower House had said that as we
were in quarantine, we were dispensed. We knew about
dispensations and understood this one. But what possible
excuse could there be for not going to mass now? After an
initial period of disorientation and apprehension, I felt less
guilt than a sense of loss. I was separated from the out-
stretched arms of Mother Church and the comforting proximity of her angels and saints. It was like another death. For
as long as we stayed at Farmingdale, there would be no
mass, no confession, no benediction, no litanies, no processions, no hymn-singing, no feasts, and, as soon became
clear, certainly no fasts. What was offered instead was the
visits of a Lutheran minister, Canon Wells of Trenton, who
came once a month to satisfy the not very demanding
spiritual needs of the community. The other children,
vexed at losing an hour of playtime, wiggled, whispered,
and pinched one another during his homily. My sister and
I, who had been trained to sit quite still and fix our attention on whoever was talking, drank in his (rather confusing)
words. When he asked who had learned the psalm he had
given out the previous month, our hands shot up. Who

were these two girls? So: Catholics. That explained it. It
was enough to make a Lutheran wistful.

Canon Wells took us for little walks after the others had
been dismissed. He asked kindly about our former life,
seemed to understand something the others did not. He
talked about God in a funny way, which made Him seem
both more intimate and more remote. When we mentioned
our Blessed Mother, whose name had been invoked a hundred times a day at the Convent, he seemed a little embarrassed.

I would have liked to talk to him about the crisis of
conscience I was undergoing, but ministers didn't hear
confessions, so I said nothing about the Friday-night showers. The children who had been in residence warned us that
on Fridays after supper there was always weight-taking,
showers, and distribution of clean clothes. They gave us to
understand that we should worry about our weight. It was
essential to show a weekly gain. Failure to do so might
mean that you would have to spend the rest of your life at
the Preventorium, eating cornmeal mush. Mush and milk,
thought to be mighty weight-builders, were the staples of
our diet. Although there was an awful lot of it, the milk slid
down easily enough. But the mush, coarse, tasteless,
lumpy, and copious, was another matter. "Eat! Eat!" the
matron admonished us.

We worried about our weight that first week when what
we should have worried about was the showers. What *was*
a shower? I wondered. At the Hedges, there had been a
garden hose suspended above a wooden platform behind
the hotel where we washed off the sand and salt after a day
on the beach. At Farmingdale, in a basement room to which
we were shown after we'd been weighed, there was a row
of ten showers without partitions. Marie and I watched with
unbelieving eyes, then looked away, as the other girls
stripped, threw their clothes into a pile, and ran naked into
the showers. The noise of their squeals and shouts at being
liberated from the itchy woolens they'd been bundled in

day and night since the previous Friday ricocheted around
the room. Innocent of any training in modesty, they were
as uninhibited as babies.

What were we to do? How could we take a shower without a bathing garment, and in a room full of other girls? We
held back and held back. When the cleaning woman came
to collect the laundry and put out the lights, she found us
in the now empty and silent shower room, limp with misery.
Why hadn't we showered like the others? We hung our
heads. (How could one explain to an atheist?) Did we want
to stay dirty? Did we realize that if we didn't do as we were
told, we wouldn't be able to go to the commissary to spend
our weekly five-cent allowance on candy? Nor would we be
allowed to see the movie that the others were at this very
moment taking places for upstairs. She would give us five
more minutes before reporting us to the matron. Charita-
bly, she withdrew. Without a word, Marie took the shower
at one end, I the shower at the other. Back turned to back,
we took off our clothes, showered, and dressed as quickly
as we could.

So it was with the cooperation of the cleaning woman
that, Friday after Friday, we waited until the others had left
and, keeping immodesty to a minimum, got clean. For
weeks, I wished there were a priest to talk to about this
dilemma, but that was just it: There *was* no priest. Squaring
this part of the Preventorium routine with my conscience
was so difficult that I took little pleasure in spending my
nickel, and sat with eyes closed during the movie. But gradually the enforced nudity began to seem not so much sinful
as disagreeable, like having to eat cornmeal mush. One had
to swallow both. It was all part of getting well, I told myself,
and before long I began to eat my candy with as much relish
as the other children ate theirs, and was no less transported
than they by Tom Mix's derring-do.

Lessons at the Preventorium, in contrast with showers,
were a positive delight. Because classes were held on un-

heated porches like those we slept on, they lasted at most two hours a day. Even dressed in coats, hats, leggings, mufflers, and mittens, the whole ball of wool enfolded in a heavy blanket so that only our faces showed, we could not be expected to remain seated for long without being bitten into by the cold. So at frequent intervals we threw off the blankets and ran single file around the room, clapping time with our mittened hands, our teacher, Miss Barnes, a ball of fur, running and clapping with us.

When it snowed or rained, a canvas drop covered the opening of the classroom and offered partial protection from the elements. If there was a blizzard, we crowded into Miss Barnes's office. With the diversions nature provided, with the physical activities, with lessons on hygiene (a very important subject in our curriculum), with the singing of the national anthem and pledge of allegiance (where formerly we had prayed to the Holy Ghost), there was little time left for reading, writing, and arithmetic. This suited me perfectly.

In late spring, when we no longer needed our blankets, we did our running and breathing outdoors. For lessons, we sat on the grass under the trees. Since it seemed to me that Miss Barnes's aim was less to instruct than to entertain, and her manner was soft, her voice pleasing, I looked forward to these interludes in a regimen otherwise devoted to eating, sleeping, and resting, and hardly thought of it as school at all.

In the springtime, when we dropped our blankets and shed a layer or two of wool, Miss Barnes was metamorphosed from a graceless bear into a flapper. From under the immense fur coat, which had a collar that reached to the top of her fur hat, and a hemline that just cleared the floor, emerged a slim young woman in a dress with a skirt to the knees and high-heel shoes. One day when I returned to the schoolroom after lunch to wash the blackboard, I heard the sound of an automobile coming down the road from the main gate. Out stepped a handsome stranger. Miss Barnes, who had been correcting papers in her office, ran to the door. She greeted the young man in a fluty voice I had never heard her use before. As I was puzzling over this, I saw her twirl around on her high heel to show the young man her new skirt, one she had never worn in class. The young man, who was perhaps less wonderstruck by this display than I was, caught Miss Barnes around the waist as she was coming out of the spin, bent her over his arm, and, before my astonished eyes, kissed her! Dropping the wet sponge, I ran back to Cottage B, my heart knocking against my ribs. Never before had I seen lovers kiss.

The Friday-night movies, worn-out prints of Westerns and slapstick comedies, had prepared me for romantic love as little as had life at the Convent. It had never occurred to me that my teacher might have a life apart from us, her students. Nor had I taken it in that she was a woman. Nuns, matrons, maiden aunts were neuter. Miss Barnes was decidedly feminine. What I had seen was . . . stirring. It gave me something to think about at night, before going to sleep. When I grew up, I, too, would have such a skirt. I would also wear high heels. With practice, I might even be able to warble the way Miss Barnes had done when she greeted "Larrryyy." I had been kissed by my father and my cousin, but only on the cheek. What did it feel like to be kissed on the lips? I thought of Jimmy and wondered how his lips would feel. Was it possible that, despite Mother Giovanna's prediction, I might not have a vocation to be a nun after all?

With the lengthening days, our playtime after supper was extended. Nonetheless we found it harder and harder to get to sleep as the sky outside the cabin remained light. Even the matron's threats to take away our movie and candy didn't settle us down. The older children were especially restless. I became aware that between the girls of Cottage B and the boys of Cottage D a lively and illicit exchange of notes was going on. Declarations of interest were made, rendezvous proposed. During quiet time, letters were written and read aloud:

Dear Milly,
    I don't believe it but Stan says you have a crush on me. Write back.

                                                                    Allen

Dear Allen,
    Stan thinks he's so smart. He thinks he knows it all. Meet me at the club house after supper.

                                                                    Milly

The club house referred to was one of the many shacks made of broken tree branches and discarded pieces of lumber the groundsmen had left and given the boys. These flimsy structures went up quickly and came down with the first strong wind. The younger children, like me, used them for playing hearts, jacks, and checkers. Or for fashioning clappers, primitive castanets on which one sounded out the beat of a popular song, the cutting, sanding, and playing of which had become a craze of even greater intensity than cat's cradle. For thirteen- and fourteen-year-olds, the shacks were trysting places. Had Jimmy been older, our play might have imitated the adolescent couples whose supposedly secret activities we were constantly stumbling upon. But except for the one kiss Jimmy gave me, in his nervousness missing my lips and hitting my nose, he was still mostly interested in running. So we ran. Or occasionally, when he and his pals were building a club house, I held the lumber and branches in place while they tried to hammer in the rusty nails they'd retrieved from a collapsed structure, a tedious business because my arm was always stretched to the limit. But I dared not complain lest a girl with longer arms be found to replace me.
    By the time the blossoms began to appear on the apple trees in the orchard behind the administration building,

there was almost no one who did not have, or pretend to have, a partner. Unlike the inflammatory effect of Larry holding Miss Barnes in a back bend, these crushes and trysts seemed to me awkward and athletic affairs, with lots of pushing, pulling, shoving, and even punching, nothing one would have thought to worry the authorities. Still, the matrons began to monitor chance encounters between the sexes in the dining room, at the commissary, and at the movies, where, when the lights were off, brazen attempts were made to change from the boys' to the girls' side of the room.

Despite this zealousness, the authorities were not able to reduce the hysteria for romance which the warm weather had brought on. A mock wedding of many couples was scheduled to take place under the apple blossoms. Some of the teenage girls took the ceremony so seriously that for days beforehand there were tears, upset stomachs, fits of jealousy, and even a fistfight or two. Luckily for the general sanity of the institution, a band of coldhearted boys, who thought that the wedding was a "dumb game," hid in the branches of the trees, and at the moment the vows and rings (of braided twine) were to be exchanged, jumped down on the nuptial couples, hooting and jeering in a way that killed the pastel prettiness of the scene.

When vacationtime came, the only change in the day's schedule was that there were no more classes. We were free to play outdoors the livelong day, penetrating deeper and deeper into the pine forest.

One night in August, about the time of my ninth birthday, we were awakened in the dead of night by sirens. From our beds, we could see that the sky above the trees was glowing red. "Forest fire! Fire! Fire! Fire!" The word was passed from one bed to another. The matrons, who had dressed quickly, came to reassure us. We were in no danger if we stayed where we were. No one was to get out of bed. Miss Barnes, who appeared with Larry in the middle of the confusion, was told to stay with us while the others went off to help the firemen. All night they passed buckets of sand and pails of water from hand to hand. Some of the big boys, who had been called on to help dig a ditch, came back exhausted and wild-eyed with what they'd seen. All night the sirens screamed as fire trucks came from towns along the Jersey shore. We were keyed up and, assured by Miss Barnes of our safety, happy to have the excitement. It wasn't until the next morning, when the fire was finally extinguished and the whole school went to look at the destruction, that we saw that what had been our limitless playground was now a bare and blackened wasteland. This was the way I had imagined the end of the world would look.

Although I had seen children come and go at Farmingdale, I began to think that we would stay on as long as we had at Dobbs Ferry. Having learned what the matrons expected of me, having become accustomed to sleeping outdoors, to the diet, showers, and even the lean spiritual life, I would have been content to remain. So it came as a great surprise to be told, after one of the monthly checkups, that we were well enough to be discharged. We had stopped coughing and had put on weight. While we were by no means plump, the milk and cornmeal mush had rounded out our cheeks, and they were no longer hectically flushed but bronzed by the sun.

Until recently, when I read the literature on the treatment of tuberculosis, I believed, as I had been told growing up, that the sojourn at the Preventorium had saved our lives. But even at that time, the efficacy of preventoria was in dispute. Many specialists thought that the money would be better spent isolating and treating affected adults. One, Dr. J. Arthur Myers, went so far as to say, "There is not one iota of evidence to show that building up a child's body through care in these institutions protects him in any way from infection from tubercle bacilli if he is later exposed to them." Preventoria, he believed, were even dangerous because they exposed susceptible children to people on the medical and domestic staffs who had been attracted to the jobs because they themselves had active cases. Whatever its therapeutic value, our stay in Farmingdale served useful purposes. We returned to New York looking so healthy that our relatives were no longer afraid we would develop galloping consumption and die on their hands, or that we would infect others with the deadly disease. It also allowed them time (although not as much as they would have liked) to struggle with the seemingly insoluble problem of who should look after us.

In the jitney, we retraced the route we had traveled six months earlier. At Lakewood, we boarded a train, the conductor promising to see that we found the relatives who were meeting us at Pennsylvania Station. What relatives would they be? I wondered. The prohibition against visitors at the Preventorium had made me forget the Sunday-afternoon ache at the Convent. At mailtime, when some of the children talked about mothers or fathers (many had lost one or the other to TB), I talked about aunts and uncles. But since I'd seen little of them since my father's death, they had become shadowy figures. The place called "home" was almost as much an unknown as the Preventorium had been on the journey out. I looked forward to it with no less apprehension.

CHAPTER 5

Inwood

"ORPHAN." I WAS beginning to hate the word. Until I lived on Academy Street, I'd rarely heard it spoken. Now it seemed to me I heard it every day: "orphan." Or, as my new classmates pronounced it, softening it by dropping the *r*, "awfin." What did it mean? That one had lost one's parents, of course. But many other things as well. Since I'd been living at home, what it meant to me was to yearn for my father so intensely that while I continued to pray for him in my night prayers, during the day I imagined him alive. What evidence did I have that he *was* dead? Only the word of adults. And I was learning that they didn't always tell the truth. I had not seen him during his brief illness in the hospital. The man in the coffin so little resembled him it could have been another patient. Or a wax dummy. Wasn't it possible that at this very moment he was trying to find

Marie and me? The next time Auntie lost her temper, and was shouting at us, he would pound on the apartment door, catch us up in his arms, put us in the old Packard, and speed us down to the Village, where we would live forever afterward.

The first thing he'd do would be to take us to Best's and buy us new clothes. In the Convent, where we'd all worn uniforms, clothes had interested me only on procession days, when there had been the excitement of wearing a white dress. At Farmingdale, when we hadn't been wrapped in wool, we'd all worn khaki shorts and white shirts. At public school, everyone wore something different. And what one wore was examined and commented upon. "How come you wear those old-fashioned shoes?" they'd ask. "How come you wear those awful stockings?" The other children went shopping with their mothers, expressed preferences and, within reason, were listened to about what was bought.

Auntie shopped alone and brought home what she thought suitable for us. The dresses were always two sizes too big "because you're growing." The woolen stockings were to keep us from catching pneumonia, and the high shoes were to strengthen our ankles. When Marie, who was far braver than I, protested, saying we wanted to dress like other girls, Auntie said we were not like other girls. Did she mean that we were orphans? Or that we were poor? Or that because we'd been to the Preventorium we needed to protect our health? One time she seemed to mean one of these possibilities; another time, another.

The clothes issue reached a crisis at Easter. At the Convent, we had prepared for the greatest feast of the year with forty days of prayer, with fasting and abstinence. At P.S. 52, a period no less lengthy was devoted to feverish talk about shopping expeditions to buy spring coats, straw hats, and Mary Jane patent-leather shoes. These "outfits" were worn on Easter Sunday and from then on for dress occasions until the hot weather. When we asked Auntie what we were going to wear at Easter, she said we'd wear what we'd worn every Sunday. To buy new clothes for the occasion, she suggested, was vulgar, lower-class, in the same category with buying cheap candy or chewing gum, and going to the Saturday-afternoon movie.

Marie and I decided that the only way to avoid the shame of appearing in our winter clothes was to hide out for the day. We told our friends that we were being taken to visit relatives in Chelsea. To avoid the children's mass at nine o'clock, we got up early and went at seven. The remainder of the day we loitered in the vestibule of a building up the street. We whiled away the hours when the others were out promenading by making up joint fantasies about the lives we'd live when we grew up. We would not become school-teachers (the profession Auntie favored for us), but dancers and, like Mert and Marge (show girls in a radio serial running at the time), we'd have an apartment of our own (Greenwich Village was the preferred site). We'd go to the movies whenever we wanted to and be taken, as were Mert and Marge, to ritzy hotels for dinner and dancing, on which occasion I would wear a white accordion-pleated skirt like the one Miss Barnes had worn.

What we hadn't counted on when we'd decided to hide out on Easter was that we'd have to follow the same routine Sunday after Sunday. Our friends became suspicious, and hiding out became tedious. We decided to go back to the children's mass in our winter clothes and pretend that in our family Easter outfits were worn only on Easter Sunday. We didn't get away with this story, but we stuck to it doggedly, praying for the hot weather to come so we could leave off lying.

Whatever would Daddy have thought of our ill-fitting, old-fashioned, ugly clothes? I wondered when I fell to day-dreaming instead of doing my homework. If he hadn't liked to see us in our uniforms, how much less would he have liked to see us dressed in a way that proclaimed to the world that no one cared how we looked, that we were—here it was again—orphans. Closing my eyes tight, concentrating as hard as I could, I said, "Daddy, *hurry!*"

Our relatives had received the news that we were ready to be discharged from the Preventorium at the moment when the family as a unit was on the point of dissolution. Our paternal grandfather, a man greatly respected in the community and much loved at home, had just died. Not only had he not amassed a fortune from his work as a contractor, as was generally believed, but no sooner had he been buried than creditors presented bills they claimed had never been paid. (As he was a scrupulous man about money, it would have been out of character for him to have left debts; yet receipts for three of the largest bills could not be found among his papers.) Auntie, who had heard her father say many times that a man's soul remained in purgatory until his just debts were paid, felt conscience-bound to honor the bills. On her salary as a teacher this would not be easy, especially since her younger sister, Lucy, whose recent separation from her husband had left her with two young children to raise (the cousins we had played with each summer at the Hedges), earned a very modest salary at the job she'd been forced to take. The Chelsea house being clearly beyond their means, the sisters decided to sell it and look for an apartment. They found one on the same street where their brother Vincent, our guardian, lived at the upper tip of Manhattan Island. Since Vincent's wife had her hands full taking care of their four-year-old daughter, our aunts agreed to take us to live with them—temporarily.

Our aunts were themselves feeling orphaned. They had lost their beloved father, lost the brownstone he had bought after he was mustered out of the Union Army, lost the comfortable style of living his income had made possible, lost a community in which they had known every house and its inhabitants, every store and its owner, lost their parish church with priests and nuns they had known since childhood. To ease the pain of separation, they told themselves they would have frequent reasons for returning to the old neighborhood (which was, after all, only a longish subway ride away), and that the new one was a healthier place in which to raise children.

What I had imagined when I'd fallen in with the Preventorium children's talk about home was the spacious parlor floor in the house on Twenty-eighth Street, and Grandpa, who had a hospitable lap and pockets full of cookies, sitting in his special chair. No one had written to say that the house had been sold, nor that Grandpa had died. Since neither he, nor his chair, was in evidence, I concluded after a few days that he had joined the "dearly departed," and added his name in my prayers. Although I had not known either Grandpa or the Chelsea brownstone intimately, both had been closely associated in my mind with the mysterious word "home" in a way in which aunts, cousins, and an apartment were not.

By contrast with the openness of the buildings at Farmingdale, the apartment (especially the closed-in bedroom) seemed small, dark, and confining. Upholstered sofas, overstuffed armchairs, velvet portieres, mahogany tables, and large standing lamps with fringed lampshades, which had been to scale in the old-fashioned, high-ceilinged rooms in Chelsea, made the new quarters look cluttered and cramped. That first year on Academy Street there seemed never to be enough air, space, or light.

The darkness, I see now, had much to do with mood. Not only were our aunts in mourning, but like many women with children to raise without the financial and moral support of husbands, they were overburdened and low-spirited. They rose early, cooked breakfast, prepared lunch boxes, tidied the house, hurried to work, returned at the end of the day to a round of shopping, cooking, and cleaning up before falling into bed at night. For relaxation and entertainment they had no leisure, money, or even heart. It was a time of raising children, two not theirs, paying debts, also not theirs, a time of fatigue, irritability, and, I suspect, sexual frustration.

Auntie, the older of the two sisters by ten years, dominated the household. With prematurely white hair, no-nonsense clothes and sensible shoes, she looked like the archetypal maiden aunt and old-maid schoolteacher. In theory, she loved children. She had been a second mother to Aunt Lucy, and when Lucy, the violet-eyed beauty of the family, married at seventeen (in the wartime acceleration that made early marriages common among girls of her generation), and had two babies to look after, Auntie energetically assisted in raising them. Now there were the two of us.

In reality, what Auntie loved was not children but babies. Signs of independence in budding personalities—"willfulness" she called it—made her apprehensive. Her defense against it was to impose iron discipline and a clockwork schedule. As we had moved to the sound of bells in Dobbs Ferry, at Academy Street we moved to the command of "Hurry!" We hurried out of bed, hurried to and from school, hurried through our meals, hurried to do our homework so we could hurry to bed. And when it looked to Auntie as though she could not possibly get through all she had to do despite a speed-up of her already demanding pace, she urged us to hurry faster.

Neither discipline nor a clockwork schedule was new to us, of course. What was different in our new life was that where formerly the dramatic action had been played out with a giant cast of characters in a large theater (latterly an open-air one), there was now a small family troupe performing on a narrow, claustrophobic stage. The other players, having been together for years, knew their parts. We, the newcomers, had everything to learn and learn quickly if we were not to provoke the director's displeasure. To help us pick up cues and learn our roles, we became mood-watchers.

What *were* our roles? Home life was so much more intricate than institutional life had been that it was very difficult to make out what was expected of us. The actual presence of parents made things more complicated. They were intimately attached to their children, and their children to them in a way that nuns and matrons could never be. Our classmates had parents. The cousins we lived with had a mother, and an auxiliary mother, Auntie. Our cousin down the street had both mother and father. Not to have parents put one at a distinct disadvantage because they made the rules and could break them. They had the power to soften the discipline, slow the tempo, make exceptions. They bestowed affection on their children, offered them special tidbits at the table, selected their clothes with an eye to what suited them, took account of their preferences, and were indulgent about defects of character (especially those that reflected their own). Parents felt no need to disguise their preferences: they unashamedly preferred their own children. Orphans were outsiders.

Nuns and matrons, on the other hand, were under an obligation to treat those in their care in an evenhanded way. They didn't always succeed, but they tried. Favoritism, where it existed, was expressed in a restrained, covert way. Demonstrations of affection were rare, a pat on the head at most. Although at Farmingdale I had missed the nuns in the beginning, and especially Mother Giovanna, it took me no longer to get used to being an anonymous member of the group than it took me to get used to sleeping outdoors or eating cornmeal mush. I had been so little aware of being a favorite at Dobbs Ferry (as Marie says I was), and had so much associated whatever special attention I received with being sick, that not having it seemed a small price to pay for feeling well and being free to play outdoors with the other children instead of being tied to the infirmary bed.

Now that I saw the point of being a favorite, however, I wanted desperately to be one. But the qualities that had made me attractive to those who had looked after me in the past were insufficiently appealing on Academy Street to counterbalance my failure in school (where it was discovered that I did not know how to read), and the turbulence this failure created at home. I dreaded going to school, and dreaded returning home. In neither place could I be anonymous. At school I was a dunce; at home, a member of a family, but a second-class member, and in very bad standing. (Marie, though a success at school, was no better off than I at home once it was discovered that she was "willful.") So I retreated into daydreams. If Daddy were alive . . .

Time passed and he did not appear. Another man, whom we called Uncle Jack, did. Uncle Jack was tall, rangy, soft-spoken, with something about his gait that permitted me to imagine he might once have been a cowboy (though such a past never figured in the bits of autobiography he offered in answer to our questions). He was a bachelor who, according to Marie, was courting Aunt Lucy. Courting or no, he seemed as much interested in the children in the household as in the adults. Marie and I understood that he had to be particularly attentive to Aunt Lucy's children because if he and Aunt Lucy married (although how could they when she had been married?), he would be our cousins' stepfather. Nevertheless, the well of affection he drew on was so deep he was able to give generous quantities of it to Marie and me as well. When we were sick with measles, mumps, or flu, a time when other adults shunned us, he ignored the quarantine and, sitting at the foot of our bed, entertained us by telling us the plots of the movies playing at Loew's Inwood, with promises that when we were well he would take us there one Saturday. When he kissed us good-night, he was infinitely patient as we clung to his neck, reluctant to let him go, and only put out the light after the second or third reminder from the living room that it was past our bedtime. I fell asleep many nights worrying about his not being a Catholic, praying for his conversion, and wishing my father had known him and made him our guardian.

The night before one of our semiannual checkups by the lung specialists Auntie was always more irritable than usual. She sent us to bed well before the usual hour so that the doctor would find us "rested." Catching her concern that he might discover "something" in the course of his examination, we, too, became apprehensive, with the result that we slept fitfully and woke up tired. On the way to the doctor's office, I felt just as I did before a test in school. My hands and feet were ice cold, my stomach was in a knot, and when the doctor put the stethoscope to my chest I was afraid that the thunder of my heart knocking against my ribs would sound to him like rales in my lungs.

The threat of what the doctor would find became Auntie's most powerful weapon in the struggle over cod liver oil, naps, early bedtimes, and how we should dress. If Marie was "mulish" about having to wear ugly shoes, Auntie's rejoinder was "Your mother caught cold and *died* because she followed her father around the golf course at Lake Placid in thin, silk, dancing slippers. That's what will happen to you if you don't . . ." What was supposed to be a cautionary tale affected us quite differently from the way Auntie intended. The scene created by the words "father . . . golf course . . . thin, silk, dancing slippers" was so evocative of the kind of life we yearned for that I used to repeat the sequence as a kind of chant. And in our joint fantasies, Marie and I added thin, silk, dancing slippers to the wardrobe we'd wear when we grew up.

Discreet as he was, Uncle Jack could not help overhearing Auntie laying down the law to us, and our struggles to be allowed the freedom enjoyed by other girls our ages. He didn't say so, but we felt he was on our side. When he knew Auntie better, he teased her lightly about the strictness of her rules. For any softening of discipline or relaxation of routine, we knew we had him to thank. (He was so commonsensical, so reasonable, I more and more thought he would have made an ideal guardian.) Certainly it was he who arranged for us to see a few selected movies that would have passed even the most severe board of censors. Usually they were Westerns, or the melting pot dramas so popular at the time, like *Abie's Irish Rose*. The one that made the strongest impression on me was *For the Love of Mike*.

Three bachelors, one Irish, one Jewish, one Italian, who run a dry-goods store on the Lower East Side, find an abandoned baby on their doorstep and decide to raise him themselves. Doting on Mike, as they call him, they compete with one another in showering him with affection and attention. The boy gives them great pleasure over his success in school, great pain over his failure in college. In the end, he marries a girl acceptable to all three, and the foster fathers look forward to having grandchildren.

It would have been difficult to find a story richer in material for my purposes. After Auntie warned us about kidnappers, with dire tales of what happened when they got hold of children, instead of being afraid of being abducted, I yearned to be. People outside the family always made a great fuss over us for some reason, so I didn't see why kidnappers should be any different. *For the Love of Mike* suggested an even more satisfactory scenario. I rewrote the script, changing the boy into a girl, the foundling into an orphan. The foster fathers would be Uncle Jack, the man in the dairy who asked every time I went to buy eggs if I wouldn't like to be his little girl, and our dentist, Dr. Glickman.

Of all the children in the neighborhood Dr. Glickman treated, and he treated them all, Marie and I were his favorites. As he told us repeatedly, he thought the most terrible thing that could happen to a child was for it to be orphaned. How could one grow up without a mother? Only she could understand her offspring, take care of them when they were sick, see that they were nourished properly so that their teeth grew in strong, only she could make them happy. How I must miss my mother! I listened to his lament for my motherless state grateful for his sympathy, but mystified. As far as I knew, I had never missed my mother. She had always been for me a celestial spirit, an angel rather than a flesh-and-blood woman. And having lived for years with other motherless children, I found it difficult to see orphanhood as a state rich in drama, or as needful of compassion as he did. And besides, it was a father I needed, not a mother. Looking gloomy, Dr. Glickman would say, "You don't understand now because you're just a kid. When you grow up, you'll see."

I tried not to be alarmed, though it always gave me a shiver, when he predicted that life would be hard for us in the future, because it was dreams of the future that made tolerable the dreary present.

Dr. Glickman treated all our relatives who lived on Academy Street and, as he frequently told me, "had the dope on them" ("Patients talk to dentists, so if they keep their ears open they learn a lot"). While he worked on my teeth, he analyzed our aunts' and our uncle's characters, and told me things about them I didn't know. He was critical of Auntie's severity (and told her so), but admiring of her intelligence and energy. She meant well. Could she help it if she was cut out to be the principal of a school and not a mother? "If your parents hadn't died, she would have had a much freer life, go traveling—the way unmarried teachers do." Aunt Lucy's marriage had been ruined by the war from which her husband returned a shell-shocked wreck. She looked like a Follies girl, but if any man made eyes at her he'd find out she was as reserved as a nun. She was a more motherly type than her sister, at least with her own kids. Uncle Vincent he openly disliked. Between the two men there was an ongoing dispute about dental bills, especially ours. "You have money of your own, you know, and don't let anyone try to tell you you don't." When I looked blank, as I always did when he said this, he'd get more heated and say, "Don't let them treat you like a charity case."

Money of our own? I would have liked to ask about this at home, but the person who would know about it, if anyone did, was Uncle Vincent, and I couldn't imagine asking him. I knew Uncle Vincent far less well than I knew Dr. Glickman. Although we called him "Uncle," and kissed him on the cheek in greeting, he didn't seem like a relative. So it always surprised me to be reminded that he was Daddy's older brother. How could he be so sour when our father had been so full of fun? He smoked cigars instead of sweet-smelling Murads, disapproved of dancing, and gave us the impression that we caused him grave and needless concern.

One Sunday during the second year we lived on Academy Street, we were summoned for a conference at his apartment after mass. Putting a light to his cigar, he said we had a relative we didn't know. Keeping us in suspense, he pulled on the cigar, puffpuff, to be sure it was lit. Another relative? Who could that be? It was a great-uncle, our maternal grandfather's younger brother. This great-uncle had been searching for us since we'd left the Convent (just as I had imagined Daddy doing!) and had finally traced us to Academy Street. He and his wife had been very fond of our mother and her sister, and had been brokenhearted at their deaths. Having had no children of their own, they had adopted the son of a distant and overburdened relative who'd been widowed. But the boy was now away at prep school and came home only for the holidays. They wanted very much to see us and asked if we might spend part of our next vacation at their house in Westchester.

Uncle Vincent, a cautious man, said he had thought it over for some time, and seeing no harm in it, had agreed. We would go for Christmas. He prepared us for the visit as if for an examination. We must remember to make our beds every morning, leave the bathroom in perfect order, tub scrubbed, towels neatly folded, sink wiped clean. Halfway through his talk I came to and realized that he was no longer giving us needless instruction about how to behave (all this we had learned in our boarding school days), but had moved on to how to answer questions our relatives might ask us. Having missed the beginning of what he was saying, I was lost. It all seemed so complicated that even when he repeated his instructions the morning we were to be called for, I couldn't take them in. Besides, I was in a state of high excitement about the visit and could think of nothing else.

At the sound of the doorbell, Marie and I sprang to our feet. Uncle Charlie and Aunt Hilda, brushing aside formalities, held us in tearful embraces. Joyfully, they exclaimed over my sister's likeness to our mother: she was her double. And was I not the picture of our mother's sister, Eleanor? My guardian demurred: I was just like my father. Yes, yes, perhaps a little of both. Well, it was wonderful to have found the children at last. It was like having the girls alive again.

While the adults, who had met only at our parents' wedding and their funerals, made polite conversation, the one side recounting the steps in their search, the other our moves since we'd left the Convent, we stole glances out the window at the bottle-green chariot that was going to carry us off. Beside it, our new cousin, Albert, was attempting to keep the more audacious children, boys mostly, from crawling over and even under its sleek, highly polished body. I wished my friends would behave with more dignity. For the first time, I saw that there was another measure by which their conduct could be judged. Already I had a hint of what it would be like to be torn between two milieus, Inwood and Westchester.

CHAPTER 6

Westchester

THE PIERCE-ARROW, its shining grille topped by a winged Mercury that promised a performance of speed and grace, pulled smoothly away from the curb, leaving behind an openmouthed crowd of curious neighbors. In the backseat sat Uncle Charlie, ruddy, jovial, a derby hiding his sandy-red hair. Aunt Hilda was in a velvet toque and a seal coat. Next to us, behind the driver's wheel, was Cousin Albert, handsome and debonair, with a profile like a movie star's. Strangers, all three. What would it be like to spend ten days in their company?

Albert, who according to Aunt Hilda had just obtained his license, was already so skillful a driver that he could steer the car with one hand, leaving the other free for smoking maneuvers. He tapped out a cigarette on the wheel, lit it with the burning ember of a lighter that popped out of the mahogany dashboard, and sent two jets of smoke

streaming from his nostrils with the drama that only someone who had recently been granted permission to smoke
could bring to these newly acquired gestures.

We had crossed into the upper reaches of the Bronx and
were speeding along the Sawmill River Parkway when Albert addressed Marie and me for the first time. "Want a
thrill?" When we nodded shyly, he put both hands on the
wheel and accelerated. The automobile flew over a triad of
rises and dips in the road, maintaining only the barest
contact with its surface. The roller-coaster effect was such
a success on this first trip that ever after, at Christmas, at
Easter, and at the beginning of summer vacation until we
were adults, Albert accelerated for the thank-you-ma'ams.
En route to Laurel Place, they made my heart swell. En
route to Academy Street, they caused it to shrivel.

Uncle Charlie, I decided even before we reached the
turnoff to his house, was going to be easy to love. He
seemed so genuinely delighted to have found us, so eager
to make up for lost time. Showing us to the pretty guest
room, which was decorated in flowered chintz and flooded
with sunlight, he made it clear in his jolly, bustling way that
vacation time was party time. For parties, girls needed
something pretty to wear, which a cursory glance into
Daddy's Gladstone made clear we had not brought with us,
so after lunch Aunt Hilda took us off on a shopping expedi-
tion. At Ware's, in New Rochelle, she unwittingly followed
our father's holiday pattern, buying us each a party dress,
taking us to the store barber and then the store photographer to have our pictures taken. On a table in the living
room from then on, next to the photographs of Albert and
Irene Dunne (a friend of the family), were the current year's
photographs of Marie and me. In that first picture, I wore
an ice-blue taffeta dress. In subsequent years, the dresses
were green velvet, yellow crepe de chine, honey-colored
pongee—I remember them all with pleasure (though the
photographs have long since disappeared)—my first evening gown and, finally, the white satin wedding dress

which, though they were by then having "financial difficulties," she had bought me to wear the day Uncle Charlie led me down the aisle at the Lady Chapel of St. Patrick's Cathedral to give me away in marriage.

Uncle Charlie was not, as we thought when we were children, a rich man. "Just comfortable," he told me once when I was older but before the shadow of bankruptcy fell over him. What he was, was an aesthete. His house was small by comparison with the sprawling mansions of his neighbors, but everything about it, from floor plan to bibelots, expressed his highly developed taste. It was, as I heard a neighbor say, "a little jewel box."

It was generally agreed that Uncle Charlie had an eye— an eye for form, color, arrangement. As a boy, academic subjects had not interested him, as they had his brothers, my maternal grandfather, who became a lawyer, and the youngest of the three, Mathew, who taught astronomy at Cooper Union. After a period of resistance, his parents allowed Uncle Charlie to pursue what had been a precocious fascination with the rings, brooches, and beads he had seen his mother and other women wear, by apprenticing him to a Maiden Lane jeweler, who in conversation was always referred to as "the Old Man." When the Old Man retired, Uncle Charlie made the mistake (a fatal one, for anxiety over the bankruptcy proceedings caused the heart attack that killed him) of buying the business. But when we first met him, he was the Old Man's chief designer, and was leading the "just comfortable" life that allowed him to have a Pierce-Arrow, and to have built not a mansion but a jewel box house.

One day while I waited in the sun room for Aunt Hilda to take me visiting with her, I leafed through an architectural magazine that was on the glass-topped table. To my astonishment, I came across a picture of the house I was staying in. Seeing Laurel Place in print, with floor plans and photographs, I became aware of a difference between the two sides of my family that I had been feeling throughout the vacation, but had not been able to articulate to myself. My mother's people cared how things looked. When the hostility between the two sides of the family became overt, as they were soon to do, Auntie and Uncle Vincent hinted that that was all they cared about. This was not true, though it must have seemed so to my father's people who (all but my father) had, where creature comforts were concerned, a decidedly puritanical streak.

Uncle Charlie was strikingly different. He was also a man who loved parties of all kinds. For our visits, he and Aunt Hilda rounded up their friends and their friends' children for luncheons, dinners, evening sleigh rides, afternoons of roller-skating at Rye Beach. In the summer, there was swimming at Glen Island and, when we were older, dancing with Cousin Albert and one of his friends at the Casino. There were picnics at Compo Beach with fitted wicker baskets, a leather case holding a silver cocktail shaker and glasses from which the adults had their cocktail. (The word was always in the singular, since they had only one, until Albert and his friends suggested that if one cocktail was good, two would be better.) It was from this cocktail shaker that I had my first head-spinning Sidecar.

Parties and outings were especially intoxicating because they were arranged—it seemed hardly possible—for us. But what I remember with even greater pleasure was everyday family life. The tempo of the day quickened when Uncle Charlie's leather heels struck the flagstones on the path leading up to the house. We ran to greet him as he came up from the city, the evening paper folded under his arm, tidbits of gossip he had picked up on the New York Central on his lips. "I'll just take a minute to change," he'd say after kissing us. We'd wait impatiently for him to come downstairs again, as he would do in an hour, his cheeks pink from a hot bath and fragrant with Pinaud's eau de cologne. (Not having lived in close proximity to a man since the holiday visits to Daddy's flat, my senses reveled in the odor of shaving cream and eau de cologne, the roughness of tweeds, the smoothness of the plush on a top hat, the softness of chamois gloves.)

The evening meal he made into a fête. It was not the fare so much as the flourishes. He readjusted the table silver, rearranged the centerpiece, shuttled back and forth from the pantry to the kitchen, supervising, interfering, getting in Aunt Hilda's way, until it was time to sit down. His carving of the roast was a mime that said: we must get as much pleasure out of this bird or joint as we can. He urged us to eat for the enjoyment of eating rather than because he wanted us to gain weight. If there was wine with the meal (sparkling burgundy was in fashion in Westchester), we must have a little in our glasses. At Academy Street, children were to be seen and not heard. At Uncle Charlie's table, they were encouraged to take part in the conversation.

If no formal entertainment was planned after dinner, and if Albert was not going to a dance, he might take us to a movie. A heady combination: the movies and Albert. Luckily he was not our *real* cousin, for how could we have resisted falling a little in love with a young man who every other night put on evening clothes and, looking like an ad in *Vanity Fair* or *Esquire* (both of which were also on the table in the sun room), went to a prom. When he began to bring a date along to the family picnics, Marie and I were still young enough to be thrilled to be invited to ride in the rumble seat of his roadster instead of in the Pierce-Arrow with the adults. Later, we hated the rumble seat and the date. Why couldn't we sit in front? What did he need with another girl when he had the two of us?

Over the years, Albert taught us a good many growing-up things: how to whistle, how to watch a football game and make appropriate remarks about the plays, how to smoke and blow rings, how to play bridge, how to drink. That first vacation he showed us how to dance the "Westchester," and taught us a new vocabulary with words like "weird" and "smooth" and "nifty." It was with Albert that we first drank too much, stayed up all night to see the dawn, went to a nightclub, saw Sally Rand's fan dance. When Albert began to have sexual adventures, he told us about them, obliquely. Later he attempted to round out our knowledge about the facts of life, inaccurately.

On prom nights, after the scene that always accompanied Albert's attempts to tie his bow tie, after Aunt Hilda's unheeded plea for him to drive cautiously, Uncle Charlie sat down at the grand piano. His fingers raced over the keys in a warm-up before playing arias from Italian operas or hit tunes from Broadway musicals he and Aunt Hilda had been to. Aunt Hilda, who confessed she was not musical, nevertheless enjoyed these evenings when Uncle Charlie played and Marie and I sang. From her place on the couch, she would come out of a doze and say, "Charlie, isn't it *just* like having the girls alive again."

Had our Westchester relatives never given us a party or bought us a dress, had they not given us an aperture on another way of life, they would still have had a privileged position in our affections because they had known "the girls," our mother and her sister. In those days, they were the only people we knew who had known our mother, known her from infancy until her death. Our Academy Street relatives could tell us a good deal, though never enough, about our father. When Auntie and Aunt Lucy were in good humor, particularly during summer vacations when they were less ground down by the pressures of life, they could be coaxed to reminisce about the old days in Chelsea. They had a fund of anecdotes about our father's school days, his brushes with the Jesuit prefect of discipline, his canoe trips with his brothers, his bachelor days reading law, his tea-dancing courtship with our mother, their brief marriage, his role as a father. Excellent storytellers, they made the past come alive with their wit and skillful mimicry.

It was Uncle Charlie and Aunt Hilda who blew a little life into our mother's statue. They had known her so intimately

they called her by a nickname we had never heard before.
To them she was "Molly." "Molly always played the piano
while waiting for a beau to take her to a dance," Uncle
Charlie would say. What would she play? we wanted to
know, greedy for details. "Now let me think." He'd flip
through the sheet music in the piano bench. "Here's one
she was fond of." Adjusting his pince-nez, he'd play Bee-
thoven's "Für Elise" or Chopin's "Minute Waltz."

Aunt Hilda, studying us in the new dresses she'd bought,
would say, "Molly and Eleanor had a reputation for being
stylish. How they could carry clothes!" When we asked
what they wore, Aunt Hilda would say, "Charlie, where are
those photographs of the girls we took at Lake Placid?"
This would call for a visit to the attic to look through old
albums. In the attic were also stored objects belonging to
our mother that Uncle Charlie had bought from our father's estate to give to us when we married. On rainy days,
we were allowed to play with our mother's table silver,
which was wrapped in plum-colored felt bags, her Art Nou-
veau dresser set with brushes she used on her "glorious
chestnut hair that went down to her waist," a pair of black-
and-white China spaniels she had used for doorstops.

Although Aunt Hilda and Uncle Charlie found it painful
to talk about their nieces' deaths—"It still seems hardly
possible that *both* should be taken so young"—it was from
them we picked up, a little at a time, most of the details
about our mother's illness. At a moment when she was
leading the heady social life, with tea dances and parties, of
girls of her set before they married, she came down with a
cold that dragged on and on. Her persistent cough, lack of
appetite and fatigue, aroused the family doctor's suspicion
that she, like her father (and perhaps from helping to nurse
him), had become tubercular. Molly must be sent away, the
doctor said.

By the time she went to the Trudeau Sanitarium on Saranac Lake, it had become world famous, and catered to a
cross section of society that included royalty, movie stars,

and gangsters. There were amenities of all kinds, but for bed patients there was little to do but look up at the ceiling, or out at the snow, or wait for the high point of the day, the doctor's visit. In the first stage of treatment, immobilization was very strict (far stricter than in Europe) and very difficult for patients to tolerate. Any activity, even reading (and crying!), was forbidden. They were washed, toileted, swaddled against the bitter cold, and fed from overloaded trays of food that arrived five times a day. Under such a regimen it was hardly surprising that many left prematurely, especially as they often were convinced that they were cured. Molly left, had a relapse, returned, left again, and, a year later, when she supposedly was well, married. She had Marie, came down with what was thought to be influenza, recovered, had me, had another relapse and eleven months later was dead. Eleanor's story was almost identical, but though she, too, married, she died so soon thereafter that she left no orphans.

Westchester holidays, especially that first one, were not without discomforts that come from a shift in milieu. An expanded social life exposed us to snobbery and prejudices of which Inwood was innocent. Clothes were an even more painful problem on these holidays than they were with our school friends. Party frocks were lovely, but one couldn't wear them every day, and Aunt Hilda could not replace everything we'd brought in the Gladstone without giving offense to Auntie and Uncle Vincent. What looked merely comically old-fashioned on Academy Street was judged by our new, bourgeois playmates (who pretended to believe that we wore them by choice!) as reflections of poor taste. And how come we were going to P.S. 52 instead of the Religious of the Sacred Heart when nobody but the maid's children went to public school?

Although Auntie had said many times that convent schools encouraged snobbery with their homogeneous student bodies, and were poor preparation for a life in which one needed to get along with people of all classes and all religions (as, she implied, orphans especially would have to do), I had a secret yearning to attend the Westchester Sacred Heart Convent. It was run by a different order from the Dobbs Ferry one. These nuns were called "madame" instead of "mother," they spoke French instead of Italian, they looked little older than the girls in the graduating class, and they seemed to cosset the ten or so pupils in each grade in a way a public school teacher, who had forty or so students to look after, could not possibly do.

When I was a little older, I realized that the deeper charm of the Westchester convent, which I visited with Aunt Hilda when she called on the mother superior to discuss "the little prize" she and Uncle Charlie offered at commencement, was that the school my mother attended was not unlike it (certainly more like it than like P.S. 52). Had I gone to my mother's kind of school, I would have studied from the same syllabus. This would have permitted me to make up imaginary conversations with her. "Didn't you hate fractions?" I could have said. Or, "Weren't you dying to get on the basketball team?" I felt sure that her answers would have made a bond between us.

At home, it was my father I daydreamed about; in Westchester, my mother. While I never looked for substitutes for her, as I did for my father, it was during these holidays that for the first time I could imagine, if dimly, that she had had an earthly existence. Tentatively Marie and I began to use the word "mother" not to signify a nun, but the woman who bore us. Playing in the attic, we'd say, "Pass me Mother's mirror." Or, of a photograph, "Which one do you think was prettier? Mother or Aunt Eleanor?" The word sounded theatrical, as if we were playacting, but I felt I had a right to use it, and every time I did it stirred me deeply.

At Sunday dinner, the final day of our first vacation, we found at our places the first of the many small velvet-lined jewel boxes we would receive from Uncle Charlie. A ring! Mine had a stone as clear and watery as the sea. An aquamarine, Uncle Charlie said, the color of the Mediterranean. It was a young girl's ring, one to look into and dream of sun playing on water, of holidays, of exotic countries, and a far-off time when she would have escaped the servitude of childhood. But since she was still just a girl, she had now to go upstairs and make ready to go back to Academy Street.

Albert backed the Pierce-Arrow out of the garage. Dusk, descending on the wintry landscape, filled me with melancholy. We were leaving behind the comfortable suburban mansions, their snow-covered lawns decorated with lighted fir trees, their glittering windows suggesting that for those not transients there was time for yet one more party before the holidays were over. As Albert turned onto the parkway, and accelerated to take the three rolls, the crisis of conscience that had been hanging over me like a black cloud, threatening to spoil the vacation from the very beginning, broke with the violence of an electrical storm.

Lies, lies, lies. Between the parentheses of thank-you-ma'ams, Marie and I had told hundreds, thousands, millions of lies. Wishing my way back to innocence, as we drove through the gritty streets of the Bronx where snow was not a sparkling entertainment but a dirty-gray burden, I tried to recall the question that had evoked the first, the capital lie that had made necessary all the others. It had begun harmlessly enough with the usual questions adults ask children to make conversation. Where did we go to school? Aunt Hilda and Uncle Charlie wanted to know. What grades were we in? What were our teachers' names? We had lost our initial shyness and had got into the catechetical swing, so we hadn't been on guard when Aunt Hilda asked us what room we slept in.

In the briefing session at Uncle Vincent's apartment, he had told us that for good reasons, but reasons children could not understand so he would not trouble us with them, we were to "pretend" that we were living with him. He gave a great many other instructions, perhaps even what to say should we be asked where we slept, but because I had been woolgathering, I missed them. Inexperienced and untalented liars that we were, we showed Uncle Charlie and Aunt Hilda by our temporizing and contradictory statements that we were inventing on the spot.

We had our own room (true).

Where was it?

Where??? Next to the kitchen, I said. Next to our cousin's, Marie said.

Aha! Just as Aunt Hilda had suspected. Our guardian was hiding something. A sweeping but practiced glance around his apartment had told her that there were only two bedrooms, one he and his wife shared, the other for their daughter. Did we sleep on a couch in the living room? No. Then we must be living elsewhere. Where? Aunt Hilda knew she shouldn't keep at us, but she couldn't resist trying "to get to the bottom of the thing," as we heard her say when Albert, seeing our mounting distress and confusion, came to our rescue, saying, "For God's sake, Aunt Hilda, *stop pumping.*"

By an unspoken agreement Marie and I didn't discuss our dilemma during the day (we were determined not to let it spoil our fun), but in bed at night, thanks to our old training in the examination of conscience before going to sleep, we could avoid it no longer. What could we do? we wondered, trying, with increasing hopelessness, to coordinate our stories for the following day. There was a straightforward way out: we had only to tell the truth. But that would mean disloyalty to our guardian and, more important, to our father's side of the family. There was nothing to do, we agreed in whispers, but to go on lying.

The Pierce-Arrow pulled up to the curb outside Uncle Vincent's apartment. We kissed our relatives good-bye and nodded, disbelievingly, at their talk about the next vacation, at Easter. Would we ever see them again? Might they not drop us, pathological liars that we'd shown ourselves to be, as suddenly as they'd taken us up? I wanted to cry out the truth (What was the truth? By this time I no longer knew for sure) and beg to be taken back to Laurel Place. Instead I followed Marie out of the car. Clutching each other's hand, we walked into the eye of the storm that was about to break over our heads.

CHAPTER 7

Hanover

THE SURROGATE COURT of the State of New York had become actively interested in the welfare of two of its wards some months before the visit to Westchester. A letter written on official paper, signed and sealed by a judge, reinforced Uncle Vincent's previously unfocused anxiety that his was not to be an untroubled guardianship. The Tully side of the family was stirring up trouble. Among other things, they were demanding the right to visit the children.

Uncle Charlie Tully had no way of knowing that his first letter, arriving in the mail at approximately the same time as this alarming missive, could not but arouse suspicion that he was in league with the troublemakers. The story of searching for his great-nieces, of wanting to do something for them, was an unconvincing fiction. Or was it? If it was fact, would it not be wise to grant his request, thereby gaining an ally instead of swelling the ranks of the enemy?

After weeks of turning the matter over in his mind, and discussing it with his sisters, Uncle Vincent decided on a compromise. He would agree to the visit, but should the "Westchester connection" be engaged in espionage, it would be given to understand, as was understood by the Court and the Other Side, that the orphans were domiciled where they were supposed to be, under their guardian's roof.

Had not children been involved in this deception, all might have gone as planned, but as became dismayingly clear shortly after we alighted from the Pierce-Arrow, children, at least two, could not be trusted. Saboteurs, they had not only poured sand in the machinery; they had also allowed themselves to be caught in the act. Aiming an accusatory finger at Marie and me, Uncle Vincent thundered, "Do you *realize* what you've done?"

That we were terrible liars we needed no one to tell us. That we had played into the hands of our father's enemies came as a sickening surprise. In the days during which the cross-examination continued—What else had Aunt Hilda wanted to know? What had we said then? And then? And then?—we learned that our maternal grandmother (whom we had not seen or heard of since our father's funeral) had turned into a wicked old woman, who with the help of the judge and the court was menacing life on Academy Street. The immediate result of her lawsuit, and our lies, was that we were in danger of losing our newfound Westchester relatives to whom we had already become strongly attached.

The Wicked Witch. The Judge. The Court. These figures, gigantesque and caricatured, like the *cabezudos* in a Spanish procession, haunted my dreams, growing more monumental and threatening every night. Then another of those small but timely miracles occurred. A new letter arrived from Uncle Charlie. With disarming compliments for the way we were being brought up, and a diplomatic turn of phrase about what from now on was called "the misun-

derstanding," he made it clear that he had no wish to inter-
fere with whatever living arrangements our guardian had
made for us. He wanted, quite simply, to be allowed to
continue seeing us, and proposed dates for a visit at Easter.

We were so overjoyed to hear that we had been invited
again, and that Uncle Vincent was accepting the invitation,
that we were less observant than usual and didn't notice
that he was as relieved and pleased by the letter as we were.
The Wicked Witch, the Court, and the Judge became characters in a storybook that was closed and, for the moment,
put on the shelf.

The home to which we returned after our guardian had
finally dismissed us, exhausted and red-eyed, at the end of
that Christmas holiday, was now headed by Aunt Lucy. It
was the same apartment, although smaller-seeming and
darker after ten days at Laurel Place, but the most important personage was now missing. Auntie had gone away. If
we were given an explanation for her disappearance (perhaps that she was on sabbatical leave?), I don't remember
it. Habituated to impermanence, and trained not to be
inquisitive, I accepted without question that Aunt Lucy
would now look after us.

Aunt Lucy's reign was in many ways more easygoing than
her older sister's had been. If Auntie's view of childhood
was that it should be a disciplined preparation for life,
which was bound to be hard, especially for children without
parents, Aunt Lucy looked upon it as a carefree time before
the crushing burdens of adulthood descended: her biography in capsule. The only thing that gave purpose to the
drudgery of her days was the sense that she was doing what
she could to make her son and daughter happy. And since
we lived under the same roof with them, we were allowed
some, but by no means all, of the simple pleasures they
enjoyed.

Near the end of the year with Aunt Lucy, I was out roller-
skating with my friends one evening after dinner when,
rounding the corner of Post Avenue at high speed, I

crashed into Uncle Vincent. With my hair flying, my blouse hanging out of my skirt, I looked, he said, when he regained his balance, "not at all like a little lady but like a tomboy." Because of his displeasure at my wild appearance, I was not surprised that in a few days Marie and I were summoned to his apartment for another conference. He was distressed, he said, to find that with a report card as poor as mine, I did not feel that I should devote my evenings to studying instead of racing around the streets with the neighborhood hoodlums. Then, addressing both of us, he said he had been thinking a good deal about our future. We were coming of an age . . . he puffed on his cigar . . .

Marie and I telegraphed each other a look: something was up.

. . . when we required closer supervision than Aunt Lucy could give us. He and his wife, had decided, puffpuff, that it was time they took us to live with them.

Marie and I sat up a little straighter.

It would require a move to a larger apartment.

No immediate threat then.

One in the building was promised for September.

This *coming* September? Whatever complaints we had about Aunt Lucy's handling of us, we suspected that it was as easygoing a regime as we could hope for, and that Uncle Vincent's supervision would be so close as to allow little freedom of movement or opinion.

We would remain with Aunt Lucy until the end of the school year and, after a visit to Westchester, would go to New Hampshire to spend the summer with Aunt Helen, Uncle Vincent's wife, in her mother's house in Hanover.

The transfer from one address to another, also on Academy Street, was accomplished with little outward fuss. Inwardly, we felt that we were being moved to a foreign country, where people would speak a new language and there would be a whole new set of laws to live by. But for the moment it was vacation time and since Aunt Helen and our cousin had gone up to Hanover before school closed,

Marie and I were to make the overnight trip, our first, on
our own. Uncle Vincent took us to Grand Central and put
us on the train. The porter promised to look after us en
route, and see to it that we detrained at White River Junction. Marie was thrilled by the adventure. I tried to be.
When I could master my uneasiness about whether Aunt
Helen would really be at our stop to meet us (what would
we do if she was not?), I enjoyed everything about the trip
that gave me a foretaste of adult life. Marie and I were on
our own, we had a little money, and there was no one to tell
us what to do except for the dignified porter who treated
us as if we were young ladies.

The night in a lower berth, which Marie and I shared, had
an hallucinatory quality that made difficult the separation
of dreaming from waking periods. The sound of the wheels
racing along the track was amplified by the pillow. In the
aisle, lurching figures made grotesque bulges against the
curtain and seemed on the verge of stumbling in on us. If
we dozed off, we were awakened by the cessation of motion
as the train pulled into a station, or, more mysteriously,
braked and screeched to a halt in the middle of nowhere,
and remained there for what seemed a very long time.
Peering around the window shade, we could see the moon
and stars, fields and forests, but no sign of life. As inexpli-
cably as it had stopped, the train would start up again with
a jerking motion, and we would be hurtled through another
state on our journey north.

Order was restored with the return of daylight, the folding away of bedding, the reassembling of Pullman seats,
and the appearance of the friendly porter to tell us that
breakfast was ready in the forward car. By midmorning, the
thrill of being treated like an adult had become eroded, in
my case, by the fears of a young girl. The money Uncle
Vincent had given Marie having been spent, we would be
arriving at our destination with empty pockets, and only the
promise that we would be met by a woman who had been
so self-effacing on the occasions when we had been called

to our uncle's apartment that she was almost a stranger.

It was just as I had imagined it would be. The porter helped us down, the other passengers were met and departed. The train pulled out, we were alone on the platform. I felt a gust of panic. In New York City if one were stranded there was always a policeman nearby who, we'd been instructed, was the person to apply to for help. At our familiar railway stations, Grand Central and Pennsylvania, there was also the Travelers Aid Society. Unlike the enclosed terminals we were used to, White River Junction was a naked mass of crisscrossed tracks, freight trains, pyramids of packing cases, baggage carts piled high with trunks, and gates that were raised and lowered by unseen signals. There was no one to turn to.

Marie, in her habitual way, was putting up a brave front. Although she must have been frantically turning over in her mind what we should do, she said if we just waited a little while Aunt Helen was bound to show up. And so she did. The suntanned woman who came running toward us, wearing a tennis dress and sneakers, her hair in a bandeau, looked so much younger than Uncle Vincent's wife that I didn't recognize her. They'd had a flat tire a mile or so away, she said breathlessly, and had had to wait for a farmer to come by to help change it. Crossing from Vermont into New Hampshire, Aunt Helen and her friend, the owner of the old Ford, giggled like schoolgirls as they described the adventure they'd had on the way over.

As became clear during the weeks that followed, a summer vacation in Hanover, the town she'd grown up in, allowed this harassed mother of an active and precocious five-year-old, this wife of a finicky and dour husband, to recapture the lightheartedness of her youth. With her own mother to run the house and look after the little girl, Aunt Helen was free to sleep late in the morning, play tennis and swim in the afternoon, and visit with her girlhood friends in the evening.

At the white clapboard house on School Street, her

mother came out to greet us. Mrs. Geery embraced us in
a way which, if translated into words, would have said,
"Poor motherless girls! How can one make up to them for
their loss?"

But after the first rush of emotion, this white-haired,
pink-cheeked woman, who in termtime ran a boardinghouse for Dartmouth undergraduates and was used to
mothering young men, treated us with the kind of absentminded solicitude familiar to us from the French-Canadian
at the Lower House at Farmingdale. She saw that we were
comfortably installed in the large front bedroom on the
ground floor, prepared for us the kind of meals that had
given her a reputation among the undergraduates of being
the best cook in town, introduced us to two families down
the street with girls our ages, and left us to come and go
as we pleased.

To be left on our own meant we were freer of constraint
than we had been since the golden days of quarantine at
Farmingdale. After breakfast, we set off for the day with
picnic lunches and no instructions except to be back at
dinnertime. The Barwood sisters, our neighbors, seemed
delighted to show two city girls around. On good days, they
took us on hikes in the foothills of the White Mountains, or
for a thrill closer to home, to the top of the ski jump, where
we sat on a shaky platform and ate peanut butter sand-
wiches washed down with grape juice, trying hard to control vertigo by not looking at the ground. They also showed
us how to sneak into Dartmouth's small natural history
museum, which was closed during the summer, so that we
could see the mummy on the top floor. They swore they
had seen it move when it thought no one was looking. We
looked at it with fascinated horror, waiting for a sign of life,
and when we thought we saw one ran down four flights of
stairs and out through the basement window to safety.
They showed us how to ride bikes; we taught them how to
dance.

The first time they invited us to go to the movies, we

asked Aunt Helen for permission with little hope of being allowed to go. Uncle Vincent did not approve of movies— at least for us. Before there could be any discussion about it, Mrs. Geery said she could see no reason in the world why not. And what was more astonishing was that when Mr. Barwood, who owned the theater, invited us to accompany his daughters to the twice-weekly showings as his guests, and Aunt Helen said that perhaps she should write her husband about this, a nod from her mother caused her to give in with a shrug and say, "Well, why not?" From then on, on Tuesdays and Saturdays, we excused ourselves from the dinner table as soon as we could, sidled out the door and ran to the Barwoods', hoping that by avoiding further conversation about the subject, we would also avoid posing our new aunt with a moral dilemma that she might have to take up with her husband in her letters addressed to Academy Street.

On dog days, when we felt too languid for any activity more strenuous than lolling in the Barwoods' hammock, Aunt Helen and her friend with the car would come by, honk the horn, and say, "Who wants to go for a swim?" In minutes, we and our friends would gather up bathing suits and towels and be bouncing up and down with excitement in the backseat, jabbering a mile a minute about what we were going to do when we got to the lake. At Fairlee, we raced to the slide, sloshed it with water from the hand pump, and, shrieking with pleasure, abandoned ourselves to its curves before being plunged down down down through what seemed like fathoms of mild fresh water until we could see the bottom and were carried up to the surface with time only to get a breath before swimming out to mount the stairs again.

On the way home, it was the adults in the front seat who did the talking, often about us. On these trips, we learned that while Aunt Helen had dreaded taking on the responsibility for two girls our ages, she had found that we were no trouble at all because we were never at home except for breakfast and dinner. Even on rainy days, the smart one (Marie), took the other one (me) off to the library, so there was very little supervising to do. (Back in the city it would be different, of course.) In a way, she had been dying to get her hands on us, she admitted to her friend, to correct the errors she had seen her sisters-in-law making. They dressed us in the winter as if we were living in the Arctic, forced cod liver oil down our throats, and made us take naps as if we were babies. Her training as a nurse had convinced her that the only way to build resistance to diseases was through a toughening-up process, so the fewer clothes we wore the better it would be for our lungs.

This was sweet music to our sleepy ears. If, the following winter, we sometimes wondered if Aunt Helen didn't go too far in the opposite direction when, on bitter days, our bare knees turned blue with the cold, we thought it worth suffering a little to be liberated from the hideous shoes and stockings, and the rest of the old regime.

More revolutionary even than her theories about health was Aunt Helen's attitude toward our sisterhood. She was an only child, so she didn't really understand about sisters, but wasn't it crazy, she asked her friend, that her husband's family had raised two girls born ten months apart, and who were different in personality and temperament, as if they were twins? Until now, the girls had had their hair cut in exactly the same way, had worn identical clothes that differed only in color, had been given identical gifts, had often been punished as if they were one person, and had even been put to bed together when one was sick (with the justification that whatever one was down with the other was undoubtedly incubating). Well, there'd be no more of that! It might not be possible to break the strong tie between us, but Aunt Helen had no intention of fostering it.

The death knell to our twinness Marie and I listened to —wide awake whenever this subject came up—with very different emotions. Marie was elated that at last someone had recognized her seniority. It had galled her that we were not only treated as if we were the same age, but also that that age had been taken to be mine, rather than hers. This had permitted the adults in charge of us to rationalize the restrictions they imposed on our lives, as to bedtime, movies, hairstyles, and, of course, clothes, as "too old" for us. If Aunt Helen recognized that there was an immense difference between a thirteen-year-old and one soon to be twelve, Marie would be allowed greater freedom, or at least we would both be treated like adolescents rather than children.

Apprehension rather than elation was what I felt when Aunt Helen talked this way. Why it was so scary I didn't know, but scary it was. I didn't like to think that Marie and I were different. There was no denying Marie was a reader and student who preferred sedentary activities, whereas I, who never cracked a book, was a tomboy. And it was true that despite twin outfits we didn't really look alike. Also I could understand Marie's wish to separate herself from me when I showed insufficient daring, was a crybaby, or a copycat. (Recently she'd found it pesky that when we went to buy ice cream cones after the movie, I wouldn't make up my mind what flavor I wanted until I heard her choice, and with maddening predictability said, "I'll have the same, please.")

As I listened to Aunt Helen talking to her friend, I couldn't see what was so wrong with people treating Marie and me as if we were alike. The tacit agreement, based on our father's wish, that we would never be separated had been the one family rule about which I had had no doubts. Wasn't what Aunt Helen planned a kind of separation? Auntie had many times told me that I was too dependent on Marie for my own good, and threatened me with the day when Marie would marry and I would have to get along on my own. That was a worry, all right, but childhood moved at such a snail's pace and adult life seemed so far away that I felt I could put this worry at the bottom of my already long list. Now it had to be moved up to the top, for Aunt Helen was not talking about the future, but the present. Also, there was no intended threat or disguised punishment behind her words. She spoke of untwinning us in the same objective, even clinical, way she had spoken of unswaddling us, and for this reason it was alarming.

My twelfth birthday, a steaming August day, brought evidence that the untwinning process had begun. Heretofore, I had been able to predict what presents I would receive because they were duplicates of those Marie had been given two months earlier. In June, Aunt Helen had given Marie a sweater, so I expected, and wished for, one just like it, but in blue rather than red. When I opened the box and found a blouse, I had to make an immense effort to disguise my disappointment. And when Mrs. Geery asked what dessert I wanted for the celebratory meal she was preparing, and I responded, "The same as Marie had," Aunt Helen, not unkindly but firmly, said that I must think of a different one. I went off by myself and brooded (very uncharacteristic behavior for me). What fun was a birthday if you had to spend the whole day thinking? It was like being given a homework assignment. The effort made my brain hurt almost as much as the growing pains I'd been complaining about lately made my legs ache. When Mrs. Geery came to find me, to hear my decision, I said with as little enthusiasm as if she'd asked me what medicine I'd decided to take that I'd have chocolate ice cream. Eating it, I was astonished to find that I really preferred it to strawberry shortcake (which had been Marie's choice).

That evening, as I swung over the gully on the Barwoods' swing, and watched the fireflies blinking below, I realized with a pang that the days were growing shorter and that this blissful vacation would soon come to an end. My birthday made me feel older in a way earlier ones hadn't. Perhaps it was because of Aunt Helen's gift, the blouse, which it would take me some time to become reconciled to, and the less obvious but more momentous one, which was making me introspective in a way I hadn't been before. A nightly examination of conscience had made me aware that I had a soul that was uniquely mine. That I also had a self that was unique had not occurred to me before. Or if it had I'd tended to deny it. Very uncharacteristically, this evening I felt a need to be by myself, a need the swing satisfied as it carried me up and away from the others to a moment of being when I thought, "I am me." The thought left me almost as quickly as the swing came down, but having had it, I knew that I would never completely lose it.

It was many years before I could put a name to the sadness I felt on going away from people I'd become attached to. On the rides home from Westchester, this bleak, forlorn, gone feeling became so strong, and the lump in my throat so large, that I was never able to respond to Albert's teasing, or his plans for what we'd do during the next visit. Would there *be* a next visit? I couldn't be confident there would be. And, besides, I was too busy struggling with the disagreeable feeling that came over me whenever I kissed Aunt Hilda and Uncle Charlie good-bye. I had had the feeling when we'd left our city friends to come up to Hanover. Now again I was having it about leaving the Barwoods and Mrs. Geery. How lucky the college boys were to have Mrs. Geery to look after them! Aside from the way she spoiled them at the table with homemade ice cream and the like, she was even-tempered, warmhearted, sensible, understanding, a little (but not too) indulgent. I couldn't imagine what qualities I'd want in a real mother, but hers made for a perfect housemother, and I hoped that when I went to college I'd be lucky enough to be in the care of someone like her.

If I wasn't drawn to Aunt Helen in the same way, it was because her manner was more detached. During Uncle Vincent's ten-day vacation in Hanover, we had learned that while her temperament was less equable than Mrs. Geery's, her bad moods were shallower and more explicable than those of other adults, and had little to do with us. During his visit, we'd tactfully not mentioned the movies or other subjects we suspected would provoke his displeasure. The best thing was to lie low, and that we did. Nevertheless, there was a tension in the air that had not been there before he arrived and evaporated after he left. In the coming months, I learned to appreciate qualities Aunt Helen had. So little did she show favoritism that I sometimes wondered on occasions when our little cousin was especially mischievous if her mother's evenhandedness did not make the child feel as if we, the outsiders, were being favored. Aunt Helen was fair, and she was just—qualities I was beginning to think rare and admirable. When it came time (far sooner than any of us could have anticipated) to write her a thank-you letter for having looked after us, I wished that I had been skillful enough in composition to tell her how I felt.

It was with a heavy heart that we hugged Mrs. Geery and said good-bye. I mustn't look so downcast, she said, not guessing how much we dreaded going back to the city. In no time at all, summer would come again and we'd be back in Hanover for another vacation. We repeated her words to our friends as we said good-bye to them. We took our last walk on Tuck Drive, passed the movie house, the museum, Baker Library, the fraternity houses, down the sleepy streets of the town we'd come to love. It was the end of our first summer in Hanover and, because of a series of dramatic happenings which would take place in the coming year, our last.

CHAPTER 8

The Trial

THE SPEEDWAY ALONG the Harlem River, though less fashionable than it had been at the turn of the century when it was the scene of horse-drawn carriage races, was a favorite place of weekend promenading for the residents of Inwood. It was there one Sunday afternoon that Marie and I escaped from our guardian's house to mingle with the families out for an after-dinner stroll.

Sunday was the heaviest day of the week at Uncle Vincent's, as heavy as the midday dinner; for it was after this meal that he took up the heavy duty of supervising his wards. It was a task as trying for him as being supervised was for us. How was he, who had little talent for the role of father substitute, to deal with two girls, little more than strangers, who were approaching adolescence? Mindful of his younger brother's defects of character—his chronic lateness and extravagance with money—Uncle Vincent set

100

himself the task of training us out of similar tendencies. If our father had been able to get away with both because of his charm (Uncle Vincent had seen their mother melt under it), they were weaknesses in the moral fiber deplorable in anyone, but which orphans especially could ill afford to develop. And while we had so far shown no sign of either, heredity made us as susceptible to developing these moral defects as, from our mother's side, we were susceptible to her physical weakness.

This particular Sunday we had had our first lecture on a subject of great importance in the secular world: money. With the privilege of receiving an allowance, which Uncle Vincent said he was instituting, came the duty of accounting for the way it was spent. It was not too early for us to learn a few simple rules of bookkeeping that we would find useful the rest of our lives. He had bought us each a five-cent notebook, a red one for Marie, a green one for me, to which he had attached a string at the end of which dangled a yellow pencil. When we received the allowance, we were to write "Amount received—25 cents" in the upper-left-hand corner of the page, under the date. Below, and to the right, we were to list three invariable items with their unvarying amounts. "Church money—5 cents," "School supplies—5 cents," "Savings—15 cents." Then a line was to be drawn to show that the total of these three items balanced with the amount received. The books would be inspected weekly. Our father had been an extravagant man, generous to a fault. To help us develop better habits, our uncle had also bought us a small metal bank in which to put the fifteen cents we might have been tempted to squander in a candy store. Through the window in the little bank we would be able to see our savings accumulate. Did we understand? Silent nods that we understood.*

Eager though we always were to escape from the house, we had found that the hours of freedom on Sunday after-

*The training had mixed results. While it is difficult for me to be late, it is easy, very easy for me not to balance my checkbook.

noons were burdensome. Our friends were often away on family outings, or lounged at home listening to the radio. If it was very cold, as it often had been this winter, after half an hour of outdoor play our hands and feet had turned to ice, making us long for the moment when it would be time to go home again, even though we knew that once there we'd be given as busywork some self-improving task, a reminder that we'd been instructed not to come a minute sooner than the appointed hour.

Sometimes after the ice-skating season had begun in the rink at the end of Academy Street, we'd sneak into the locker room to warm ourselves in front of the Franklin stove. Through the window, we watched skaters in short, fur-trimmed dresses whirl around to the sound of Victor Herbert waltzes. They appeared as impervious to the cold as figures in a glass globe who, when the globe is shaken, become covered with fake snow. Occasionally, when we had a gift of money from Uncle Charlie—"Not a word of this to anyone, eh?"—we'd borrow skates and join the gliding figures. But since we weren't supposed to have the money, we skated furtively, one eye on the wire fence that enclosed the rink, lest by some unlucky chance Uncle Vincent should pass by and see us.

After the MacBride sisters moved in across the street from our house, we found a warmer and even more agreeable alternative. If Mary and Clara didn't have to go to visit their grandparents, we would have a dancing class in the entrance hall of their building. What they had learned on Saturday afternoon at the Non-Pareil School of the Dance on Nagel Avenue they taught us the following day. Divesting ourselves of our outer garments and shoes, we warmed up at the barre (the refectory table on which we had piled our coats). We ran through the five graceful arm and leg movements, *ronds de jambe, pliés, battements tendus,* counting and humming the Chopin waltz the piano lady for the class at the Non-Pareil had played on the aged upright. The highly polished marble floor, the mirrored walls, and the staircase down which we made our entrances created an ideal practice room. We would happily pass two hours of playtime in this way if the Polish janitor didn't come along and put us out, or worse, threaten to tell on us.

The March Sunday of the bookkeeping lesson, the first day, mild and windless, to give one hope that the winter was finally over, was too agreeable to squander indoors. As Marie and I stood on the street gulping in the fresh air in an effort to throw off the oppressiveness our guardian's lectures unfailingly produced, we speculated about where to go. Marie suggested the Speedway.

Although close to home, the Speedway was not an everyday play place for unaccompanied children. If it was not out-of-bounds, neither was it in. Occasionally our teachers took us there on nature walks to study the trees that grew along the slope under Fort George. What interested us city children more than wild flowers and tent caterpillars was the raffish waterside that bordered the Harlem River. While our teachers were searching for specimens, we slipped away to watch the lively and ever-changing river traffic. There were tugboats, barges, rowboats, and canoes. There were shells manned by the Columbia crew, and sculls, whose solitary oarsmen glided through the water. College boathouses, their wooden balconies festooned with pennants, came to life in the spring when handsome young men in black sweaters with giant *C*'s in blue on their chests lounged about after a workout on the river.

More interesting still were the houseboats which nestled between the club houses, where men, sometimes even families, lived. What kind of people were they? We wondered. "Drifters and tax dodgers," our teachers had said censoriously. This label didn't satisfy Marie and me. As we leaned over the railing to study the houses more closely, we saw that they varied greatly. Some were so dilapidated they provided only the flimsiest shelter from the elements. Others were built with care and were appealingly cozy. Our favorite, we decided, the one we'd like to live in, had red-

and-white-checked curtains at the window and smoke coming out of a twisted comic-strip chimney.

What would it be like to live on a houseboat? As we
walked along past women with baby carriages and men
sitting on benches reading the rotogravure section of the
paper, we indulged in the narcotic to which we had become
addicted. Before we fell asleep at night, when we were sick
in bed, on our walks in Inwood Hill Park, now on the
Speedway, we shared our when-we-grow-up daydreams.
These years of waiting until we could take control of our
lives were like the tunnel we'd traveled through the previous summer on the way to White River Junction. The dark
came suddenly, frighteningly. Fear subsided into a neutral
period of waiting, which was not scary really, but blank,
empty, colorless, and, above all, long.

We had fallen so deeply under the spell of the delightful
possibilities offered by our present fantasy (we would
marry brothers and live in neighboring houseboats) that
before we knew it we had walked much farther than we'd
planned. Wasn't that the 181st Street Bridge ahead? Never,
not even with our teacher, had we come so far. Surely this
was out-of-bounds. And wasn't it time to turn back? Plenty
of time, Marie said. We were so near the bridge it seemed
a shame not to see it up close.

Neither the builders of houseboats nor the Sunday strollers had ventured as far as we had come. Except for an
occasional passing car, the Speedway was empty. Now the
tree-covered slopes on the right rose sheer to Washington
Heights. The water side was bare except for, here and
there, a dock or a tied-up barge. A light wind blowing down
from Spuyten Duyvil at our backs made walking easy. Occasionally there was a gust so strong it made us skip. Laughing at the wind's playfulness, pushed by it into a run, we
were at the bridge in no time. As we looked up through the
impressive steel girders, we saw that the sky overhead had
darkened. Without our having been aware of it, the weather
had changed. It was beginning to snow. Large, papery

flakes fell softly on our eyelids. They melted on tongues we put out to catch them.

As we turned toward home, the wind, coming head-on now, made us button our coats, turn up our collars. When we tried to talk, we found we had to shout to be heard. We fell silent, communicating by gestures until our hands became so cold we had to keep them in our coat pockets. The passing boats looked farther away and had become covered with polka dots. The opposite shore was no longer visible. There were no Sunday strollers now, no automobiles.

From time to time, we looked back to check our progress. The bridge seemed to be following us. The playful wind had turned mean. The papery snowflakes had grown teeth. The teeth, biting into our cheeks, felt as if they were drawing blood. The sidewalk had become as slick as glass. My feet danced away from each other in a crazy jig. When I fell, Marie pulled me up. Her eyes pleaded: Please, *please* don't cry. I saw that she, too, was on the verge of tears. Arms linked to keep us from slipping, we battled the wind and the waves of panic that rose between us.

We were on an escalator now, moving in the wrong direction, surrounded by undifferentiated white. We were alone. Stories of children lost in the snow crowded my mind. One, a fairy tale I'd heard my first year in public school, had given me a nightmare. It was about two girls lost in a blizzard. Sisters they were. A farmer discovered them the morning after the storm. Their arms entwined around one another in an effort to keep warm, they had frozen to death.

A question floating on an icy wave of terror drove the cold down my spine. Hadn't the children been orphans? They had been put out of the house. Or they had run away. I hadn't listened carefully, so I couldn't remember the details, but it seemed to me that their death had been a punishment, an unjust punishment for a crime they hadn't been aware of committing.

Was it possible that our lives would end now, that we would never see the longed-for days when we would be free and living on our own? Was it possible that for us, as for the sisters in the fairy tale, there was no future?

When it seemed the escalator would go on into eternity, the storm abated as abruptly as it had blown up. Marie pointed to an elephantine mass in the distance. With wild joy we recognized the familiar outline of the Dyckman Street elevated station. As we came closer to it, our joy was dissipated by a new anxiety. We were late. To our guardian, lateness, at least ours, was a serious offense. What excuse could we give? We could tell the truth, admit to poor judgment in having walked so far, explain about the storm. Would he believe us? Not likely. Why was it the truth had a way of sounding like a lie? It would be better to invent a lie. But it better be a good one, and well rehearsed, so we wouldn't get caught out.

At Dyckman Street, we ran into the station to see how late we were. The moonfaced clock on the wall told us that if we raced home as fast as we could, we'd get there on time. Turning down Academy Street, we saw with astonishment that there was little trace of the storm here. How could it be that what had seemed like a blizzard on the Speedway had left this more protected street with only a light dusting of snow? The malice of nature was new to us. How right we had been to see the danger of telling the truth! What storm? Uncle Vincent, whose afternoon nap had coincided with it, would ask. Were we trying to dupe him? Did we take him for a fool?

Our burning cheeks were the only evidence we had that our adventure on the Speedway had been more than a runaway daydream turned nightmare.

Lies such as we fabricated were transparent and unimaginative by comparison with those I was afraid we would be required to tell in a court of law. Not long after the freak snowstorm we heard that the Other Side of the family was again stirring up trouble. In affidavits and petitions, they were charging Uncle Vincent with misconduct.

The latest bulky communication from them was so threatening our guardian dared not ignore it, as he had done their previous letters: He sought counsel. Charges and countercharges flew back and forth between the lawyers of the two sides for five months. At the end of that time, the judge decided that since there seemed to be no possibility of an amicable resolution in sight, the case should be brought to trial.

Each night after Marie and I were told that we would appear in court, the *cabezudos* marched again in my nightmares. No one had said what role we'd be asked to play in the proceedings, but if we had been instructed to tell our Westchester relatives we were living in one place when we were in fact living in another, what might we be told to say before the Other Side, who, if the nervous electricity at home was any indication, must be threatening to put Uncle Vincent in jail? It would have been nice to be able to enjoy being the subject of a dispute, but I was learning that I didn't have a strong stomach for family quarrels, and certainly didn't want to be the cause of them. (How, without doing anything, could Marie and I have stirred up so much trouble?)

One day in early June, we were kept home from school. Dressed in clothes bought for the occasion, we accompanied Uncle Vincent, who was more taciturn than usual, on a subway ride to Lower Manhattan. As we emerged at the Brooklyn Bridge station, he came out of his brown study long enough to give us a little lecture on the government buildings surrounding what is now called Foley Square. The one we headed toward, the Surrogate Court, was designed to impress citizens. Its neoclassical façade and marble entrance hall with majestic stairway (a replica of the one at the Paris Opera House) not only impressed but also intimidated two minors whose modest affairs the state was keeping an eye on.

Lawyers carrying briefcases, their leather heels clicking on the highly polished floor, rushed to and fro on urgent business. Melber Chalmers, Uncle Vincent's lawyer, a dapper man with a small moustache and a self-important air, led us to the court where our case was to be heard. Movie trial scenes had not prepared me for the splendor of this room with its mahogany paneling, ornate Italian fireplace, and windows draped in garnet velvet curtains. The only reassuringly familiar note was the American flag that stood on a pole in a corner of the room. If I focused my attention as hard as I could on counting the stars and stripes, I might succeed in governing my inner turmoil.

The whispered consultations between Uncle Vincent and Mr. Chalmers stopped abruptly when the lawyer for the Other Side appeared. Behind him came a tall man with a woman almost equally tall on his arm. She was dressed in mauve and was wearing a hat with a chin veil. Over her arm she carried a fur piece. There was something regal about her posture. Indeed she bore a striking resemblance, though she was taller, slimmer, and handsomer, to Queen Mary, whom I'd seen in Pathé newsreels at Loew's Inwood. Was it . . . ? Yes, it was our grandmother. Marie and I stood up, and not knowing how to greet her, curtsied as we had done the last time we had seen her five years earlier in the Convent parlor.

"My darling granddaughters," she cried, in a voice that cracked with emotion and sounded theatrically loud. "They've kept you from me." I felt her cool cheek next to mine, and caught a whiff of the delicate scent she was wearing.

What a tumult of feelings! Here was our mother's mother, our closest relative, and yet a stranger. If I responded to her embrace—oh, it was tempting!—I would be a traitor to our father's family. And weren't the tears I saw under the veil "put on," as we said in Inwood? If she loved us, why hadn't she come to see us in the Convent after Daddy died? Or during the long years since then? She was the enemy, wasn't she? And yet . . .

Everything that followed during the trial was an anti-climax to the meeting with Grandmother. It was a long time after her embrace before my heart stopped jumping and came to rest in its berth, a long time before I could concentrate on the proceedings. During the reading of affidavits, objections by lawyers, and calling of witnesses, when I wasn't worrying about what I would say when I was called upon to testify, I speculated about the woman in mauve, the press of whose cool cheek I could still feel against mine. What were her feelings on seeing us after so many years? Questions about her, which we had long ago given up asking our father's relatives, had always been answered elliptically. She wasn't dead, we knew that, but that was all we had known until the letters began to arrive from her lawyer. Then she became the subject of agitated dinner conversations between Uncle Vincent and Aunt Helen in which she was depicted as a cold, sharp-tongued troublemaker who had done something very very wicked. Since Uncle Vincent's ideas of wickedness and mine didn't always coincide, I wondered what it could have been. The worst thing I could imagine was her having taken so little interest in her granddaughters that she had made no attempt to see them. But if this was so, what had she meant when she'd said, "They've kept you from me"?

The tall man who greatly resembled her must be her brother. He frequently conferred with another member of her entourage, who, Marie whispered, was Uncle George, Daddy and Uncle Vincent's older brother. What was Uncle George doing on the Other Side? When he took the stand, he angrily read out a list of figures. Uncle Vincent's lawyer kept interrupting and objecting. They were arguing about money. *Our* money. (So Dr. Glickman had been right!) Uncle George was accusing Uncle Vincent of mismanaging our estate. The judge seemed to be agreeing that the accounting was unsatisfactory. I imagined that Uncle Vincent had a little green book with a yellow pencil hanging from a string, such as the one he'd given me. Frequently when he examined my book, he found that it was not in order. As he reprimanded me for carelessness, so the judge was now reprimanding him.

Uncle George left the stand looking pleased and returned to his seat next to Grandmother. I knew more about him than I knew about my grandmother because of the stories his sisters, Auntie and Aunt Lucy, had told us about life in Chelsea. He had been the intellectual star of the family, earning his Ph.D. from Georgetown University before he turned twenty. His sisters had sometimes found him overbearing in his role as older brother and had had a serious (and to us mysterious) disagreement with him after their father's death.

As Grandmother rose to take the stand, a moment I had been awaiting with impatience and dread, I forgot about the others in the room, intent on hearing every word she said. But I was not to hear. During her swearing-in, a woman I had never seen before took me rather too firmly by the elbow, and before I knew what was happening, I found that Marie and I were out in the hall, the courtroom door closed behind us. There was no need for us to be present, the woman said. Her husband, Mr. Gonzales, had been appointed court guardian. He would listen on our behalf and testify in our place. Relieved as I was to learn that we would not be called to the stand, I could not imagine how Mr. Gonzales could represent us. Nor could I understand what his wife meant when she said, in an unctuous way, that we must become friends because we were going to see a good deal of one another from now on.

At the end of the long, confusing, and emotionally exhausting day, there came a stunning surprise. This time when Mrs. Gonzales took us out into the hall it was to lead us down a corridor to the Clerk of the Court's office. There, to our astonishment, we found Auntie. Offering no explanation for her two-year absence,* behaving, rather, as if

---

*Where had she been? Her manner forbade our asking. When I was older and began to wonder about her life, I broached the subject of her long absence. She'd been traveling, she said. An unsatisfactory response, but such was the limit of our

we'd seen her the previous day, she said that as a concession to our mother's side of the family, Uncle Vincent had been removed as guardian, and she had been appointed in his place. Instead of going to Hanover for vacation, we would spend the summer with her at the Long Island cottage she had bought. In the fall, we would transfer to a new school, the one to which she had been assigned. To ease the transition, we would continue to live on Academy Street, in an apartment she was taking for the three of us. On the advice of her lawyer, she was not going to adopt us.

The word "adopt" filled me with alarm. While I felt rueful when I learned the reason for the lawyer's advice ("One can never tell how orphans will turn out"), I was relieved to hear that he had advised against it. I didn't understand all the implications of adoption, but I suspected it would somehow have made us less our father's daughters, and that the change of relationship might have required us out of politeness to call Auntie "Mother."

Nevertheless, we could rest assured, Auntie said, that from now on there would be no more changes of authority. We would remain with her until we came of age. There was one other important result of the trial we should know about. Judge O'Brien had given our grandmother visitation rights. Six times a year she would be allowed to see us. At the insistence of our father's side of the family, we would be accompanied on our visits to her house by a court representative, Mrs. Gonzales.

intimacy that I didn't feel I could press her further. The year before she died (at age eighty-five), on my weekly visits to her in the hospital where she was confined, I frequently tried to get her to talk in an autobiographical vein, with little success. About this absence, she added only that she'd been in California.

CHAPTER 9

Grandmother

THE NEW REGIME was in many ways more benign than the old one had been. Auntie worried less about our health as we got older, less about my schoolwork as my grades improved. Her financial situation was easier, and she was happier at the school to which she'd been transferred. From now on, there were summers on Long Island, which we loved because of the beach and the friends we made there. During our high school years, classes and extracurricular activities kept us away from home so much there was little need for supervision—until we began to go out on dates and to parties. Then the clashes became sharp again, especially between Auntie and Marie.

If Auntie's moods continued to be inexplicable, and it was no less clear than it had been in the beginning that she was not temperamentally suited to the difficult task of raising someone else's children, we remembered with gratitude that she was the only one who had come forward to take the responsibility. "Not even your darling Uncle Charlie or your grandmother offered to raise you," she'd say when she was angry at us, and imagined that we were comparing life at home with life in Westchester, or as it might have been in our grandmother's house.

No, Grandmother had never asked to raise us. Her plea had been to be allowed to see us. Once every two months, on a Saturday afternoon, Mrs. Gonzales called for us at Academy Street and took us for the court-sanctioned visits. After the deaths in rapid succession of her husband and daughters, and then her mother, Grandmother had sold the house they had lived in and moved into an apartment, with windows overlooking the garden of the Jumel Mansion, in the building she and her brother Joseph owned jointly. On the floor above, she had Joseph, his wife, and their three children, our new cousins, or cousins-once-removed, who frequently dropped in to keep her company and see that she wasn't lonely.

When I first met the youngest of these cousins, who was close in age to Marie and me, I marveled at his affectionate, teasing relationship with this woman who seemed, in the days when our visits with her were achingly uncomfortable, too queenly to be a blood relative. There was her cool cheek in the kiss of greeting, after which we took our invariable positions—Grandmother in her wingback chair, Mrs. Gonzales by the curio cabinet, Marie and I on the couch.

It had been a long time, Grandmother said, studying the way we looked on the first visit. She was delighted that Marie was even more the picture of Molly than she had been as a little girl, and that I greatly resembled Eleanor. She hoped we two were as close as her two girls had been. It would have been our salvation in the years since she'd seen us. Mrs. Gonzales looked at us hard to see what we made of this. I made little of it, confused by the secular use of the word "salvation."

Grandmother's blond hair had turned pure white. It was

coiffed in a coil at the back of her head, exposing the tip of her ears and the pearl earrings she always wore (and which I decided I, too, would wear when I grew up). She had not lost the peaches-and-cream complexion Uncle Charlie raved about when he said she had been a great beauty.

Could we not address her more informally? she asked. We had called her "Grandmother." Her brother's children called her "Nan." Her grandsons called her "Granny." (How long they had known her! How intimate they were! I thought with a pang. Had they sat on her lap when they were little? I wondered.) We didn't feel cozy enough to call her "Nan." We tried "Granny," but after a while all three of us got used to "Grandmother" (although not completely used to it. The word, like the word "mother" continued to sound theatrical to my ears, and I had to remind myself that I wasn't inventing the relationship. It was real).

Grandmother's living room substituting for the Convent parlor, and Mrs. Gonzales taking the place of Mother Superior as auditor, our conversations were as wooden as they had been when we were in boarding school. And now we had the added inhibition that so few things were safe to talk about. Even school, that serviceable subject, was risky. Grandmother made it clear that she disapproved of the way we were being educated. Ignoring Mrs. Gonzales's move to the edge of her chair, she said that the Preventorium Uncle Vincent had sent us to had been run by atheists. Upon investigation, she had discovered that no provision had been made for us to go to mass, or receive the sacraments while we were there. Surely Mrs. Gonzales—who was a Catholic, was she not?—must agree with her that it had been an improper place for two Catholic girls. And what Vincent could have been thinking of when he put two fragile children in an institution made up of flimsy, unheated buildings, she could not imagine. It was a miracle we had survived, morally and physically. And now these public schools. What had been the number of that P.S. (she bit out the initials) we had gone to? Auntie and her modern ideas

about public education! There was money for private
schools and we should be going to an academy as our
mother and her sister had done. Our father had been a—
Here Mrs. Gonzales cut her off.

Why did Grandmother talk in this inflammatory way?
Was it, as Auntie claimed, because she had "a tongue" and
couldn't control it? Or because, smarting under the court
chaperonage, her pride directed her to show how con-
temptible she thought the arrangement? Whatever the reason, she paid little attention to the mime Mrs. Gonzales put
on as she pursed her lips, shifted her weight, snapped her
pocketbook open and closed. I admired Grandmother's
boldness, but I couldn't afford it. I wanted only innocuous
things to report, as report we must, when we returned
home. And I wanted Mrs. Gonzales's accounts to the judge
to be so dull he would doze over them. Above all, I didn't
want the case to be reopened. Uncomfortable as the visits
were, it would have been worse not to have them. I didn't
want to lose my mother's side of the family again. So while
I would have given a great deal to ask Grandmother how
she knew about Farmingdale, and to question her about
our money, I did what I could to steer the conversation
toward bland subjects, hoping to distract her and make
Mrs. Gonzales forget she'd heard Uncle Vincent and
Auntie criticized.

What were the objects in the curio cabinet? Pleased to
find that Marie and I were interested in her collection of
family memorabilia, Grandmother brought out a pair of
Waterford salt holders her father had brought from Ireland. Their tublike, palm-filling shapes had the weight of
time. We liked to hold them in our hands, to catch the light
in the diamond-cut crystal. There was a pair of eyeglasses,
so tiny they looked as if they'd been made for a child, which
had belonged to our great-great-grandmother, and a black
lace fan that our great-grandmother (the ancient woman
dressed in black that Daddy had taken us to call on during
the Christmas holidays) had used on hot summer days.

These objects would come to us when she died, Grandmother said, and she hoped our children would keep them
for their children.

Later, when I found out how bitter Grandmother had a
right to feel toward our father's family (all but Uncle
George, who was her ally), I realized that her criticisms
were mild by comparison with what she would have liked
to say. But our overalert ears picked up every nuance, and
we felt we had to have a supply of safe subjects at the ready.
One that soothed her, and gave us great pleasure, was to
ask to look at family photographs. The walls in the corridor
between the living and dining rooms were lined with them.
After high tea (with real tea, forbidden at home, served in
china cups that came from London), we dallied to look at
the pictures. There was our grandfather behind a desk in
his law office. We thought he looked like Adolph Menjou.
Grandmother was amused. It was the moustache and an air
of urbanity both men had. There was our mother, her sister, and their Brooklyn cousins, who all summered together
on Long Island. Weren't they lovely, Grandmother asked,
with their long hair hanging down their backs and tied with
colored ribbons, ribbons that matched the sashes on their
white lawn dresses?

I learned a little about how long one could grieve when
Grandmother talked about the loss of her daughters. Unlike many mothers, she had preferred her girls to her boys.
"When boys marry you lose them. Girls remain close to
their mothers, as I did to mine. Unless, of course, they die."
Years later, she often wondered aloud to me if God had
taken the girls so early as a punishment for her having
shown that she favored them. There was poor Jim (her
firstborn), so big and healthy-looking, still in a sanitarium,
still alive.

If we lingered over the photographs long enough, the
time passed quickly. Mrs. Gonzales would look at the watch
that hung from a black ribbon around her neck. Time to
leave. The visit—part ordeal, part treat—was over. At the

door, Grandmother would say, "Now it will be another two months before I see you again." How she felt when we left I don't know. I was always so churned up inside that I couldn't eat at dinnertime and unfailingly vomited during the night, as I had done after the day in court. (When it was said of me at home that I was "high-strung," what was meant was not that I was spirited, or hard to handle, but that I was quick to tears, and had a hypersensitive digestive tract.)

Sometime after we were both in high school, we finally got rid of Mrs. Gonzales. How or why this happened remained as mysterious as did the reasons for the court battle. Once a year until we were eighteen, we returned to the Clerk of the Court's office to sign our names in a large black book. The woman with unnaturally red hair, who was always there, reminded us each time that we were agreeing to the continuation of Auntie as guardian and to Catholicism as our religion. This seemed implausible. What choice did we have about either? I wondered what would have happened if I'd said I wanted to become a Jew, or asked to have Uncle Charlie as guardian. Nevertheless the act of signing gave me a certain pleasure. It made me feel that although I didn't see the judge, it was not outside the realm of possibility that I might do so, and that I would be able to tell him how much we hated Mrs. Gonzales spying on our conversations with Grandmother. But we were not asked to sign that we agreed to her presence, so how, I wondered, had we got free of her?

Without Mrs. Gonzales's intrusive presence, our visits gradually became more relaxed. Sometimes we joined Uncle Joseph's family upstairs for tea, or our cousins came down and entertained us with accounts of deb parties, balls, and preparations for a family wedding to which we would be invited. On nice days, Grandmother often took us to sit in the garden of the Jumel mansion. Or we went to a matinee at the local movie, stopping on the way home at her church for benediction. Our relationship with her con-

tinued in this way until Marie married and, four years later,
I began life on my own.

Marie's elopement, at age seventeen, shook Auntie violently. Although she had never shown any sign of it, I realized, as perhaps she did for the first time, that Marie had
been her favorite. Now Auntie wondered aloud whether
her severity had accelerated Marie's impatience to be an
adult. Since I had copied my sister in so much else, would
I, too, try to leave home? Reminding me that Marie and I
now inhabited different worlds—she was a married woman,
living in the suburbs, while I was a schoolgirl, living at
home—Auntie put so many obstacles in the way of our
meeting that months would go by without our seeing each
other. Wouldn't I like to go abroad? Auntie would take me.
While she didn't keep that promise, she took me on winter
cruises and summer travels. In the city, we moved from one
apartment to another, even for a time to a hotel, living, as
she said, like Gypsies, because she couldn't settle down.

If the loss of Marie unsettled Auntie, it was devastating
to me. I became listless, lost weight, began to walk with a
posture so twisted that there was no hiding that there was
something seriously wrong with my back. As Auntie took
me from internists to orthopedists to osteopaths to chiro-
practors to physiotherapists, and none of them seemed to
know what caused my pain, she became convinced they
were paying insufficient attention to my family history.

A neurologist who listened to her report of my childhood
malnutrition and stay in the Preventorium said, after studying the X rays, that while those early years had set the stage
for my present symptoms, it was not tuberculosis of the
spine that was causing them but a herniated disk. Auntie
was briefly reassured, but after she rejected his recommendation of a spinal fusion, and saw that months of phys-
iotherapy did nothing to make it easier for me to stand or
walk for more than a few minutes, her suspicions returned
in full force: I even *acted* tubercular.

I was dragging myself on what were supposed to be di-
verting travels, unable to enjoy them because Marie wasn't
there to share them with me, dragged myself to doctors'
offices, to classes, and to the library, where I stayed until
closing time with the excuse that I had research to do for
term papers, putting off until the last possible moment the
time when I would have to go home. Had Auntie taken me
to the one specialist who could have seen what ailed me, he
would have said that I was grieving for Marie. Her loss had
been like a death to me, and though I didn't recognize it,
I was in mourning.

Auntie had warned me that the time would come when
Marie would marry, and if I hadn't learned to be independent of her, I wouldn't be able to stand on my "own two
feet." From one day to the next, that time had come. As
Auntie had predicted, I wasn't able to stand alone. The
herniated disk was real enough, but my bereavement undoubtedly aggravated my symptoms.

Time gradually cured me. I took a year to recover. When
I did, I threw myself into college life, developed sisterly
relations with my friends, and spent so much time in the
houses of the three I was closest to that their parents
treated me as if I were a member of the family. These
fathers of daughters seemed to be looking for another
daughter (instead of a son, as I would have expected), and
the mothers, feeling sure I must be yearning for mother
love, made much of me.

In the Hunter College lunchroom, where my classmates
and I spent hours reenacting domestic psychodramas, and
advising one another on how to deal with problems at
home, I became aware how many of them suffered over
agonizing relationships with their parents. They loved
them and hated them; they rebelled and felt guilty; they
wondered how they could have been born to people who
were so alien to them; they felt stifled by constraints imposed upon them, and counted the days until they could
get away. As the young men I was going out with felt my

orphanhood gave me an aura of mystery and glamour, so my college friends envied me my parentless state. "If only I were an orphan . . ." one or the other would say. Or, "Do you realize how lucky you are?"

It was true that no matter what difficulties Auntie and I had (and they increased as, learning to be independent, I became more spirited), I suffered less from them psychically than my friends suffered from disputes with their parents. I could say to myself, and for the comfort it gave me frequently did, that Auntie was not my mother, or my father. If my parents were alive . . . There followed a daydream of an idyllic homelife, of perfect accord.

My parents were safely dead. I had never heard them quarrel (whereas some of my friends' parents lived in a constant state of war). My mother was never irritable, unreasonable, or unloving. She was never a nag, never talked too much, never voiced prejudices I found shocking. Above all, she never showed a preference for another of her children. She was forever young, without defects, her image untarnished by time. So, too, with my father. If the picture of him I carried around with me was more lifelike, he was not a bully, an alcoholic, a cold or embittered man like some of the fathers I heard described. His gravest defect was that he was chronically late.

After I had my first job and could afford to live on my own, I told Auntie I planned to leave. I picked a moment when there was a natural break (she was going off on a summer vacation to the West Coast and Alaska), rehearsed my speech a hundred times, and prepared what I would say if she challenged me. She listened impassively, as if she had been anticipating this moment for some time. She had trained me to be independent, she said, so she would not hold me back. Legally I was of age, and I could just about support myself. Now that my inheritance had been spent, I would have to manage my salary carefully. I must remember, however, that if I was lonely, lost my job, or fell ill, I could not do what other young women did when the going got rough. I could not "run home to Mama." From now on, I was solely responsible for the way I conducted my life, and would have to take the consequences of my actions.

My friends' parents, distressed to learn that I was looking for a furnished room, urged me to join their households. I declined as gracefully as I could, but I knew they found my resistance to their kind invitations incomprehensible. How could they know that I was on the verge of fulfilling a childhood fantasy? I had found a small room in a Village brownstone (around the corner from the scene of the holiday seesaw rides and dancing lessons in my father's flat). I was on my own, traveling light (no heavy family baggage). Free!

One of the freedoms of my new life, which I hurried to take advantage of, was that I could go to see Grandmother whenever I liked, not once every two months, as it had been during the Mrs. Gonzales era, nor once a month, which later Auntie had felt was sufficient. In the years before I married, Grandmother and I settled into a routine of having dinner together once a week. She would pour me a glass of sherry from the decanter that had stood on the dinner table next to my grandfather's place when they'd had the house, and ask me what I'd done since our last evening together. So much of my life was beyond her comprehension—a girl living alone in a furnished room in the Village, going out at night with young men who came from families one had never heard of (and who probably weren't Catholics), working in offices where she was thrown into contact with all sorts of people—that I sketched my activities with a few quick strokes and asked her what she had been doing. She might describe a stylish funeral she'd been to, a movie she'd seen, or report on a sermon her pastor had preached. Then we settled down to the subject that was of unfailing interest to both of us: the past. I wanted to know everything she could tell me about her youth, her marriage, her children, and, especially, about my mother.

It had been a grand life, in a happier, more leisurely era, she said. They had lived well. James had always been generous with money. He was proud that she and his daughters dressed smartly, and that they had a well-run house, for James (like his brother, Uncle Charlie) had the Tully eye and taste. He worked hard at his law practice, but not the way young lawyers nowadays had to work, so he was always free for family parties and outings. When two of his trust cases took him abroad, he had taken her with him. She knew that people had criticized her for leaving the children, but there had been Bridget to look after them, and Mama (her mother) to see that all went well. One of the things James had loved about her was that she was always ready "to go." In winter, they'd had an active social life with the Cathedral crowd (the parishioners at St. Patrick's), and summers the various branches of the family rented neighboring cottages on Long Island so that the cousins could be together. Then . . . then it was all over. Over so quickly that for years she had been too stunned to take it in. First there was James's illness, then the girls being sent to Saranac, their three deaths, Jim's hospitalization, the loss of Mama, and, when she thought she could bear no more, the loss of Marie and me.

At the mention of this last loss, I found that I would try to steer the conversation onto safer ground as Marie and I had done in the old days. While I no longer gave credence to the story that Grandmother had stopped coming to see us at the Convent because she was a cold, egocentric woman who was afraid that our upbringing would be foisted upon her if she had, I didn't know what to believe. Unable to imagine what her motive could have been, I decided it was not up to me to judge her. I had a perfect mother. What I wanted in a grandmother was not another angel but a flesh-and-blood woman, an ancestor and a family historian. During these evenings together, I found her.

My visits were a party for which she prepared a special meal (though, as she said, she was not one to spend time in the kitchen, having had cooks most of her life), a party at which she sketched with a lively tongue the personalities of people she wanted to describe. When it was time for me to leave, we embraced far more freely than we had in the past, and while she was always sad to see me go, she knew it would be a week rather than two months before we met again. Each time, she made me promise that as soon as I got down to the Village I'd telephone her, to let her know I was safely home (the only overt sign she gave of uneasiness about a life-style so foreign to any she had known).

As she grew older and her activities became more circumscribed, I worried about her living alone. The time came when she no longer went to the movies, or took the Fifth Avenue bus down to Washington Square to look from the upper deck at the shop windows as she had done every year at Christmas, or even went to funerals. Her mourning clothes, as she said, were worn out. All her friends had died. Nevertheless, with surprising independence for a woman raised as she had been, she couldn't consider living with anyone. She said she cherished her freedom too much. She had her prayers to say, the radio to listen to, and her reveries about the dead.

Some years after I married and moved to Princeton, I had a late-night telephone call from her daughter-in-law, Uncle Jim's wife. She had been summoned because Grandmother had had a heart attack. To see that she was properly looked after, Bessie was moving her to a hospital near where she lived, in Poughkeepsie. Grandmother was out of danger, but her mind was a little cloudy, as I would see when I went up to visit her.

Since Grandmother belonged to a generation that thought to be sent to a hospital was a shameful experience, I dreaded what I would find. At the reception desk, I was told to go through a complex series of buildings to Ward D. In one of the courtyards on the way, I was arrested by the spine-tingling voice of a woman, well-trained and powerful enough to fill an opera house, singing *"Vissi d'arte."*

So thrilling was it to hear a voice of this quality emanating from granite walls that I didn't take in immediately that the singer repeated the first few phrases of the aria over and over again. Looking up, I saw a pair of hands clutching the bars of an open window. Behind it, the faceless perseverator sang out her madness. What had initially been thrilling became, with ceaseless repetitions, unnerving. It was like listening to a defective record with no way to lift the needle. Heart pounding, I understood that, for the first time in my life, I was in a mental hospital. Grandmother had been put in the senile ward.

The head nurse admitted it had been a misdiagnosis. High fever from a flu that followed the heart attack, and the move from New York, had temporarily disoriented the patient. She was "clear" now, but unfortunately there wasn't a bed free in the medical ward and it was thought unwise to move her to another hospital. The nurse complained to me that my grandmother was a rebellious, stubborn patient. She refused to get out of bed even though she was well enough to walk. Her daughter-in-law had had no luck in trying to get her up. Would I see what I could do?

Never having seen Grandmother's hair anything but perfectly arranged, I was shocked to see it hanging loose on her shoulders. Her peaches-and-cream complexion was dead white. She had lost weight. Her blue eyes looked at me for a few moments without recognition. Then she smiled. She pointed to a flowering apple tree she could see through the window near her bed. "Isn't it beautiful?" She was distracting my attention from her distasteful surroundings like a woman who has been caught by a visitor in an untidy house. She asked after Marie, her children, and my husband. When I said Marie had received her Ph.D. in psychology and that I was working in a clinic, she said, "How strange that both my granddaughters spend their time in a darkened room listening to people's troubles." And then, philosophically and, more to herself, "Perhaps it's because of the childhood you had."

Shortly before leaving, I asked why she refused to walk. She said placidly that since the nurse had taken her possessions—her nightgown, bed jacket, hairbrushes, comb, and mirror—she didn't see why she should. I could take a message to the head nurse for her when I went out. "Tell her that a woman who isn't well enough to have a mirror isn't well enough to walk." As Grandmother turned her cool cheek, and we kissed for the last time, she whispered conspiratorially, "You know, there's nothing to see here anyway, so why bother to get up?" No reason at all that I could see. At eighty-four, surely a woman had a right to stay in bed if she liked.

A week later she was dead. Hers was not, to use her words, a stylish funeral. For one thing, it was too small. She might have said she had lived too long. Only two cars drove behind the hearse down from Poughkeepsie, past the Convent in Dobbs Ferry, and out to Queens to what, when my grandfather was buried there, had been countryside, and was now a tangle of highways. We had no sooner left the cemetery than the conversation turned to Grandmother's possessions. I closed my ears to the genteel bickering about who would get what.

After Uncle Charlie died, and the objects belonging to our mother he had been holding for us were sold, together with the contents of his house, in the bankruptcy proceedings, Grandmother had become concerned about the things she was planning to leave Marie and me. She had a feeling, as she put it, that for some reason we were not meant to inherit. Something would always happen. She knew that Uncle Joseph (who had a seat on the New York Stock Exchange) had recently suffered losses in the market, and since he took care of her affairs that meant she must have lost money too. She wasn't sure if there would be any left by the time she died, so she'd decided to have identical rings made for Marie and me from the diamond brooch James had given her on their twenty-fifth wedding anniversary. She wanted to put them on our fingers herself, so she'd know for certain that we had something of hers. Nowadays when I hold the ring up to the light, I fancy I see the diamond cuts of the Waterford salt holders. The contents of the curio cabinet, the only things besides her photographs I would have liked to possess, disappeared at the time of her death.

Grieving over the loss of my grandmother, I at the same time felt grateful she had lived so long. The years had allowed me to get to know her. Nevertheless there was still a good deal I didn't know. Auntie had told me some things about the dispute between my mother's and father's people. So, too, had Uncle Charlie. Still, there were mysteries.

A desire to clarify them sent me back to the Surrogate's Court a few years ago. At the familiar Clerk of the Court's office, I asked to see the records of the trial and the files the judge had kept on Marie and me. I was told that it was impossible, that the request was highly unusual, that it would require a judge's permission, and, once that was granted, that the files would probably prove to have been destroyed. When it became clear that I wouldn't leave until a search had been made for them, I was sent to the file room. A man who looked to be retirement age, wearing a green visor and cardboard cuffs to protect the sleeves, became interested in helping me when he heard that I was not an investigative reporter but an orphan looking for her past. In a few days, he found the record "and not a moment too soon. It was with the batch about to be destroyed." (Not true. When I returned recently to check a detail or two, there was a very businesslike system for requesting the files and, after a two-week interval, those I had asked for were retrieved from storage.) Opening the manila folders, I felt a rush of panic, and, when the thought that it might be dangerous to delve into the past subsided, a residual nervousness, reminiscent of my feelings on that day in court.

As I pieced it together, the trouble had begun with the reading of my father's will. Grandmother had taken it for granted that his eldest brother, George, would be named guardian. (From the time of our weekly dinners, I knew George was her favorite. *"There* was a charmer," she'd say. Had she hoped, I'd wondered, that my mother would marry him?) According to Uncle Vincent's testimony, Marie reported Grandmother's having said, "Your father was a fool to have appointed Vincent." This was the wicked thing she had done.

The word "fool" flew off the page at me, reviving a suppressed memory. Marie and I were sitting in the Convent parlor. Grandmother, who was ordinarily so self-possessed, was pacing the floor. She had just come from the reading of the will, from learning that not George but Vincent was to be our guardian. Stopping in front of the couch, towering over us, she threw up her arms in a gesture of exasperation and said, "Your father was a *fool* to have chosen Vincent. What could he have been thinking of?" I was frightened by her anger. Marie, who was upset by what she heard as an attack on Daddy, reported the scene at home, hoping for clarification.

According to Grandmother's testimony, the next time she went up to Dobbs Ferry to see us she was shown not into the reception room but into Mother Superior's office. Was there another medical crisis? Was Eileen sick again? No, we were both well, Mother Superior said. She was distressed to report, however, that she could not call us in from the playground. Our guardian had written that on no account was our grandmother to see us.

Not allowed to see her own grandchildren? How ridiculous! Surely Mother Superior would not honor so absurd and unnatural a request.

Mother Superior, whose rapport with Grandmother had always been better than with our father's family, was truly sorry. There was nothing she could do; her hands were tied. On the ride back to the city, Grandmother, between tears and rage, mentally composed a letter to Vincent. It is not in the file. His, in answer, is:

Dear Madam:

Replying to your letter of the ninth instant, I wish to say that inasmuch as I am convinced that you did your utmost to create confusion in the minds of the children as to the propriety of my guardianship over them, I am compelled, in their best interest, to withhold my permission for you to see them.

The following week, when George accompanied Grandmother to Dobbs Ferry to see if he could exert his influence over Mother Superior, he was handed a letter Vincent had sent to be delivered to him should he appear. It said, in part, "It is deemed best for you not to see the children in order to keep them free from family quarrels and rancor."

Could this be his younger brother addressing him in this insolent way? It took George some time to think of a way to retaliate, according to Auntie. When he did, he convinced Grandmother that, working together, they should go to law. She was the widow of a lawyer, and the friend of many others who had been her husband's colleagues. To go to law was not a difficult step for her to take. Through her cousin who was a judge on the State Supreme Court, she hired an attorney. He wrote Vincent, demanding an accounting of the way the money in our father's estate was being spent. George, convinced that Auntie had mismanaged their own father's estate, now suspected that she and Vincent were lining their pockets with the money our father had left us. (This was the first I knew that a member of the family had also believed my paternal grandfather had died a rich man. I'm sure George and the others were wrong. There was never any sign of money except what Auntie earned and frugally managed. As her executrix, I know that at her death, after her medical and hospital bills had been paid, there remained only a few thousand dollars.)

In the matter of Uncle Vincent's mismanagement, George accused him of "juggling and manipulating the figures." Was Vincent charging our estate with the price of a ticket every time he went to see us at Dobbs Ferry? Item dated December 18, for two dolls at $8.16: was the estate paying for Christmas presents he had given us? Where were the receipts for the dental bills he had supposedly paid? And did the court not think that the amount he was charging the estate for room and board was exorbitant?

What Judge O'Brien thought of the accounting is not recorded. By comparison with the cost of the trial, and of having Mrs. Gonzales accompanying us to Grandmother's, what our estate paid for these items was small. But together they ate a giant bite out of the inheritance that was to have provided for us until we were twenty-one, and made it necessary for me to take a job working evenings during my last year in college. What I felt when I studied the accounting of the way our money had been spent was—what?—embarrassment such as a child feels at catching an adult in a shabby act. If I felt resentment, it was rather at having been made to believe all those years that Marie and I were a financial as well as emotional burden. How differently I would have behaved (or I think I would have) had I understood that our supposedly extravagant, improvident father had died at the age of thirty-one leaving an estate large enough to support us until we were out of college, with ample money for the kind of clothing and modest entertainments we had craved.

The rage I felt, which exploded in my heart like a time bomb with a fuse coiled deep in the past, was not over these mean revelations, but over another I found in the file. On those interminable Sundays at the Convent after Daddy died, when we waited in vain during the visiting hours for our names to be called, Grandmother had been in Mother Superior's office *begging* to be permitted to see us. Week after week, accompanied by first one male relative and then another to help her plead her cause, she attempted to storm the Convent. It must have been an immense relief to Mother Superior to be able to say, one Sunday, that we were no longer there; where we had been taken she didn't know.

Hiring a detective, Grandmother traced us to the Preventorium. Again she was turned away. The detective's investigation furnished the material for her inflammatory remarks on our first visit to her apartment after the trial. Vincent had put us in an institution that made no provision for our religious education, an institution so primitive we slept in unheated shacks. Alarmed by the detective's report, frustrated by her inability to do anything about it, and exhausted by the emotional strain of the year-long struggle, she acknowledged defeat in a final letter to Uncle Vincent. His behavior, she said, was "cruel, heartless and inhuman toward me, and will instill in the children's youthful minds a feeling of neglect and abandonment."

"A feeling of neglect and abandonment": that describes perfectly what we did feel. It is for those long-ago Sundays when Marie and I waited in vain, and for the needless anguish Grandmother suffered, that I saved my retroactive anger. I was so overwrought by what I had found in the files that I raced down four flights of stairs, through the marble entrance hall of the Surrogate's building, and out into the air.

A few days later, when I had recovered sufficiently to continue my research, I learned that the judge had appointed Mrs. Gonzales as chaperone to insure that Grandmother "would not attempt to create confusion in the children's minds, or say anything derogatory about their father." Grandmother was also forbidden to tell us her side of the story. And she never did!

Recently, when I returned to the Clerk's office again to check a detail or two before writing this chapter, I found myself rereading the file dispassionately. So much that I had been critical of in our upbringing, I saw, had been motivated by a lack of understanding of what goes on in the heart of a child, and fear—fear that we would become tubercular, fear that we would be kidnapped (and not by strangers but by relatives), fear that we would not be strong enough to look after ourselves when we were older, as well as the unarticulated fears that orphans stir up in the breasts of those responsible for them. I had made Uncle Vincent the villain because his temperament was foreign to mine. The real villain was Fate.

What remained incomprehensible was why Grandmother hadn't rebelled against the injunction not to tell us her side of the story. More than once, she repeated that Daddy had been a fool to have appointed Vincent as guardian, but she never told me about her attempts to see us at the Convent or Farmingdale. *Why?* I ached with regret at not having known these crucial details during the years when she and I saw each other alone. I had tried not to judge her, and had mostly succeeded, but there had always been awkward moments when my unposed questions hung in the air.

What I like to think, now, is that she hadn't been aware of my awkwardness, perhaps hadn't realized that I still didn't know her side of the story and, in any case, felt that explanations were no longer necessary. It no longer mattered. Her longevity—oh, blessed longevity!—had made it possible for us to know one another as grandmother and granddaughter, to build a bridge over the missing generation and the irretrievable years.

PART II

AT A RECENT film seminar, I saw again George Cukor's
Gaslight (1944), with Ingrid Bergman and Charles Boyer.
After the screening, as I listened to the long and erudite
lecture, I was surprised that while the critic examined the
picture from every conceivable angle, he never once mentioned what I think is crucial to an understanding of the
heroine's situation: she is an orphan. It is her being alone
in the world that puts this romantic and susceptible young
woman in a vulnerable position, it seems to me, for she has
neither parent nor relative to warn her away from the
suavely seductive older man who, once she marries him,
will drive her to the edge of madness for his sinister purposes.

Had I been struck by the heroine's parentless and unprotected state when I saw the film for the first time? I don't
think so. It was only after my awareness of my own orphanhood had been reawakened that I reread the autobiogra-
phies, the masterpieces of imaginative writing, and the

133

popular comic strip, which I talk about in the chapters that follow, with a heightened sensitivity to aspects of these works that had escaped me earlier. It was as though I were now reading with eyeglasses, the lenses ground to a prescription which picked up details my naked eye had not seen before, and which others who wear no glasses, or have a different prescription, would be less likely to see.

CHAPTER 10

Orphanhood: A History

> If ever you do wrong then, and they cry out to me, I will
> surely hear their cry. My wrath will flare up, and I will kill
> you with my sword.
>
> —Exodus 22:23–24

To BE REASONABLY LUCKY, an orphan should have a brother
or sister close in age, a modest inheritance (large ones
cause trouble), and hospitable relatives. What to do with
the unlucky ones has become the concern of society whenever one of the giant orphan-makers—wars, mass migra-
tions, economic depressions, epidemics—caused their
number to rise abruptly. Especially at such times children
without parents have been subjected to the exploitation
their vulnerability seems almost to beg for.

Although there were attempts to protect waifs from
being sold into slavery in Rome under benevolent rulers,
in the asylum established by Trajan and Marcus Aurelius's

home for girls, it wasn't until the outlawing of infanticide by the early Christian Church that there was a felt need for institutions where the abandoned and the orphaned were looked after together. (Was this, one wonders, when the stigma attached to the one began to be transferred to the other?) By the twelfth century, when life expectancy was only thirty years, so many children lost their parents early that a French monk, Guy de Montpellier, established the Order of the Holy Spirit to look after them. When Innocent III arrived in Rome, he was so appalled by the number of babies' bodies he saw floating in the Tiber (undeniable evidence that infanticide continued to be practiced despite the Church's interdiction) that he summoned Guy to spread the work of his Order in Italy.

In foundling homes and orphanages like Florence's famous Innocenti (which today tourists visit to see Della Robbia's medallions of swaddled infants), babies were nursed by peasant women either inside or outside the walls. After being weaned, they lived in the institution until they were seven or eight, at which time they were either adopted or bound out as apprentices and servants.

Until the Reformation, it was the clergy, or lay workers under the supervision of priests and nuns, who took care of orphans. Afterward, in countries where convents and monasteries were shut down, they again became vagrants. In England, with the passage of the Poor Relief Act under Elizabeth I, the state took responsibility for them, and placed them under the jurisdiction of community nurseries, where they were looked after until they were old enough to be farmed out.

During the Industrial Revolution, which produced an explosion in the orphan population of record proportions, this system broke down. As a result of the migration from farms to cities, unemployment, poverty, and overcrowding in fetid tenements, orphans "swarmed the streets like locusts," where, joined by the Hansels and Gretels of their day (children turned out by indigent parents), their numbers made them menacing to the gentry. Although they died like flies, they yet remained so numerous that Swift (a posthumous child who felt abandoned by his mother because she turned him over to a nurse and rarely troubled to see him until he was an adult) suggested with bitter wit that the only solution to the question of how to get rid of urchins was to fatten them up and serve them at the tables of the rich at Christmastime.

In response to the clamor for them to be put away, they were thrown into almshouses with impoverished, insane, and depraved adults where, according to one reporter, quoted by Lawrence Stone, they were looked after by

> filthy and decrepit women, three or four [children] to one woman, and sometimes sleeping with them. The allowance to these women being scanty, they are tempted to take the bread and milk intended for the poor infants. . . . The child cries for food, the nurse beats it because it cries. Thus with blows, starving and putrid air, with the addition of lice, itch, filthiness, he soon receives his quietus.

The youthful orphaned king, Edward VI, acting on the advice of Bishop Ridley, had already recognized the need to institutionalize children separately when he established the Blue Coat School at Christ's Hospital in the middle of the sixteenth century. The school went through phases during which the governing of the inmates was benign or brutal, depending on the interest the reigning monarch took in its management. In the early years, the boys were treated like the paupers they were. The patronizing attitude of the public toward these orphans is suggested by the custom of using them to swell funeral processions. One eccentric Londoner made provision in his will for the Blue Coat boys to march every Good Friday to All Hallows Church, where, after the service, each was given a penny and several raisins. The raisins they undoubtedly gobbled up on the spot. But did they hold on to the penny? I wondered, remembering the crisp dollar bills we Convent girls were given for singing a funeral mass, and what happened to them.

By the late eighteenth century, when Coleridge, Lamb, and Leigh Hunt went to Christ's Hospital, the six hundred to one thousand boys who were accepted were considered to live privileged lives in a classless society that now included children whose parents were alive but abroad in the colonies, or who, for some other reason, could not keep them at home. The inmates slept in airy dormitories, were fed in a magnificent dining hall, and those deemed sufficiently intelligent were taught by superior masters who prepared them for a university education. So privileged were they that Lamb looked down on the altogether inferior type of boy "with abject countenance, squalid mirth, broken-down spirit, crouching or else fierce and brutal deportment" who went to "common orphan schools."

The recollections of these men give us a rare view of the institutional orphan's life. Lamb was in a favored position because he had relatives living nearby whom he was allowed to visit frequently, and whose maid brought him hot rolls and tea for breakfast. Although Coleridge later composed an anthem for the boys of Christ's College to sing—

> Seraphs around th'eternal seat who throng
> With tuneful ecstasies of praise:
> Oh! teach our feeble tongues like yours the song
> Of fervent gratitude to raise

—*his* feeble tongue needed coaxing. While he was grateful for the education that had prepared him for Cambridge, he continued to be haunted throughout his adult life by painful memories of his school days, when he was "a depressed, moping, friendless, half-starved, poor orphan." The diet the boys ate in the magnificent dining hall—"dried bread and some bad small beer" for breakfast (no hot rolls and tea for him)—was enough to dampen but not satisfy a grow-

ing boy's appetite: "I never had a bellyful." Even more
painful to one starved for affection was the lack of emotional nourishment. The weekly day of freedom, which
Lamb passed happily with his relatives, was for Coleridge
a cause for chagrin:

> The long warm days of summer never return but they bring
> with them a gloom from the haunting memory of those
> whole-day leaves, when, by some strange arrangement, we
> were turned out for the livelong day on our own, whether
> we had friends to go to, or no. . . . We would sally forth and
> go swimming, but having eaten our crust of bread, were
> building up an appetite that by noon we had no way of
> satisfying . . . the very beauty of the day, and sense of liberty
> setting a keener edge on it. How faint and languid, finally,
> we would return, toward nightfall, to our desired morsel,
> half-rejoicing, half-reluctant, that the hours of our uneasy
> liberty had expired. . . .
>
> It was worse in the days of winter to go prowling about
> the streets objectless . . . shivering at the cold windows of
> print shops.

Had the author of *The Ancient Mariner* been orphaned a
century earlier, it is unlikely that he would have ascribed his
physical and emotional deprivations to his expulsion from
family life. As historians and demographers like Lawrence
Stone, Philippe Ariès, and Lloyd de Mause have demon-
strated, the family as we know it evolved very slowly from
the end of the feudal period to the modern era. Until the
seventeenth and eighteenth century, its structure remained
loose and its emotional tone cool (especially in England).
Infants were routinely placed in the care of wet nurses. At
age seven, dressed and treated like undersized adults, they
moved into "the great community of men." Until childhood had been carved out as a stage of life between infancy
and maturity, and the family unit had been consolidated,
neglect and ill treatment of the young were so common-

place that the child without parents was little worse off than the one with them. And so many were orphaned early (according to Stone, in Bristol of 1696, one-third of all children had lost their parents) that their situation was hardly noteworthy.

By Coleridge's day, the contrast between the care and affection a middle-class child received at home and in an institution was so sharp that a precocious, imaginative, hypersensitive boy who had been made much over by his many older brothers and sisters (if not his mother) would have felt the difference acutely, so acutely that he developed—and this is new—an orphan's sensibility. By the middle of the nineteenth century, when, with the cult of domesticity, the bourgeois family reached its sentimental peak, and middle- and upper-class children were cosseted as never before, the orphan's lot became sufficiently poignant to make it a subject of novelistic interest and attract the attention of social reformers.

To instruct "the thirty thousand naked, filthy, roaming, destitute children of London," Lord Shaftesbury established the Ragged School Union (named after a model orphanage established in 1695 by August Francke in Halle, Germany). Dickens, whose novels and journalism did more than any social reformer could have done to expose the evils of almshouses, the corruption of the heads of orphanages, the stupidity of those who instructed the inmates, and the cruelty of couples to whom children were bound out, was a staunch supporter of the Ragged School movement, which he hoped would rescue orphans from slum streets, "that vast hopeless nursery of ignorance, misery and vice."

With the opening of the New World, vagrant children had been rounded up by agents and exported to the Colonies to provide inexpensive labor. Almshouses and orphanages were opened by the states, and by religious orders, when the need for them grew as a result of epidemics of yellow fever, cholera, and typhus. The Civil War, as a result of which the number of orphans in almshouses increased 300 percent, together with wave upon wave of immigration, produced another explosion in their population. Whereas in 1825 there had been two orphan asylums in New York State, by 1866 there were sixty, with a like increase in Eastern Seaboard states where immigrants landed. And even these were not enough to take care of the homeless children. Again they swarmed city streets. Again they menaced the gentry.

Charles Loring Brace, who was head of the Children's Aid Society, described the homeless boys he and his staff of volunteers gathered up for the Ragged Schools and lodging houses he opened in New York as "little Arabs," who "slept in hallways, under stairs and in cardboard boxes." They had little to eat but what they stole or bought with money they got from begging. The girls, "barefooted, bonnetless, ragged, and dirty, had, many of them, singularly wild and intense expression of eye and face, as of half-tamed creatures with passions aroused beyond their years."

There was no better way to cool the passions of the girls and shield the boys from a life of crime than to send them to work on farms, Brace believed. With a reformer's energy, he organized "orphan trains" to transport city waifs to families out West who were willing to take them in. When the orphans went off singing a song composed by Brace for the occasion—

> No more complaining fills the street,
>   Of children who deserted roam,
> For here the houseless vagrants meet
>   A benefactor and a home.
> And girls defenceless, wretched, poor
>   Snatch'd from the haunts of vice and care
> From ill examples here secure,
>   Instruction and protection share

—there was not a dry eye in the crowd of well-wishers who had financed the trip and were on hand to see them off. (Singing, together with work, prayer, and study, was a part of the daily routine for asylum orphans. The children regularly performed for visitors who, marveling that those so ill favored were *able* to sing, were moved to tears. Sung expressions of gratitude reminded benefactors that they didn't have to wait for the hereafter to be rewarded for their generosity, and prodded them to dig deeper into their purses.)

On arrival at their destination, the orphan-train children were greeted by a crowd of applicants who looked them over and made their selections. Then, according to Henry W. Thurston,

> . . . if the child gave assent, the bargain was concluded on the spot. It was a pathetic sight . . . to see these children, tired young people, weary, travel-stained, confused by the excitement and the unwonted surroundings, peering into those strange faces [of the applicants] and trying to choose wisely for themselves.

From 1854 to 1924, an estimated 100,000 children were sent West on orphan trains. Brace was well pleased with the success of the program. He admitted that many of the foster parents were exigent and had little or no tolerance for the childish imperfections of character in their charges that parents might take for granted. Some of them attempted to "thrash the boys," but these tough city kids, "muscular orphans," fought back. If life proved intolerable, and the local agent who helped arrange the pairing learned about it (usually from neighbors), the child was transferred to another home. Some ran away, but the majority stayed on until they were able to strike out on their own. A fair number were adopted.

Had the orphans written accounts of their feelings, they would have admitted to fear of leaving the familiar, if disorderly, city for the unknown faraway country; to sadness and loneliness at leaving friends, siblings, sometimes even a parent; to apprehensiveness over the possibility of not being selected and, when they were, of going off to isolated farmhouses with total strangers—feelings they expressed to one another, to the agents with whom they traveled, and to those who interviewed them as adults.

For years, a controversy between "wholesome indenture" and institutionalization raged, neither side being willing to admit that while a good foster home was better than an asylum, a poor one was worse. One veteran of both, E. J. Henry (who as an adult became a superintendent of an orphanage), says that even in the superior orphanage where he was raised, there was never enough to eat—a complaint rarely heard from farm children but heard from all orphanage children from the days of Coleridge on (unless the child was sickly and the food so unpalatable, as it was in the Convent, that even the too little seemed too much):

> There was mush and milk for breakfast; soup, bread and water, and once in a while chopped meat made into a gravy and put on bread. At night we would have bread and milk —and only one helping.

Henry, who learned well the lesson that he must be grateful, permits himself only a mild protest about the life he led after he was sent to a farm to live: "I had to work very hard as I was the only man on the place." The "good people" who took him in, like many others, were looking less for foster children than for farmhands and servants. They therefore allowed their charges little time for schooling, believing (as did many others, directors of asylums among them) that it was a mistake to educate orphans above their station. Orphans, on the other hand, longed to go to school, to get away from the burden of doing a man's work on a farm or escape the drabness of institutional life. The intelligent ones hoped by being model students to attract attention to themselves. The important thing was to be singled out, whether through brains, beauty, or winning ways, to elicit from women teachers a little maternal affection.

Protests about serious mistreatment of orphan-train children at the hands of foster parents reached agents slowly if at all. Rumors of mismanagement of asylums circulated continually and sometimes grew so loud an investigation was called for. One such was undertaken by the Strong Commission appointed by Governor Whitman of New York State in 1916 to look into the management of asylums that received state subsidies. The testimony of board members made tabloid headlines. The stories told of "little children with hair cropped . . . sitting at wooden benches and eating out of tin plates . . . some without anything to eat at all." Or, "forced to do drudgery, working eight or nine hours a day, with only one hour for schooling, and that often at night." Asylum directors hurried booklets into print that showed carefully dressed children seated at well-set tables, or playing around a Maypole, but as one alumnus of an orphanage said:

> Even in 1913 all the homelike things and kindness of such an institution were but a show and a sham to allay the suspicions and idle curiosity of visitors and social workers (that radical and hated class.)

A social historian wanting to know what life had been like for children a hundred years earlier would have found his answer inside asylums, where attitudes of directors and staff toward the inmates lagged by that many years behind child-care practices in the outside world. Orphans were expected to work harder and be better than other children, or not to be children at all, as a sign posted in one institution makes clear:

WHAT EVERY GIRL SHOULD BE ABLE TO DO: To sew. To cook.
To mend. To be gentle. To be patient. To value time. To
dress neatly. To keep a secret. To be self-reliant. To avoid
idleness. To respect old age. To hold her tongue. To keep
the house tidy. To make a home happy. To avoid gossiping.
To control her temper. To take care of the sick. To sweep
away cobwebs. Above all to attend to her religious duties.

Overworked and underfed children were more tractable
and posed less of a threat to their custodians, many of
whom lived with the conscious or unconscious fear of the
evil innate in their charges, as well as the fear of insurrec-
tion. To avoid both, regimentation was essential, and even
minor infractions of the rules had to be punished severely.*

Michael Sharlitt, another asylum inmate who became a
director, was at the Hebrew Jewish Orphanage of New York
(one of the ones I used to pass on my way to school as a
girl) during a period of transition in attitudes toward the
orphans. When he entered in the 1890s, food rations were
"kept close to a daring minimum . . . and this was reflected
in the weirdly small stature of the boys who left . . . at the
legal age of 14 years." The staff was made up of "escapees
from competitive life, ill equipped to look after love-hun-
gry children of whom at one time there were 1500." He
remembers not cruelty so much as incompetence, repres-
siveness, denial of individuality and of family ties (brothers
and sisters were separated and rarely had a chance to
meet). Inmates wore ill-fitting hand-me-down uniforms,
often with shoes a size too large or too small, marched two
by two in silence from one activity to another, had no personal possessions, no time to play, and could look forward
to only one day of the year that was out of the ordinary—
Orphans' Day at the circus (at other asylums it was Christmas Day).

*The rigors of orphanage life were so well known, or vividly imagined, by
those outside the walls that many a desperate mother used the threat of incarcera-
tion to subdue an unruly child.

By the time Sharlitt became a director, the question began to be asked: What do orphans need? When social workers, who had joined asylum staffs, conducted follow-up studies to find out how alumni felt about the way they had been looked after as children, and how they had fared after they were discharged, they learned that they had to proceed with caution. Many whom they hoped to interview were as furtive about their past as if they had been in reform schools, and were unable to rid themselves of the feeling that they were somehow responsible for having been institutionalized. Others were afraid of being discriminated against professionally or patronized socially ("unfortunate little ones"). Successful alumni expressed gratitude for the care they had received, and especially praised the orphanage librarians who had encouraged them to read and had recommended books. Not a few felt a strong responsibility to help other former inmates less fortunate than they.

Some who didn't land on their feet (in pre–World War II days when jobs were often difficult to find) had known years of financial insecurity. They described themselves as being unworldly, dowdy, ill at ease with people who had grown up in families, and, above all, solitary. From having been "in the same boat" with so many others at the orphanage, they felt isolated when they were living on their own. A few admitted to having had daydreams in childhood that were so far removed from the reality of their adult lives that they felt disillusioned. One man said that since he had known nothing outside of the institution but the houses of wealthy patrons he and the others visited during the holidays, he had supposed that that was the way life outside would be, and couldn't reconcile his boyhood fantasies with the dreary life he lived as an adult in a seedy furnished room.

One well-educated man's memory of his arrival at the orphanage remains vivid: "At first, utter despair and loneliness gripped me." To add to his misery, his hair was sheared close to his scalp (a defense against lice). As if afraid he has overdramatized his feelings, he continues self-deprecatingly, "Like Coleridge, we orphans are apt to be unduly imaginative."

At the sesquicentennial celebration of the Hebrew Jewish Orphanage, Art Buchwald says of his time there:

> I think I was seven years old, when confused, lonely and terribly insecure, I said to myself: The hell with it. I think I'll become a humorist. From then on I turned everything into a joke . . . and I found I could survive. I had my bag of laughs, I had my fantasies, which I must say were really great. Would you believe that I dreamed I was the son of a Rothschild and I was kidnapped by gypsies when I was six months old, and sold to a couple going to America?

The couple going to America were his parents. After his mother died, his father, finding that he could not keep his son and three daughters at home, put them in the orphanage, where they remained until they were placed in separate foster homes. After he left HJO, Buchwald missed the comforting sense of being one of many "in the same boat" (how frequently orphans use that expression!), and while he expresses gratitude to his foster parents for taking him in, admits that he ran away from them to join the Marine Corps. As an adult, he has had the immense satisfaction of seeing his childhood dreams of glory come true:

> In Paris I decided to make up for my deprived childhood by becoming the food and wine expert of the Paris edition of the *Herald Tribune.* I lived it up with the International Set, sailed on Onassis' yacht, played roulette with King Farouk, and danced until dawn with the Duchess of Windsor.

(What he does not say on this celebratory occasion, but discloses elsewhere, is that despite his successful career and the family life he created with a wife and children, he suffered from depression. It was caused, he learned through psychoanalysis, by his early losses.)

In pre-Freudian days, if sympathy was expressed at the death of a parent, it was offered to the surviving relatives who would be burdened with raising someone else's child. Orphans went numbly where they were told to go, with the admonition that they should be grateful to be fed, clothed, and sheltered. What directed the attention of child analysts to children who lost their parents prematurely was the onset of World War II. In England, the government called upon Anna Freud to organize nurseries for infants whose fathers were mobilized and whose mothers had joined the work force, as well as for those evacuated during the blitz.

In the Hampstead Nurseries, which offered a unique opportunity for close, round-the-clock observation and recording of reactions of children from birth to four years of age, there was no denying the effects of separation. When mothers left these "artificial orphans" (many of whom became biologic orphans by the end of the war), they cried incessantly, refused to eat, slept poorly, were alternatingly clinging and detached, refused to recognize their mothers when they reappeared, and only accepted a substitute for her, when they did so, because their need to be looked after was so great. That their grief was deep and serious, that they felt despair, was beyond doubt.

Separation from fathers (for whom the nurseries could offer no substitute) the children seemed to tolerate well. When one came to visit, he was adopted by all (in a way that a visiting mother never was), the children begging to sit on his lap and be carried around. One might have predicted from this promiscuous substituting of a stranger to play the role of father that the children would not be deeply affected when they were told that their own fathers had been killed. Such was not the case. They continued to talk about the dead parent as if he were alive; or, when they grasped the reality of death, as the older ones did, seemed to accept their loss one minute, and the next deny it with fantasies of reunion at the end of the war.

In 1945, Anna Freud was asked to look after another group of children without parents. They were survivors—the rare survivors—of concentration camps who had lost mother, father, relatives, homeland, and native language: the most orphaned of orphans. Among the thousand who arrived in England were six three-year-olds (some a little younger, some a little older) whose parents had been exterminated soon after their births. As babies, they had been hidden by other inmates in camp dormitories and passed from one woman to another for care until, at ages six to twelve months, they were placed in a ward for orphans in Terezín. The women detailed to look after them there, also inmates, were so enfeebled by malnutrition that they were able to make only a minimal effort on behalf of their charges. The six remained together until the camp was liberated by the Russians in 1945, when they were taken to a Czech castle for medical attention before being flown to England.

On arrival, they reacted with such acute anxiety at finding themselves in a strange, and to them hostile, environment —ignoring the solicitous adults who tried to look after them, rejecting food, sleeping fitfully, weeping, having temper tantrums, clinging to one another for comfort— that Anna Freud decided to keep them together, to allow them time to adjust to their new surroundings.

The Bulldogs Bank six (so named after the house donated for their use by an English family) reacted to loss as the Hampstead children had done, only more dramatically, more violently. But there was a way in which they were strikingly different from both children raised at home and those in the nurseries, which taught analysts something about orphans it would have been difficult to learn in any other way. Although the six reacted negatively to adults, they were strongly attached to one another, so strongly that they refused to be separated (even when the infectious disease of one made it essential). More astonishing to their nurses was the solicitude those in the little band showed toward one another. They resisted being singled out for treats, did not have to be urged to take turns, never told on one another, lent their possessions willingly, and at the table made sure that their neighbors were served before they ate.

Mothers worn down by daily battles between their children would find the behavior of these concentration-camp children extraordinarily unchildlike. But to me it had a familiar ring. It was the way Marie and I had behaved with each other as children. And we did so for the same reasons. Adults played so little part in our affective lives that we did not compete with each other for their favors and attention. The Bulldogs Bank children, having been deprived of parents and family life, created a tightly knit group in which the members were free of the competitiveness, envy, rivalry, and possessiveness siblings feel in relationship to their parents, teachers, and nurses. It was only after some months, when they began to respond to mother substitutes, that they displayed behavior typical of other children their age. While this was a healthy sign, and a necessary step in their development, it was their having been kept together, and the comfort and support they gave one another, that explained their having survived as well as they did. For while they were restless, aggressive, difficult to handle, and some showed the beginnings of neurotic symptoms, none was autistic or as disturbed as had been anticipated. The "experiment provided by fate" raised questions in the minds of those who had taken care of these orphans about the effects of early maternal deprivation that they felt only follow-up studies could answer.

René Spitz was impressed by reports that when the mortality rate in large German orphanages dropped 75 percent as a result of improved hygiene and medical practices, those who lived beyond infancy showed a high incidence of severe psychiatric disturbance. For his 1946 study of the effects of institutionalization, he compared two groups. In one, which he called "Foundling Home," infants born of women so poor they couldn't afford to keep them were looked after by professional nurses. In the other, "Nursery," infants born of delinquent girls in prison were allowed to be with them for several hours every day. The nurses saw that their charges were fed and that hygienic standards of care were met. The delinquents, deprived of all other pleasurable activities, lavished attention on their babies.

After the first three months, the infants in "Foundling Home" showed no serious psychological damage. By the end of a year, however, they had developed what Spitz called "hospitalism." They were highly susceptible to illness and infection, and their intellectual and social deterioration was striking when compared with the development of the "Nursery" children. Their deficits could be blamed on only one thing: extreme emotional deprivation. A nurse, even a "baby-loving" one who took care of seven infants, could not give each of her charges the visual, auditory, tactile, and postural stimulation required for normal development. This is what the eighteenth-century Spanish priest quoted by Spitz meant when he said that many infants in the foundling home he directed sickened and died from *"tristeza"* (sadness).

This sadness that leads to death used to be so well known that to place an infant in a foundling home was called, in common parlance, giving it "to the angels." Yet today it is so painful for us to contemplate that even psychologists and analysts try to deny it. I did. What about the Bulldogs Bank children? I wondered. But I knew the answer. They were the remarkable exceptions who had not only survived but somehow *had* had mothering despite the desperate circumstances into which they were born. The women who looked after them would have had a fierce desire to protect and comfort them.

From Spitz on, all the studies have shown that where there is no mother, or mother substitute, there is no possibility of a normal child. What it meant for 65 to 90 percent of those who were placed in foundling homes, especially after the bottle replaced the breast and babies were deprived of the close contact that had been necessary during nursing, was that they received a death sentence. What it meant for the few who survived was that they would be physically, intellectually, and emotionally damaged.

In 1950, Bowlby became interested in the effects of maternal loss when the World Health Organization asked him to report on the mental health of homeless children. As a result of his observations, he believed that infants become attached to their mothers at six months (other analysts put the age at nine months). If the attachment is broken (by absence or death), an infant will cry in protest, hoping to bring her back. If she doesn't return, his protest turns into despair. He may continue to cry, but what is more likely is that he will become withdrawn and make so little demand for attention that the adults looking after him mistake this phase as a sign that distress has diminished. The kind of attachment formed to the mother will determine the emotional tone of relationships children develop with others throughout life. If mother goes away, or dies, or is unresponsive, they will become either "anxiously attached" or "cold and inhibited."

By age four, children are capable of mourning, Bowlby believes. If they are to develop normally, they must be told the truth about the death, be permitted to ask questions about it, and go through the same stages adults go through —from numbness to yearning, from yearning to despair. "The greatest terror in childhood," William James said, "is solitude." In the period of despair, children know this terror. Only when they have accepted the finality of death will they be free to establish a relationship with a surrogate.

The child who is not permitted to mourn, or doesn't have a sibling close in age with whom to share the experience, will pay a heavy price later in life. Aborted mourning is the cause of many psychiatric disturbances in adults, whose symptoms are disguised forms of yearning for, and rage against, the parent who died. The loss of a close friend or, especially, of a spouse is likely to reactivate emotions suppressed at the time of the earlier loss, when the bereaved appeared to be detached and behaved as if nothing had happened.

The reason I had found Bowlby so disturbing to read was that he writes not about those grossly deprived (Anna Freud and René Spitz's subjects), but ordinary children, such as I was. Implied in what he says is: Once an orphan, always an orphan (though he uses the word "orphan" only once, and then in a footnote). This clashed with my tenaciously held view that my orphanhood had ended when I ceased to be a minor, and that I suffered no sequelae. How often is it possible for a child to have the perfect circumstances for bereavement? For most, as with me, mourning will be aborted by circumstances, or by relatives (behaving as relatives have behaved for centuries) who are too grief-stricken themselves to cope with their own emotions, much less the child's, or who underestimate the complexity of the young child's sensitivity to death.

In the imperfect circumstances following my father's death, I remember vividly the period of yearning. Aching disappointment was what I thought I had felt when he didn't come to take us home at Christmastime. Disappointment was a concept I understood. I had experienced it before and could identify it, whereas I didn't know the word "despair." It was Bowlby's insistence on the feeling of having been abandoned, and the rage that follows abandonment, that especially made me anxious. Theoretically I could accept what Bowlby said, and had seen it in children, yet I stubbornly refused to admit that I, too, must have had these feelings.

During the period of my profound orphanhood, at the height of the crisis, I had an experience that told me I could go no further with self-analysis: I needed help. One night, I was jolted out of sleep even more violently than usual by the uncanny feeling that there was someone by my side.

Lying stock-still, moving only my eyes, I made out the contours of a figure: a head encased in a helmet; a body, rigid, hands clasped on the chest. *What was it?* In a convulsive movement, I leapt up and switched on the overhead light. The apparition had vanished.

I sat in a chair, huddled in a blanket, though it was not cold. Was I feverish again? (Only recently had I recovered from a long bout of pneumonia—pneumonia, for the first time since childhood. It had taken me back to age five, four, three.) No, no fever. The blanket was for comfort. As I waited for dawn—harbinger of good sense and clear vision —I realized that the visitation/hallucination was a combination of a Dürer etching (the helmeted head) and a tomb sculpture of a nobleman such as one sees in the crypt of European cathedrals (the clasped hands and the body). It was Death. Whose? My own? Was it bringing a message? Or was it just a silent reminder?

The psychoanalyst I consulted surprised me by asking frequently about my writing. My apparatus of self-deception firmly in place, I said I didn't have what some called a "writer's block." I hadn't come to talk about my work, and implied that I didn't have time to waste. Mildly (but with the shadow of an ironic smile?), he suggested that perhaps we should consider the effect my subject, and the reading I was doing for it, was having on me. It was forcing me to do what Freud called "the work of mourning" that I had not done at the time of the death of one parent in childhood and the other in infancy. As I came to see my feelings of helplessness, isolation, and middle-of-the-night terror as the reactions of an eleven-month-old—"I feel as though I were trapped in a cage. No, a crib!" I was astonished to hear myself say—and not of a woman competent to look after herself (and others), I began to recover.

While I had not produced all the symptoms Bowlby had threatened me with, I had had a good many of them. Not delinquency (too late for that), nor suicidal tendencies (although in the blackest period, hadn't the shriek of brakes and the angry honking of horns warned me that I was flirting with death at street crossings?), but severe separation anxiety, psychosomatic complaints, and, for the first time in my life, undisguised depression.

What happened, I wondered, almost afraid to ask, to the concentration-camp orphans? In 1954, Anna Freud reported that those who had been at Bulldogs Bank maintained their "precarious normality" until adolescence, at which time they showed symptoms of delinquency, depression, and withdrawal far beyond the incidence expected in puberty. In the late seventies and early eighties, Sarah Moskovitz tracked down and interviewed twenty-four men and women who had been at Bulldogs Bank and Lingfield (another English home where the band of six joined a larger group of refugee children after their period of adjustment was over).

Memory for most of those interviewed began with the airplane flight to England. In the early days of the new lives, two pairs of sisters who had been at Auschwitz provided each other with security, especially at night, when they clung together in bed. One pair was among the fortunate few whose daydreams came true. Their mother survived Auschwitz, their father was released after six years in a prisoner-of-war camp, and the family was reconstituted. Both girls married, had children, and although the younger one said she thinks she is sadder and more introspective than her friends, both seem remarkably well adjusted.

The other pair of sisters also did well. They, like many of the orphans, had not wanted to be adopted, and when they went to live with a family were so unhappy they called the director of Lingfield and asked to be taken back. A man who as a boy of nine at Auschwitz protected these four girls had lived through a stormy adolescence during which he became delinquent and was sent to jail. After his release, he migrated to Israel, and at the time he was interviewed was managing reasonably well.

The children who were adopted spoke of having had a difficult time after they left Lingfield. They missed the other orphans and the sense of belonging they had had when they were looked after by a staff alert to their needs. In foster homes, they had been alone, and were taken care of by surrogates who had no experience with children (some, themselves refugees, seem to have been suffering from depression). They tended to blame themselves, rather than their foster parents, for their poor adjustment to homelife, saying that they had not been easy to manage. When they did express disappointment and disillusion-ment, it was over what they had felt as shattering abandon-ments that occurred when psychoanalysts with whom they were in treatment while at Lingfield, and nurses on the staff there, left to go to the United States, or died, leaving "a wake of longing and turmoil behind them."

Lingfield children, like all institutionalized orphans who talk about what made their early years more tolerable, said how important it had been to them to have had a sponsor in the world outside, someone who occasionally wrote, sent packages, visited them.

What is striking in all those who agreed to be interviewed (and here, as in other studies, one suspects that it's those who fared best who are willing to talk) is the striking lack of self-pity, anger, or bitterness—even against the Nazis! Rather, they expressed strong feelings of compassion for others, and gratitude for their good fortune. A high pro-portion of them turned to religion.

A man who as a little boy at Bulldogs Bank had gone from one nurse to the other in the days after he arrived asking, *"Bist du mein?,"* obviously yearning for an unrecog-nizable but longed-for adult to whom he had once been attached, said,

I feel I am terribly lucky to have come out of it all right
. . . to have survived . . . to have found Alice, [the director
of Lingfield]. . . . Why me? Why do I have so much? This
beautiful house, a nice wife, children . . .

Moskovitz concludes, and one would have to agree, that
these concentration-camp survivors grew up to be sounder
psychologically than anyone would have predicted (especially those on hand to greet them in England who were
afraid they might not be "human"). But their orphanhood,
as perhaps Moskovitz does not realize, is not over. Their
"exquisite vulnerability" to separation and delicate equilib-
rium had not had the ultimate test when she talked to them:
the loss through death of those to whom they have become
deeply attached—the "nice wife, children . . ."

CHAPTER 11

Orphans in Autobiography

SINCE LIFE IN an orphanage suppressed individuality, I should not have been surprised to find so few accounts of what it was like to grow up behind asylum walls, nor that those I found were for the most part uninflected and repetitious. The regimentation and dreary routine did not provide a milieu stimulating to the development of a sense of self. For that, I turned to those whose circumstances in childhood had allowed them sufficient freedom to think of themselves as "I," and who as adults were interested in exploring the drama of their budding egos: writers of autobiography who happened also to be orphans.

From Jean-Jacques Rousseau's autobiography one might expect to learn a good deal about how it feels to be an orphan, for the orphaned writer of the *Confessions* (1770) was a master of psychological analysis who promised to write "true to nature," and did so with a candor many of his readers found disconcerting. Rousseau's mother died of puerperal fever soon after his birth. When he was ten years old, his father went into exile from which he never returned, making the boy in effect a full orphan. A closer look at the relationship between father and son suggests that Isaac Rousseau had abdicated the parental role even earlier. Whatever affection he gave his son in "kisses" and "convulsive embraces," the boy had promptly to return. To him fell the burden of comforting a bereaved husband:

> "Ah," he [Isaac] would say with a groan; "Give her back to me, console me for her, fill the void she has left in my heart!"

When Jean-Jacques learned to read, which he did early, it was he who read to his father. The two stayed up so late over their books that:

> Sometimes my father would say with shame as we heard the morning larks, "Come, let us go to bed. I am more of a child than you are."

The "elderly child," as Rousseau called himself, became so because he had a childlike father.

In adolescence, when he made a bid for the absent Isaac's attention by running away from an apprenticeship he found tyrannical, neither Isaac, nor the uncle in whose care he had been placed, made any effort to look for him. At fifteen, he was homeless, penniless, on his own.

If Rousseau writes with a sensibility that is sometimes startlingly modern about his erotic feelings, he is a man of the eighteenth century when he talks about his childhood, a man who has not even read his own book, *Émile*. Self-pitying though he is about much else in his life, he not only does not pity himself for the losses he sustained in his early years, but also seems unaware of the effect they had on him. His, he says, was a happy childhood. While he lashes out with paranoid intensity at erstwhile friends and benefactors who he feels failed to return his affection, or who behaved treacherously toward him, his tone when he speaks of his father's failures as a parent is mild, muted. He records Isaac's reason for going away (the threat of imprisonment following a quarrel with a landowner) without comment, makes no judgment on Isaac's having left him behind, or failure to send for him once he had established himself in his new home, beyond saying, "He loved me dearly but he also loved his pleasure." While Rousseau claims to have been greeted affectionately by Isaac whenever he went to visit him (a claim his biographer Jean Guehenno questions), he admits dispassionately that Isaac "never made any great effort to keep me with him."

It is only about the treatment his older brother received at their father's hand that he permits himself to be critical. François was alternately beaten and "somewhat neglected" until he ran away from home. Rousseau considers this neglect of his brother to have been "very wrong," but rather than see it as a sign of irresponsibility and shallowness of paternal feeling, he prefers to believe that it was the result of Isaac's having lavished so much affection on him that there was none left over for the older boy. We are not convinced.

Perhaps the greatest disservice father did son was to make the boy feel that his birth was a "misfortune." Isaac did not say, "We both suffered a great loss, you of a mother, I of a wife." Rather, "Your birth caused my wife's death. Make it up to me."

What made Rousseau's childhood happy was the loving attention his aunt and nurse gave him. In an effort to make up for his motherless state, they may also have spoiled him. The sense he had of himself as exceptional he undoubtedly got from them; whereas it was the pleasure-loving, undisciplined Isaac who encouraged his intolerance of restraint and passion for freedom.

In his relationships with women, Rousseau sought mother surrogates throughout his life. The compassionate

Mme de Warens (herself an orphan) put an end to his wanderings by taking him in. "Dear Maman" gave him the affection he craved, and indulged his need for a protracted adolescence in which to read, dream, and educate himself in preparation for the work that would one day declare his genius. When she thought it was time for him to have a mistress, she proposed herself. So much was this thirty-three-year-old woman like a mother to him that when he accepted her offer he felt he was committing incest.

Their relationship, which he claimed gave him "the greatest happiness" of his life, has been a puzzle to historians and biographers who have struggled to sort out what Guehenno calls "the profound yet subtle distortions of reality" in pages of the *Confessions* that have to do with the years he spent with her. As Rousseau claimed to have been adored as a child, so he gives the impression of having lived an idyllic life as the favorite of Mme de Warens. The favorite he was, but for a briefer period than he remembered. Separation from her, unless he initiated it, was so painful that when, on returning from one of his absences, he found himself displaced by a "brother," her new favorite, he pleaded with "dear Maman" less like a rejected lover than like an abandoned child, begging her to "arrange things so that I need not die of despair." When she responded by offering him a cottage an hour's drive from where she lived, he swallowed his pride and accepted. For two years he lived there, mostly alone, seeing her when he did in the company of his rival, communicating with her for the most part by letter.

Once he became famous, other women, both cultivated and wealthy, offered him hospitality (which they sometimes had reason to regret, so demanding was their guest). While he remained susceptible to the "rustle of silk skirts" until the end of his days, and periodically felt a need for romantic love, the companion of his adult life was an uneducated serving girl who devoted herself to looking after him.

The mother he talked about rapturously, however, was

not a woman. It was mother earth—the woods, fields, and streams of the countryside to which he retired periodically to work, to heal his wounds, and to reestablish his precarious psychic balance. The therapy he found most comforting in periods of acute anxiety when he was tormented by paranoid delusions was botanizing. "Oh nature," he cries in the *Confessions.* "Oh my mother!" Those like Voltaire who attacked him for retiring to the country did not understand the symbolic nourishment he received from the bosom of mother nature.

Voltaire's most damaging attack on Rousseau was an anonymous letter directed at the author of *Émile* for setting himself up as an authority on how children should be cared for when he has abandoned his own children, the

> unfortunate creature whose mother died because of him, and whose children he abandoned on the door-step of a poor-house, after refusing to allow a kind-hearted person to take care of them. . . .

The secret was out. Rousseau was devastated by the exposure that made him appear a hypocrite, and which he was afraid would dishonor him in the eyes of his public. Remorse, and the need to win the public to his side, drove him to write the *Confessions.* His way, in contrast to Augustine's, was to confess a sin and then rationalize it in a way guaranteed to make his readers grant him absolution. He justifies his having made his mistress give away their first child by saying that he was following "the custom of the country." It is true that at that time men took a far more cavalier attitude toward their offspring than they do today. (Guehenno, citing a statistical study which shows that in 1772 over a third of infants born in Paris were abandoned, calls Rousseau's sin "venial.")

The "custom of the country" justification didn't satisfy even the unwilling father for long. To strengthen his case, he hints that through his mistress's line any child of theirs would have a poor inheritance. Later, he asks how he could be expected to write in tranquillity "if my garret was filled with domestic cares and the disturbance of children." He did not want to seek some "base employment" or "stoop to infamous acts" to support his offspring. "Would I nourish my children and their mother on the life-blood of the needy? . . . It is better that they should be orphans than that they should have a rascal as their father."

These "base and ignoble" sentiments, as Guehenno calls them, bring us closer to the truth. As does still another justification Rousseau offers, his remorse allowing him little peace. Had he kept his children at home, he says,

> they would have been led to hate, and perhaps betray their parents. It is a hundred times better that they should never have known them . . . I could have wished, and still do wish, that I had been brought up and nurtured as they have been.

Rousseau's callousness, which so repels modern readers, is less mysterious (if no less reprehensible) if one remembers that the model of fatherhood he had before him was Isaac—Isaac who drove away his elder son and gave away the younger. If Jean-Jacques's wish that he had been brought up by the state was genuine, it may well be the most powerful criticism (albeit still covert) of the way he was raised. "A father has no right to be a father if he cannot fulfill a father's duties," he says, suspecting that he would have been no better, perhaps worse, than Isaac in the role. His need for a mother was so great that he must have known instinctively that he would be incapable of sharing his mistress's attention with a child. *He* was the child.

One does not feel rivalrous toward a fictional child, nor does one beat it, abandon it, behave toward it as a rascal. The elderly child who grew up to write *Émile* revolutionized education with his plea to "allow childhood to ripen within the child." His bill of rights for children led many to refer to him as the spiritual and intellectual foster father of generations of children. He himself made no such claim. Even to be a foster father would have been too close for comfort. He was not a father, but a tutor. The child Émile was not his son, but an orphan.

Tolstoy, another orphan (he lost his mother at age two, his father, age nine), was a great admirer of the *Confessions*. But, unlike Rousseau, he made no claim that *Childhood* (1852), *Boyhood* (1854), and *Youth* (1857) were true to life (and was vexed with his editor for suggesting that the title of the first volume be changed to *The History of My Childhood*). His original plan was to write a novel about a family he knew, but autobiography and the history of his own family wove their way into the fabric of these books until it became what he called "an awkward mixture of fact and fiction." If Rousseau's *Confessions* often reads like a picaresque novel, Tolstoy's first novel reads like an autobiography. What is striking is that whereas Rousseau never refers to himself as an orphan, Tolstoy, writing seventy years later, sounds the orphan theme early.

On being awakened by his tutor, the ten-year-old narrator of *Childhood* invents a dream to tell the old man in which his mother dies and is being buried. The kindly Karl Ivanych comforts the boy. The boy, in turn, feels compassion for this "poor poor old man" who is an orphan, without family, and living in a foreign country, in contrast to the young hero's privileged life with parents and siblings in a country house suffused with love. Through descriptions of games, hunts, picnics, and family meals, the "happy, happy, never-to-be-recalled days of childhood" are evoked. Especially sweet are the scenes, full of tender exchanges and affectionate embraces, between the boy and his mother, in which her "lovely" face, her "gentle" hands, her "dear familiar" voice, her scent, her pensiveness, her concern for his well-being make the boy cry out, "Oh dear dear Mamma, I do love you so!"

This is the novelist, in his twenties, giving his younger

self the mother he had in reality lost before his second birthday. Though Tolstoy was able to recall episodes which occurred before her death—being swaddled and bathed—he could not remember her no matter how hard he tried. There was no picture of her in the house, only a silhouette made when she was a young girl. And those he questioned about her enumerated her virtues, but left her image as lifeless and opaque as the silhouette. After a time, she became a mythical being to whom he had recourse in periods of distress and upon whom he relied for supernatural assistance. Throughout his long life he continued to yearn—"Maman, hold me, baby me!"—for what he had so briefly had and lost.

The intensity and endurance of his yearning is noteworthy in one who had as a mother surrogate a woman ideally suited to the role. Aunt Toinette, an orphan who had been taken in by the Tolstoy family, devoted herself to serving others. She doted on Leo and taught him "the spiritual joy of loving." Life at Yasnaya Polyana, the family estate, continued under her direction to be so happy that despite the loss of his mother, Leo felt, according to his biographer Henri Troyat, "that a current of love was passing perpetually between his family and the rest of the world."

The creation of a fictional mother who lived eight years longer than his own had served a literary as well as emotional purpose. In order to portray a child's reaction to death, he needed a protagonist old enough to experience grief. From family reminiscences he knew that when he was taken to his mother's bedside he screamed in terror at the unrecognizable "livid mask" her face had become, and only calmed down after his nurse took him back to his room and comforted him. Wishing to expand the scene, he gave this primitive reaction to a little girl (about the age he was) who when held over the coffin by a peasant woman beats her fists, throws back her head, and, staring with dilated eyes, "utters a succession of dreadful frenzied shrieks." The more complex reaction he reserves for the ten-year-old hero, who imagines his mother in alternating visions as alive, gay, smiling, or as the "pale yellow translucent object" she had become, until he reaches a state in which he is oblivious of everything but a "kind of exalted, ineffably sweet, sad happiness." After this moment, the boy realizes that self-pity and self-love permit him to enjoy his unhappiness in such a way as to stifle real sorrow. He is so aware of his own feelings that he becomes angry at the expressions of sympathy the mourners offer his father. Above all, he resents their readiness to refer to him and his siblings as *"orphans.* Probably (I thought), they enjoyed being the first to give us that name." When his sense of loss returns, he goes to his mother's old nurse, who, unlike his father and the others in the household whose grief makes them unapproachable, is capable of selfless sorrow. She comforts him whenever he goes to her room and allows him to have "a good cry." When it comes time for the family to move to Moscow, the boy's thoughts turn to the future. Excitement about the trip replacing sadness, he feels guilty at being so easily able to put aside his bereavement.

As for a dual purpose Tolstoy created a mother who remained alive until his protagonist was ten, so he also created a father who remarries, returns with his family to his country estate, and is alive at the end of the book, when in reality Count Nicholas Ilich Tolstoy died suddenly, and away from home, when Leo Tolstoy was nine. No sooner had the orphan become aware of his new state than his dear old tutor (the model for Karl Ivanych in *Childhood*) was dismissed. The hated new tutor punished Leo for an act of insubordination by banishing him to a dark boxroom. The author of *Boyhood* gives his hero "imaginings" for companionship during the long hours of his confinement. Among them is a fantasy immensely appealing to children with parents—those who believe that the quite ordinary man who claims paternity cannot possibly be their father (Goethe's case), those like the boy in the boxroom, who are being punished and speculate about the cause of their mistreatment:

> "Perhaps I am not the son of my mother and father, . . . but a poor orphan, a foundling adopted out of charity," I said to myself, and this ridiculous notion not only afforded me a certain melancholy consolation but even seemed quite plausible. . . .

Upon his release, the boy confronts his father ("Papa, there is no point in hiding the secret of my birth from me") and says that now that he knows the truth, he has no choice but to leave the house.

Young Leo, with no father to turn to, spent twenty-four hours in such bitter reflections that, according to Troyat, he wanted "to die and fly away to dwell with pure souls." This desire continued to be so strong that "one day he could stand it no longer and jumped out of his third-floor bedroom window." He was found on the ground, senseless but, miraculously, with no bones broken and suffering from only a mild concussion. After eighteen hours' sleep, he woke up refreshed and as though nothing had happened.

Troyat, who offers no interpretation of this extraordinary episode, seems to accept Tolstoy's explanation, given years later, that he had been motivated by a need to impress others, to attract attention by performing some spectacular deed. Boyish histrionics seems an inadequate explanation. While it is difficult to judge how serious a suicide attempt this was, the crisis with the new tutor followed closely on the double, and unprepared-for, losses of father and father surrogate. Is it not possible that the leap of the freshly orphaned boy may have been an unconscious wish to follow a mother and father who had left the earth while he was still so young?

More deaths were to follow. Tolstoy's maternal grandmother, matriarch of the family, died a year after Count Nicholas, the aunt who became his guardian soon thereafter. At sixteen, he and his brothers were sent to Kazan to live with another guardian. Adolescent exuberance, his closeness to his siblings, and correspondence with Aunt Toinette kept him from suffering what might otherwise have been a painful dislocation. Five years later, when he came into his inheritance, he broke off his education, returned to Yasnaya Polyana, which was now his, and installed Aunt Toinette as chatelaine. He was back in what V. S. Pritchett called "the prefeudal culture of kinship" which had enriched his childhood and mitigated the effects of his early losses. And he was living once again close to nature, to mother earth, to the land he loved so passionately.

Throughout his life, Tolstoy was as preoccupied with his health as Rousseau had been with his, and no less obsessed with death. At intervals throughout Jean-Jacques's sixty-six years of life (a good age for a man in those days), he was so convinced that he was going to die that he rewrote his will and prepared for the end. With Tolstoy, the "terrifying" happiness of the early years of his marriage seemed to bring the threat of death closer. As he wrote in his journal:

> There are times when one forgets it, *it*, death, and then there are others, like this year, when one keeps very quiet around those one loves and watches with terror as *it* strikes here and there, cruel and blind. . . .

The preoccupation with *it* reached a dramatic crisis when he was convalescing from the labor of writing *War and Peace*. To fill in the time he had previously devoted to composition, he read philosophy "gluttonously." This reading plunged him into ruminations over questions of life and death. He complained to his wife that "his brain hurt, some painful process was going on inside it, everything was over for him, it was time for him to die." At a moment when he seemed to have everything—wife, children, Yasnaya Polyana, success as a writer hailed as a genius—he became afraid he would lose it all. "To fortify his defenses against this peril," Troyat says, he set out on a journey to buy more land. En route he became so anxious he decided to spend the night in the town of Arzamas. The only inn, far from hospitable, increased his foreboding. Awakening during the night, he asked himself in panic what he was afraid of:

> "Of me," answered Death. "I am here." My whole being ached with the need to live, the right to live, and at the same moment, I felt death at work.

Was he to die, Tolstoy must have wondered, like his father —on the road, far from home? (At age eighty-two, in a tragic scene worthy of his fiction, he fled his wife and the nightmare his marriage had become, fell ill, and died in a room at a railway station.) He tried to govern his terror by thinking of his family, his work. To no avail: Death was *there*. Remembering his prayers, he began the Our Father, broke off, impatient to be on his way. While waiting for the horses to be harnessed, he fell into a deep sleep. In the morning, he awakened refreshed, unable to believe the nighttime phantasmagoria. The protagonist of his unfinished story about this crisis (from which Troyat took these quotes) says in the end, "I went on living as before, but the fear of this despair never left me again."

Following the publication of *Anna Karenina*, Tolstoy underwent another profound crisis. This time, it was not fear of death but desire for it. Having reached his fiftieth year, he saw nothing ahead but "the lie of freedom and happiness, nothing but suffering, real death, complete annihilation." He brooded about how to take his life. One day, walking through the woods on his estate, he had an epiphany: he must accept God not through reason but with the faith of a child.

Troyat links Tolstoy's despair with the *mal du siècle* and a suicide epidemic that was raging among students, and the wealthy, who were killing themselves "out of lassitude, nausea, imitation, braggadocio or plain curiosity." This seems wide of the mark. Geniuses don't follow fashions. They start them. The deaths of three of his children, of adored Aunt Toinette, and of another aunt within a three-year period, together with the labor of writing the novel, left him in a psychically weakened state, with little energy to deal with the feeling of emptiness, of bereavement that even minor artists feel upon giving over their work to the public. The new bereavements, as is their wont, stirred up the old ones. V. S. Pritchett says of an earlier loss, the death of Nicholas, Leo's favorite brother, that it planted the terror of death that haunted him the rest of his life. But that terror had been planted many years earlier, in Tolstoy's orphaned childhood. The shadow that had been dogging his footsteps since then caught up with him on his journey to buy more property. It loitered by his side, tugging at his sleeve, taunting him to hurry, after *Anna Karenina.*

Some years after these crises he wrote "The Death of Ivan Ilich." What made Tolstoy able to create a short story about a man whose soul comes to life as his body is dying, which many critics consider one of the greatest ever written, was his night of agony at Arzamas, and the lifting of his despair through the revelation that came to him in the woods at Yasnaya Polyana.

A genius of a different order, Bertrand Russell early lost not only his parents (mother, age two; father, age three), but also his sister (age two) and the grandfather with whom he had been living (age six). In his autobiography, he says that as a child he used to lie awake at night thinking how dreadful it would be if the grandmother with whom he lived, a formidable woman who was "deeply, but not always wisely, solicitious" of his welfare, were also to die. He was fortunate in having, like Tolstoy, the attention of the staff on the family estate—housekeeper, cook, butler, gardener, as well as his nurse—all of whom played a larger role in his early life than did his family.

Although he thought of those years as having been "on the whole happy and straightforward," he realizes he must have felt "some kind of unhappiness, as I remember wishing that my parents had lived." When he expressed this wish to his grandmother, she told him bluntly that he was better off without them. Suppressing the questions he would have liked to ask, but knew would be rebuffed, he made up daydreams of what life would have been like had they lived. (It was only when he was an adult that he solved the "dark mystery" about his mother and father: their advanced ideas on sexual freedom and politics had scandalized their Victorian families.)

What happiness Russell had known as a child vanished in his preadolescent days, when he was plunged into a period of aching loneliness. One as intellectually precocious as he could no longer count on the companionship of servants. He had no school friends because he was being educated at home. And the adults in his milieu showed such a "remarkable incapacity for understanding a boy's emotions" that he learned to keep his own counsel. Outwardly he appeared "good-natured and well-behaved"; inwardly he despaired of ever finding anyone to whom he could express his true feelings. Some time during this period, when he was afraid he would never be happy again, his brother (seven years his senior and so rarely at home he couldn't be counted on for fraternal closeness) came to his rescue in a surprising way:

> At the age of eleven, I began Euclid, with my brother as my tutor. This was one of the great events of my life, as dazzling as first love. I had not imagined there was anything so delicious in the world.

Two of the three passions that he says governed his life, "the longing for love, and the search for knowledge," declared themselves early. (The search for knowledge, "the wish to know more about mathematics," on more than one occasion was a powerful defense against the temptation to commit suicide.) His third passion, "an unbearable pity for the suffering of mankind," was triggered by the horror he felt over the Boer War, and by intense but frustrated sympathy and love, which had to remain hidden, for the wife of his collaborator, Alfred North Whitehead.

In *The Philosophers,* a biographical study of creativity and morbidity in the lives of outstanding thinkers who lost one or both parents early, Ben-Ami Scharfstein does not go so far as to say that to be a philosopher one must be orphaned early, but he certainly thinks it helps. Early loss by death or separation generated in his subjects, of whom Bertrand Russell was one, a precocious interest in questions of being and existence, life and death. If "the child is father to the philosopher," as Scharfstein believes, budding thinkers exploit the helplessness, lovelessness, despair, and, especially, fear of their own early death that follow upon their loss by embarking on the risky and dangerous search for truth that others would be too fearful, too anxious, to investigate. While the excitement of their intellectual pursuits does not spare them the familiar symptoms of early loss—they suffer the full array—it makes them tolerable by giving them immense pleasure and often power.

Scharfstein believes that during Russell's crisis over the war and his frustrated love for Mrs. Whitehead, he projected the unhappiness he had suffered in his orphaned childhood onto mankind. What in a lesser personality would have led to unproductive self-pity, in Russell motivated his lifelong commitment as a political activist (for which from time to time he paid a high price, once with a six-month jail sentence in Brixton prison).

Nowhere, however, are the marks of his orphan childhood so clear as in his endless quest for love and affection. At age twenty-two, he ceased being the well-behaved Bertie he had appeared to be to his family when he announced his intention to marry an American woman five years his senior, and gave evidence of being on his way to adopting his parents' shocking views on sexual freedom. So diligently did his grandmother, aunt, and the family doctor fight against what they saw as a misalliance that they drove him to the edge of madness with horror stories of psychological instability in his family history, which they claimed made him unfit to have children. In the end, the young couple had their way, but Russell never completely shook the fear of insanity implanted in his mind at that time.

Although he was at first "divinely happy," and counted the early years of his marriage as the most productive of his life, from the beginning he felt, like Tolstoy, that "when joy is purest, it seems to transcend itself and turn suddenly to haunting terrors of loss." For the most part, it was the women who suffered the loss, and suffered terribly, as he moved away from them through four marriages, two long-term affairs, and countless brief flings that his biographer, Ronald Clark, sees as attempts to "assuage an insatiable appetite for personable and intelligent young women." What accounted for the insatiability? In an effort to explain his feeling to one of his mistresses, Russell wrote:

> The centre of me is always and eternally a terrible pain—a curious wild pain—a searching for something beyond what the world contains, something transfigured and infinite— the beatific vision—God—I do not find it, I do not think it is to be found—but the love of it is my life—it's like a passionate love for a ghost. At times it fills me with rage, at times with wild despair, it is the source of gentleness and cruelty and work, it fills every passion that I have—it is the actual spring of life within me.

If the ghost is the ghost of his dead parents, as Scharfstein believes, and as seems likely, any affection Russell received would have left his hunger for love unassuaged. But, astonishingly, at the age of eighty he was finally able to put the ghost to rest. In his last marriage, he found not only love but tranquility.

In the dedicatory poem to his wife, Edith, which prefaces his autobiography, he recalls the ecstasy, anguish, madness, loneliness, and pain of his life and says:

> Now, old and near my end,
>   I have known you,
> And, knowing you,
> I have found both ecstasy & peace.
>   I know rest.
> After so many lonely years,
> I know what life and love may be.
> Now, if I sleep,
> I shall sleep fulfilled.

Not as close to the end as he imagined, he lived another eighteen years and died serene.

Bertrand Russell's account of his growing up is poised between the innocent days when autobiographers accepted the myth of childhood as a happy time, even for orphans, and the Freudian era, which turned a searchlight on these early years looking for psychic wounds. While Russell gingerly uses an occasional word from the vocabulary of psychoanalysis like "latency," and even questions how happy the happy days were, he, like Rousseau, feels little need to understand the source of the passions that governed his life, nor the reasons for behavior that to others was inexplicable. With Jean-Paul Sartre's *The Words* (1964), however, we are jolted into the modern world. With its interest in motivation, character development, and symptomatology, *The Words* reads like the autobiography of an analysand (despite the author's avowed anti-Freudianism) who, having decided at some point in the treatment he's every bit as skillful at reading his past as his analyst, and far better equipped to write about it, has said, Here, now, let *me* tell this story.

Sartre, a half orphan whose father died when he was a

year old, became in effect a full orphan for a four-year period when, at age eleven, his adored and adoring mother remarried and abdicated the maternal role when she left Jean-Paul to be looked after by his grandparents. Readers who know only *The Words* are surprised to learn of this second marriage, nowhere hinted at in its pages, and of the period following the abrupt separation from his mother which he elsewhere confesses was the worst time of his life. But the shadow of this loss is cast over the book in the nostalgic recall of the days when Anne-Marie (as he calls his mother) and Jean-Paul shared a bedroom, exchanged conspiratorial winks at the rest of the world, were each other's date on semiclandestine outings to the local movie house, and lived in such intimacy that, as Sartre himself says, their relationship resembled the chaste incestuousness of a brother and an older sister.

The Words begins like a sardonic fairy tale. After a rocky infancy during which baby Jean-Paul "applies himself to dying of enteritis and perhaps resentment" when he's put out to nurse while Anne-Marie tends her gravely ill husband, he returns home to find that he has had the great good luck to lose his potential rival. His father is not only out of the way, but he had the grace to disappear from the scene so early that his son has had no time to wish for his death and therefore feels no guilt over it. Not only is he incurious about the defunct, but he also feels free to patronize the "frank-looking little officer" whose picture his mother shows him.

What luck to have his mother all to himself! And (when she returns with him to live with her parents) to be the center of the household! Here, indeed, is a lucky orphan, living in the bosom of a complacent bourgeois French family in which "life is cloudless":

> It was Paradise. Every morning I woke up dazed with joy, astounded at the unheard-of luck of having been born into the most united family in the finest country in the world.

Paradise, reexamined years later by the analysand/ analyst, is found to have had its dark side. If there was no troublesome father to worry about, there was a grandfather who treated Anne-Marie like a child, and the child Jean-Paul like a cross between a budding genius and a ventriloquist's dummy. (It is this patriarch who took the little prince with golden curls to the barber, returning him to his mother looking like "a toad.") The price the boy paid for being the center of attention was that he had to perform for his audience of two women and one old man. If the actor was docile, intellectually precocious, and clownish, they applauded. So well did he succeed in playing these roles that he became "a fake child." Tutored at home, discouraged from playing with others his age, he was forced into "a proud exile which quickly turned to anguish." What increased the anguish was that he became aware that he was *not* the center of the grown-ups' lives. "Idolized by all, rejected by each," they tell him to run off and amuse himself if they have adult things to talk about.

When family friends point out to Anne-Marie that her Jean-Paul looks sad, she laughs and says to her son:

> "You who are so gay, always singing! What could you possibly complain of? You have everything you want."

The author/analyst agrees: "A spoiled child isn't sad. He's bored, like a king. Or a dog."

Sartre, another of Scharfstein's subjects, became obsessed with death at the age of five. It prowled on the balcony outside his bedroom every night, pressing its nose to the window. The gay-bored child lived in a state of terror until he developed the defense of becoming "an honorary corpse" whose future date with the Prowler, fixed but unknown, protected him in the meantime from "derailments, congestion, and peritonitis." (This defense gave him a kind of armor which years later his university friends, who were having their first real encounter with fear of death, were to envy.) By age seven, he lived in a world of fantasy. He buried himself in books, became a writer of heroic tales in which he rescued female orphans ("a thin disguise" for the author), and was well on his way to becoming a philosopher/novelist.

Halfway through the book, Sartre drops the sardonic tone of the narrator and in his own voice blurts out, "Besides, the reader has realized I loathe my childhood and whatever has survived of it."

At age seventy, this *cri de coeur* must have sounded shrill in his ears, for he distanced himself from *The Words* by saying of it, "It is a kind of novel, a novel in which I believe, but still a novel." Yet he was unable to deny that the supposedly lucky orphan came to yearn for the father who, whatever his defects, would have protected his son from the falsity of the roles he was made to play in childhood, and continued to play as an adult. After Anne-Marie's second husband died, she asked Sartre, now forty, to move in with her again. When he did, she said contentedly, "This is my third marriage." (If marriage it was, she shared Sartre with Simone de Beauvoir, who made their affair of the head and the heart so famous in *her* autobiographical books that the French pounced on each new volume as it appeared in the bookstores.)

One finishes *The Words* thinking how different the childhood of a half orphan is from a full orphan's. The strong lopsided pull that joins parent and child, especially if the parent is of the opposite sex and there are no other children, is so unlike what a full orphan experiences that one wishes another term had been coined to designate the difference.

Closer in time, place, and circumstances to my experience as an orphan are the fragments of autobiography which Mary McCarthy published originally in the *New Yorker* and other magazines over a decade before Sartre's *The Words* appeared. In the preface to the collection called

Memories of a Catholic Girlhood (1957), McCarthy says that she was accused many times of having written fiction rather than autobiography—so improbable do the circumstances of her early life seem to some readers—when in reality she invented little. So eager is she to hug the facts that in the commentaries between chapters, she is at pains to point out changes of names, of details, and where her investigations into the past provided her with conflicting evidence, doubtful memories. One feels that today she, unlike Sartre, would stand unequivocally behind what she wrote thirty years ago.

Mary McCarthy lost both parents at age six when the influenza epidemic of 1918 hit the family as it was traveling from Seattle to Minneapolis. She and her three younger brothers recovered from their bouts with the disease to find themselves in greatly altered circumstances. Their idyllic early years of a happy homelife with attentive and loving parents who provided all kinds of little treats—"the May baskets and the valentines, the picnics in the yard, and the elaborate snowman," which "conspired to fix in our minds the idea that we were very precious little persons, precious to our parents and to God . . ."—came to an abrupt end when they found themselves in the house of their paternal grandparents. Here they were treated like "pieces of furniture." The sense of "wondering, grateful privilege" they had had was replaced by a growing awareness of what it meant to be orphans:

> We had not known what it was . . . to take medicine in a gulp because someone could not be bothered to wait for us, to have our arms jerked into our sleeves and a comb ripped through our hair, to be bathed impatiently, to be told to sit up or lie down quick and no nonsense about it, to find our questions unanswered and our requests unheeded. . . . The happy life we had had . . . was a poor preparation, in truth, for the future that now opened up to us. . . .

The most important questions that went unanswered were about their parents. At first, Mary and her brothers were told that their mother and father had gone to the hospital to get better. The children's wishes to know more were so little encouraged that they soon stopped asking about their parents, and gradually "without tears or tantrums, we came to know that they were dead." Once in possession of this knowledge, they felt not grief, which was also not encouraged, but numbness.

Although both sets of grandparents were well off, the children were treated like poor orphans, especially after they were sent to live with the couple who became their guardians. In Aunt Margaret and Uncle Myers's house (which was just a few blocks away from their grandparents'), life became a series of coercions and punishments as these surrogate parents managed to reproduce, on a small scale, the life lived in orphan asylums. Their house was a crude box, their furniture drab, the food at their table unpalatable. The children came to look, with their patched and faded clothing, raw hands, scarecrow arms, and "elderly faces," like institutional children. Also like institutional children, they were lectured on how they should be grateful for what they had, were denied privacy, and were deprived of individuality.

So unhappy were Mary and her brother Kevin that they separately conceived an identical plan: to escape to the red brick asylum that, from their vantage point, appeared like "a haven of security." Periodically one or the other ran away. From their truancies they were taken by the police to their grandparents' house, where they had a brief taste of a better life before being returned to their guardians.

The first third of the book ends with the termination of the hated guardianship and the separation of Mary from her brothers. The boys are sent to boarding school, while she goes to live with her maternal grandparents in Seattle, where she is treated like the only child, now adolescent, of a wealthy and elderly couple.

What saved her during the bad years, McCarthy believes, was religion. Architecturally ugly though the parochial school and church she attended were, they provided her with an aesthetic outlet. The Latin mass, the litanies and hymns, the altar decorations, rosaries, and ornamented prayer books fed the sensuous needs starved in Uncle Myers's house. The nuns' method of education, which was based on competition, permitted her to excel. And her superior abilities undoubtedly made her a favorite among them, feeding her hunger for affection. What also saved her was the strength she gained from the loving care her parents had given her during the crucial first six years of her life, and from having had siblings, especially the brother closest to her, with whom she shared the Minneapolis experience.

CHAPTER 12

Literary Orphans

How FREE THE author of imaginative writing is in depicting orphanhood struck me anew as I read Tolstoy's *Childhood* with his biography in mind. Psychoanalysts no matter how perceptive remain at a distance as they report their observations of infants and young children. Autobiographers are limited by amnesia for what occurred in infancy, and by repression of events from childhood too painful to recall. The commandment to honor parents, and the injunction to express gratitude toward surrogates, inhibit their candor. Writers of fiction, poetry, and plays are unencumbered. Guided by intuition, guided also by experiences in their own lives that approximate the orphan's, they are free to imagine. When they imagine with genius, they extend our knowledge of reality.

With the development of the novel as a genre, orphans became heroes and heroines whose feelings readers could identify with, whose orphanhood was not merely stated (as it is in Shakespeare's plays and in picaresque tales), but described as if from the inside. As the streets of nineteenth-century London swarmed with orphans, so, too, did the fiction of the period, supremely, of course, in the works of Dickens.

Charles Dickens's biography begins to read like a Dickens novel when, at age twelve, he felt himself abandoned by his parents. His father, whose only serious defect of character was that he could not live within his means (whatever they were), went bankrupt. He and his wife, who could see no way of supporting their children, accepted the well-intended offer of a friend to place their eldest child, Charles, in a job at a blacking factory. From having had the attention of mother, father, aunt, nurse, and the company of siblings, young Dickens was suddenly turned out on his own. He was made to work a twelve-hour day and to look after himself completely. Not long after he began his apprenticeship, his father went to debtors' prison, taking his family with him. There, each Saturday, the blacking-factory waif went to visit them (and took in everything he saw). When his father was released, and the family again had a home, Charles expected to continue his education, but his mother, seeing no reason why he should leave the factory, was content to let him stay on in his job. What made the boy especially bitter toward her was that she arranged for his sister Fanny to go to music school while he continued to work.

The blacking-factory period lasted four months. To the twelve-year-old it seemed an eternity. The life he led during that time was one common to orphans and children of the poor. But to the boy who had lived in a middle-class family and because of his precocity, physical attractiveness, affectionate nature, and high spirits had been its star, the rupture was a brutal shock. So painful was the experience that he never told anyone about it, not even his wife and children until, late in life, he confessed it to his biographer and close friend, John Forster. How this traumatic experience informed Dickens's fiction we can see in *Oliver Twist* (1838) and in the most obviously autobiographical of his novels, *David Copperfield* (1850), to take just two with the orphan theme.

Oliver Twist had been as difficult for me to read as a girl as had fairy tales, and when I took it up recently I understood why. It would be hard to imagine a less auspicious beginning in life than Oliver's. Born in a workhouse of a woman who dies in childbirth, he is looked after by a bibulous pauper woman until he is farmed out, with other unfortunates, to Mrs. Mann. In her house, "not one kind word or look had ever lighted the gloom of his infant years." Yet when, at age nine, he is taken away, he is thrown into an

> agony of childish grief, as the cottage-gate closed after him. Wretched as were the little companions in misery he was leaving behind, they were the only friends he had ever known; and a sense of his loneliness in the great wide world sank into the child's heart for the first time.

The great wide world, he finds, is peopled with malevolent adults like Mr. Bumble, the meanspirited parish beadle, and Mr. and Mrs. Sowerberry, the undertaker and his wife for whom he works and from whom he runs away, only to fall into the hands of the monstrous Fagin and his gang of criminals, who subject him to every kind of mistreatment adults can inflict on a child. Along the way, he meets and is briefly mothered by kindly women, like Rose Maylie (herself an orphan).

Are the attentions of these women, which come late in his childhood, sufficient to explain his remaining tenderhearted, open, and loving, so that when he is adopted by Mr. Brownlow he is able to enjoy the happy life that is projected for him? Modern readers, at least the adults among them, will say no. Even if "nature had implanted a good sturdy spirit in Oliver's breast," we feel he would pay a heavy price for so much emotional deprivation and brutality.*

Critics have suggested that Oliver's story should be read not as a realistic novel but as a fairy tale. Even better, I found, was to read it as a collection of nightmares and daydreams of orphan children, or indeed of all children. We don't necessarily feel, as some of Dickens's contemporaries did, that the violence of Sikes and the villainy of Fagin are exaggerated. What is difficult to accept is that a child subjected to them survived unscathed. Only in the dream world is this possible. In sleep, children are tormented by Bumbles, Sowerberrys, and Fagins. Awake, they comfort themselves by imagining scenes of maternal tenderness:

> Oliver's pillow was soothed by gentle hands that night; and loveliness and virtue watched over him as he slept.

When life becomes intolerable for children, they solace themselves with daydreams of being dead:

> As he [Oliver] crept into his narrow bed, he imagined that it was his coffin, and that he could be lain in a calm and lasting sleep in a churchyard ground, with the tall grass waving gently over his head, and the sound of the old deep bell to sooth him to sleep.

In *David Copperfield,* Dickens's favorite among his novels, he gives us a less sentimental, more convincing view of orphanhood. The book might have had for subtitle, *Orphans All,* for it contains a veritable anthology of degrees of the parentless state. The hero is born posthumously to a

---

*Remi, the young hero of Hector Henri Malot's French classic, *Sans Famille* (1878), has a far better time of it growing up. Until the age of eight, he is raised by a loving peasant woman who gives him maternal care. Even when his foster father sells him (a not uncommon practice at one time in France), he has the good luck to be bought by a kindly old musician in whose company he has many adventures and meets an equal share of good as well as villainous adults.

"mere-baby" of a woman, herself an orphan, who remarries, abdicates her role of parent in favor of her second husband, then dies. Ham and Emily's mother died early, their father was lost at sea. Tommy Traddles, Martha Endell, and Rosa Dartle have neither parent, while Steerforth, Uriah Heep, Annie Strong, Agnes, and Dora have but one. "The Orfling," who comes from the workhouse, is so without family connections that she has no other name.

After happy years of early childhood with an affectionate mother and a devoted nurse, David suffers from one separation after another. With tender farewells, he is taken away from his mother (while she is being courted by the man who will become his stepfather), becomes attached to little Emily, whose orphan state makes a strong bond between them, and suffers "agony of mind . . . that is piercing" when he has, in turn, to leave her. Returning home, he finds that under the domination of her new husband, Mr. Murdstone, his mother has become distant and unmotherly toward him. Having been convinced by her husband that her son has "bad passions in his heart," she agrees that the boy should be sent away to school. Although David while at school lets out "a desolate cry" when he hears that his mother has died, and feels "an orphan in the wide world," she had already died for him when she gave him over to Murdstone's domination. Seeing her in her grave permits the boy to remember what she had been like, and restores to him her loving image so that he can think of her ever after as "the mother of my infancy."

The full orphan is now at the mercy of the Murdstones, who treat him like a pariah. First they put him in solitary confinement, then send him to work at age ten, in the Murdstone and Grinby warehouse. Sadistic as had been Mr. Creakle, the director of the school he attended, David had been able to tolerate Salem House because he had had the company of other boys. At the warehouse, his associates are so foreign to him that he feels lonelier than ever before in his life.

No words can express the secret agony of my soul as I sunk into this companionship . . . and felt my hopes of growing up to be a learned and distinguished man crushed in my bosom. The deep remembrance of the sense I had, of being utterly without hope now; of the shame I felt in my position; of the misery it was to my young heart to believe that day by day what I learned, and thought, and delighted in, and raised my fancy and my emulation up by, would pass away from me, little by little, never to be brought back any more; cannot be written.

Sobbing "as if there were a flaw in my own breast, and it were in danger of bursting," he gives way to despair.

The "secret agony" paragraph Dickens gave David appears almost verbatim in a fragment of autobiography. The world-famous and much beloved writer, who has made his fortune and fathered nine children, continues:*

My whole nature was so penetrated with the grief and humiliation of such considerations that, even now, famous and caressed and happy, I often forget in my dreams that I have a dear wife and children; even that I am a man; and wander desolately back to that time in my life.

What to the grown man looking back was the most painful and impoverished period of his childhood was to the artist the richest. His genius permitted him to mine the experience, and fiction freed him from constraint about describing his parents as the rejected boy had seen them. He came away from the factory job fired by ambition to succeed, and create for himself the kind of bourgeois family life he had yearned for during his months of isolation and despair. He also came away a reformer whose novels were

---

*Edmund Wilson, who quotes these passages (to a different purpose) in his essay "Dickens: The Two Scrooges," says the blacking factory period lasted six months. Edgar Johnson, in *Charles Dickens: His Tragedy and Triumph* says it can have been "little over four months."

the most powerful propaganda weapon for social change in the latter half of the nineteenth century.

Charlotte Brontë's *Jane Eyre* (1847), which falls chronologically between *Oliver Twist* and *David Copperfield,* shares with them many features of the poor orphan's reality as well as orphans' daydreams. They all suffer from poverty, isolation, and despair in the great wide world; coldness and cruelty at the hands of parent surrogates; semistarvation, neglect, and humiliation in asylums run by hypocritical directors. The daydreams begin with the nursing they receive during a grave illness at the hands of compassionate strangers, recovery to full health, and to the revelation that the orphans not only have relatives (the very strangers who've nursed them), but also have inherited money.

What Charlotte Brontë added to the delineation of orphanhood is a clearer picture of what goes on in the mind of a flesh-and-blood child. Where the recipe called for sugar, she substituted salt. Jane is rebellious, high-strung, and capable of expressing anger. Here she attacks Mrs. Reed, the aunt-in-law with whom she lives and who has been mistreating her:

> My Uncle Reed is in heaven, and can see all you do and think; and so can papa and mamma; they know how you shut me up all day long, and how you wish me dead.

A few pages later, there is this astonishing dialogue between the two. Says Mrs. Reed:

> "Is there anything else you wish for, Jane? I assure you, I desire to be your friend."
>
> "Not you. You told Mr. Brocklehurst I had a bad character, a deceitful disposition; and I'll let everyone at Lowood know what you are, and what you have done."
>
> "Jane, you don't understand these things; children must be corrected for their faults."

"Deceit is not my fault," I cried out in a savage, high voice.

"But you are passionate, Jane, that you must allow; and now return to the nursery—there's a dear—go and lie down a little."

"I am not your dear; I cannot lie down. Send me to school soon, Mrs. Reed, for I hate to live here."

Jane wonders at her boldness in speaking up in this way. So do we. Her outbursts are surprising from one in her dependent position. But even if we suspect that a child situated as she is would not dare address a surrogate parent in this way, we understand that she has said these things to herself many times, and would *like* to be able to say them aloud. This takes Jane beyond the sentimental treatment of the orphan that was so tempting for novelists of the period to fall into.

That Jane is a complex child, with an introspective turn of mind, we see from these reflections that followed the verbal battle quoted above:

> I was left there alone—winner of the field. It was the hardest battle I had fought, and the first victory I had gained. . . . A child cannot quarrel with its elders, as I had done—cannot give its furious feelings uncontrolled play, as I had given mine—without experiencing afterwards the pang of remorse and the chill of reaction . . . half an hour's silence and reflection had shown me the madness of my conduct, and the dreariness of my hate and hating position.

Years later, when she goes to work as a governess in the house of Mr. Rochester, we wonder what has happened to the strength of character she displayed with Mrs. Reed, for with the man she loves she is compliant and painfully self-deprecating. The limit to which she will deny her own personality is reached, however, when she is confronted with a moral dilemma. The orphan girl's daydream of marriage to a rich, powerful, and sought-after man is blasted on the way to the altar by the revelations that Rochester has a living wife. Jane rejects his proposal that they become lovers, saying "I will never be your mistress . . . I could not without incurring the miseries of self-hatred." At Rochester's reminder that because she is an orphan she can live outside the rules of society—"Who in the world cares for *you?*" he asks her—she flares out, *"I* care for myself . . . The more solitary, the more friendless, the more unsustained I am, the more I will respect myself."

As the child paid for her outburst, so the woman pays for her moral stance. Wrenching herself away from Rochester and the semblance of family life she has created at Thornfield Hall, she wanders off—solitary, friendless, unsustained. When, after many vicissitudes, she and Rochester are reunited, and are free to marry, the dashing figure she had fallen in love with has been transformed into a blind and crippled man to whom she will be nurse as well as wife.

Although *Jane Eyre* was published originally with the subtitle *An Autobiography,* it is only loosely based on Charlotte Brontë's life. The novelist, who became a maternal orphan at age five but had a living father, two sisters, and a brother, made her heroine a full orphan. The boarding school she and her sister attended for ten months is the model for Lowood Institution, an orphanage where Jane spends eight years. Where novelist and heroine most closely resemble each other is in their precocious intimacy with death and profound sense of bereavement. After Brontë's mother died, what mothering she had came from her older sister, Maria, who died (as did another sister) when Charlotte was nine. Helen Burns, the girl at Lowood who befriends Jane, is modeled on Maria. When Helen falls gravely ill and is preparing to go to "the mighty universal Parent," Jane goes to her sickroom. Promising not to leave the dying girl, Jane gets into Helen's bed with her. Their arms clasped around each other, they fall asleep. The following morning they are found, Jane with her face against Helen's shoulder (as in a child's sleeping embrace of its mother)—Jane asleep, Helen dead.

Jane, and other orphans, are not only pulled toward death—"deathwards," to use the English poet Stevie Smith's word—because it is in heaven that their dead live. They are also pushed toward it by the hymns they sing in orphanages, and by ballads sung to them, such as the maid Bessie sings to Jane. In it the "poor orphan child" wanders "footsore and weary" over the moors where:

> Men are hard-hearted, and kind angels only
> Watch o'er the steps of a poor orphan child.

Or, in another stanza:

> Still will my Father, with promise and blessing
> Take to his bosom the poor orphan child.

Or:

> Heaven is a home and rest will not fail me;
> God is a friend to the poor orphan child.

It is a triumph of health over morbidity, life over death, that Jane, who has felt the push/pull so strongly, rejects it when it beckons to her seductively as an adult. St. John Rivers, the clergyman who becomes her tutor, exercises an almost hypnotic power over her. Whatever he asks, she finds difficult to refuse. Yet when he proposes marriage so that she can accompany him to India to do missionary work, and even coerces her, she summons the strength to fight free of what would be a "premature death." "If I were to marry you, you would kill me. You are killing me now." And when he taunts her with being afraid of herself, she rallies, "I am. God did not give me my life to throw away; and to do as you wish would, I begin to think, be almost equivalent to committing suicide."

If *Jane Eyre* can be said to have a happy ending (her marriage to Rochester), it is a muted one—one prepared for by the heroine's early life, one more suitable for an orphan than Oliver's.

Kipling, whom T. S. Eliot called "the greatest English man of letters of his generation," was, like Dickens, a temporary orphan. Born in India, he had the attention during his early years of his parents, a nurse, and a body servant. Life changed radically for him when, at age six, his parents took him and his sister to England and, answering the newspaper advertisement of a woman who specialized in looking after the children of British civil servants stationed abroad, left them with her in Southsea.

In "Baa Baa, Black Sheep" (1888), an early short story, Punch and his sister, Judy, are left in the care of a woman who asks them to call her Aunt Rosa. The children are so unprepared for the separation from their parents that when Rosa tells them their mother and father have gone back to India, they race to the sea in panic, hoping to catch the boat. The boy, who had been a little rajah in Bombay, becomes a black sheep in Southsea. Aunt Rosa bullies, beats, and humiliates him. She punishes his efforts to resist her interrogations by forcing him to wear to school a placard with the word "Liar" on it. By favoring the little girl and separating the children as much as possible, Rosa makes trouble between the brother and sister, insuring that Punch has no ally. So abandoned and despairing does he feel that it does not occur to him to complain to his parents in his letters home, or to expose Rosa to the relatives with whom he spends vacations. His years in the "House of Desolation" are brought to an end when he develops serious eye trouble and has a kind of nervous breakdown. His mother, summoned from India, takes the children away from Rosa and in time wins back their love. Although Punch says, "We were just as much Mother's as if she had never gone away," the author, unwilling to end on so sanguine a note, protests: "Not altogether, oh Punch!—for when young lips have drunk deep of the bitter waters of Hate, Suspicion and Despair, all the love in the world will not wholly take away that knowledge."

The story fails because Kipling's memories of his temporary orphanhood were still so painful to the fledgling writer than he had neither the distance nor the skill necessary to transform them into fiction. When he returned to this period in his life in his autobiography, *Something of Myself* (1937), he prefaced his recollections with the quotation from the Jesuits, "Give me the first six years of a child's life and you can have the rest"—by which we take him to mean that he survived the horrors of life in the House of Desolation because of the loving care he had during his early years in India. At least two sequelae of the Southsea years, defective vision (which was in part due to neglect), and intractable insomnia, plagued him for life. What he gained from the "constant wariness" necessary to survive under Aunt Rosa's totalitarian regime was "the habit of observation, the attendance on moods and tempers . . . the automatic suspicion of sudden favor," which were useful preparation for adult life. A less predictable response to the abuses he suffered was to "drain me of any capacity for real, personal hate for the rest of my days . . . so close must any life-filling passion lie to the opposite."

Kim (1901), Kipling's most popular novel, thought by many critics to be his prose masterpiece, relates the adventures of a precocious, impish little charmer of an orphan in India. His mother having died of cholera when he was an infant, and his father of alcohol and opium when he was three, Kim is left in the care of a half-caste woman. By the time we meet him, he is a cheeky and self-confident waif who is not only able to look after himself, but delights in meddling in the affairs of men.

What begins as a picaresque novel turns into a quest for identity of a parentless boy who lives between two cultures and wonders, "Who is Kim-Kim-Kim?" He attaches himself to a series of father figures. From his Indian mentors, he learns the ways of the Orient; from the Sahibs, the ways of the West. To an old, holy man, a lama, he forms an attachment so strong that "to see him, to be in touch with him was necessary to Kim's heart." The lama, for his part, has to make strong efforts not to become too attached to the boy until he finishes his education, at which point the two will be free to go off on pilgrimages together. He urges Kim to go back to school when he's tempted to leave, follows his progress there, and pays his tuition.

In the final third of the book, parallel with the adventure story, Kipling develops the growing mutual dependency of the two. The old man becomes "mother and father" to the young man, while he becomes son and nurse to the lama. Their roles shift as they grow older. Kim, like Aeneas with Anchises, carries the increasingly feeble sage on his back—the son becoming father to the father.

Kipling's exile from India lasted ten years. One can imagine the homesick and heartsick temporary orphan living in a dreary English seaside cottage daydreaming about the paradise he had lost, and the delights of a life such as Kim led—Kim's joy in awakening every morning to the sights, sounds, and smells of the bazaars and the Grand Trunk Road, his dropping off to sleep at night, tired from the adventures of the day. The boy in England must also have yearned for the waif's freedom from restraint in a man's world at a time when his every move was being controlled by a tyrannical woman. The lama's efforts to keep Kim at his side are not unlike the effort a stoical English father in the colonial service had to make in following the time-honored tradition of sending children back home for their schooling.

The six-year-old child living in the House of Desolation could not have known about this tradition and must have wondered why he had been abandoned. He could either have blamed his parents for being irresponsible and unloving, or blamed himself for some wrongdoing (though what?) that had led them to hand him over to a punitive woman. (It would seem, from his later relationship with his parents, that Rudyard chose the second explanation.) What sustained him during the black years were the letters his parents wrote him, the packages of books that arrived regularly from his father, and the vacations he spent with affectionate and cultivated relatives. He did not complain to anyone at the time, he says, because "children tell little more than animals, for what comes to them they accept as eternally established."

As one might suspect, the transplanted boy who felt himself abandoned was a difficult child for Aunt Rosa. Kipling's biographer, Charles Edmund Carrington, says she found him restless, clumsy, undisciplined, and somewhat spoiled, whereas his sister, Trix, won the hearts of everyone. Trix's continuing to live in the House of Desolation after Rudyard was sent to school suggests that Mrs. Kipling decided that while Rosa was an unsuitable parental substitute for her son, she was a satisfactory one for her daughter.

When Kipling returned to India at age sixteen, he was pleased to find that his parents were every bit as attractive and interesting as he had imagined them to be during the years of their separation. The three delighted in one another's society and "when my sister came out, a little later, our cup was filled to the brim. Not only were we happy, but we knew it." What the seventy-year-old writer seems to have forgotten was an uncomfortable period of transition. Trix reported that their mother was concerned about him during this time because he was "strangely moody." Nevertheless, it is true that he became a devoted son, and developed an especially close relationship with his father, whose advice on writing and on his literary career he sought and followed.

Mark Twain's best-known and most-loved novels, *The Adventures of Tom Sawyer* (1876) and *The Adventures of Huckleberry Finn* (1884), have as heroes boys who are orphans. In the earlier of the two companion pieces, Tom and his younger brother, Sid, are being raised by warmhearted and guileless Aunt Polly, their mother's older sister. She is no match for the imaginative, quick-witted, and mischievous Tom, the ringleader of a little band of boys who delight in playing hooky and sneaking out of their houses after bedtime for nocturnal adventures. Huckleberry Finn, one of the band, is homeless. Having been abandoned by his father, he is unwashed, unschooled, and unsupervised—the town pariah. While his contemporaries envy his "gaudy outcast condition," he is ostracized by their parents, who are fearful of his influence on their children.

When he and Tom and Joe Harper are away on one of their adventures for longer than usual, they are taken for dead and a funeral service is held to mourn their loss. How much more orphaned Huck is than Tom becomes clear when the boys return to town. Tom is greeted by tears of joy from Aunt Polly, Mary, and even the pesky, virtuous, little informer, Sid. For Huck, there were no mourners, and now there is no one to rejoice that he is alive. The book ends with a seeming solution to the waif's situation as he agrees, reluctantly, to be adopted by the rich and benign Widow Douglas, who will see that he is properly looked after and educated so that he can become an acceptable member of the town society.

Life with the Widow Douglas turns out not to be a solution, we learn in *Huckleberry Finn,* for the ragamuffin resists her efforts to "sivilize" him. When his father turns up, Huck goes to live with him, but life with the alcoholic and abusive Pap becomes so intolerable the boy runs away. After staging his own death, which he hopes will convince any who might come looking for him that a search is pointless, he starts down the Mississippi River on a raft with the runaway slave, Jim, for companion.

On his travels, Huck represents himself to people he meets as a full orphan even before Pap dies. Varying his early history to suit his audience, he says that after the death of his parents he was bound out to a mean old farmer; or that, his mother and siblings having died, he was left alone with his father, who, shortly thereafter, also died; or that, while going down the river on a raft, his brother and father were run over by a steamboat. From time to time, he permits kindly women he meets on his travels to mother him. He accepts their attentions, briefly lives a family life in their houses, but before long becomes restless and pushes off again. When last we see him he is escaping yet another motherly woman's attempts to adopt and domesticate him as he "lights out for the Territory."

Why did Mark Twain make both Tom and Huck orphans? The obvious explanation is that a boy without parents is an ideal protagonist for an adventure story (as those far more adventurous orphans Tarzan and Superman show). The orphan is free in the way those living with families cannot be. The lack of parental discipline, the absence of a dominating male figure in the house, allow Tom the liberty, to which Aunt Polly applies only a gentle and ineffectual brake, to play the role of a picaresque hero.

The far more complex *Huckleberry Finn*, which critics agree is Twain's masterpiece, is an adventure story on only one level. Adult readers are not far into the book before they realize that this melancholy and anxious thirteen-year-old suffers from his orphanhood in a way only hinted at in the earlier novel in the scene where the supposedly dead boys return to town. As they are being smothered with kisses by their relatives, Huck, abashed and uncomfortable, starts to slink away. Tom seizes him and says to Aunt Polly, "It ain't fair. Somebody's got to be glad to see Huck." The compliant Aunt Polly's demonstrations of affection only make "the poor motherless thing" feel more uncomfortable than he had before.

In *Huckleberry Finn*, when the runaway orphan is separated from the runaway slave, we see what goes on behind his "gaudy" façade. His fantasies are filled with images of isolation, illness, death, bereavement, and of parentless children left alone in the world. When his loneliness becomes acutely painful, he wishes that he, too, were dead. Death—the yearning for and fear of it—is so omnipresent in the novel that it is like an off-stage character poised to make an entrance:

> There was them kind of faint dronings of bugs and flies in the air that makes it seem so lonesome and like everybody's dead and gone; and if a breeze fans along and quivers the leaves it makes you feel mournful, because you feel like it's spirits whispering—spirits that's been dead ever so many years—and you always think they're talking about *you*. As a general thing it makes a body wish *he* was dead, too, and done with it all.

The earlier staged death may have fooled Pap and the townspeople of St. Petersburg, but gory self-murder though it was, it neither propitiated the spirits nor fooled them. They know Huck is alive and give him little peace.

The vagabond's reasons for rejecting foster parents, who would provide him with a homelife and protect him from loneliness, are unconvincing. It is not only that he is intolerant of their efforts to civilize him; it is also that his own dead rest so unquietly in their graves that they don't permit him to accept replacements for them, especially the one who died "ever so many years ago"—his mother. It's mother substitutes Huck is drawn to, they who are drawn to him. Restlessness is his defense against the temptation he feels to succumb to the care they offer. He "lights out for the Territory," on his way to new adventures which, one presumes, will alternate with periods of isolation and loneliness during which the murmuring of the spirits will be difficult to silence. Huck seems fated to remain a wanderer, living outside society: the eternal orphan.

* * *

In a chapter from his autobiography published in the *North American Review,* Mark Twain, who became a paternal orphan when he was twelve, claimed that when his family moved from Florida, Missouri, to Hannibal, they absent-mindedly left him behind. Albert Bigelow Paine, who worked closely with Twain on the official biography, says the memory is a false one. His subject's vivid imagination sometimes played him tricks, in this case causing him to "transpose to an earlier time an incident that happened later and somewhat differently." It would indeed be an absentminded family, Paine says, "if the parents, and the sister and brothers ranging up to fourteen years of age, should drive off leaving Little Sam, age four, behind."

The evidence the biographer offers for his contradiction is that it was not Sam but his older brother, Orion, who was left behind. He quotes Orion as having said:

> The sense of abandonment caused my heart to ache. The wagon had gone a few feet when I was discovered and in-vited to enter. How I wished they had not missed me until they had arrived at Hannibal! Then the world would have seen how I was treated and would have cried, "Shame."

Distracted parents have been known to forget one of their children for a time, a time that to the child may seem an eternity. Into John and Jane Clemens's loveless mar-riage had come more offspring than they could support, and a move, especially a move down (such as this was, one of the many in the downward spiral from landed gentry to grinding poverty), is always trying, and frequently fraught with family tensions.

The incident that happened to Sam later is less easily explained. One Saturday, a year or so after the move to Hannibal, Jane Clemens took her children to her brother's farm for the weekend, leaving Sam behind to be brought by his father the following day. When John Clemens arrived on Sunday afternoon, he admitted, aghast, that he had completely forgotten the boy. Jane Clemens's brother rushed back to town, where he found Sam "crying with loneliness and hunger. He had spent most of the day in a locked deserted house."

Paine has told us how Orion, at age fifteen, felt at having been left for the brief time it took for the wagon to go a few feet, but not what five-year-old Sam felt at having been left behind by his mother, and awakening to find that his father had gone off, leaving him alone.

Father and son were temperamentally incompatible, the one taciturn, the other volatile and difficult to manage. When John Clemens died, Sam was stricken with remorse at the trouble he had given him through the years. Overcome with grief and guilt about surviving the man for whom he had been unable to feel affection, he tearfully berated himself for his defects of character. The night of the funeral he walked in his sleep (as he had done for the first time the night his sister died). Following the burial, his mother, in an effort to comfort him, said, "What's done is done, and it doesn't matter to him any more. . . . Only promise me to be a better boy. Promise not to break my heart." (Her words may have had a sobering effect but were not likely, with their implication that Sam *had* behaved reprehensibly, to have been comforting.)

At this time, it was also agreed between mother and son that Sam should be apprenticed to a printer. The way Twain puts it in his autobiography is that he was "taken" from school. The implied reluctance seems misplaced, since he disliked school and was eager to get out of going there. Still, it is one thing to be relieved of the necessity to continue one's formal education and another to be sent away from home to work for a man who offered his apprentices "more board than clothes, and not much of either." To fill out the meager diet, Sam pilfered food from the larder. About the clothes, he could do nothing. The boss's hand-me-downs, what he was given in place of two suits promised by contract, were so much too big for him that he "had the uncomfortable sense of living in a circus tent." (By the time Twain wrote these words, he was able to take this humorous tone about his adolescent discomfort at having been dressed like Huckleberry Finn. He now had a wardrobe filled with expensive, if sometimes eccentric, costumes, which included silk dressing gowns, a beaver hat and coat, and the famous white suits.)

How he felt about being sent away from home, what his feelings toward his mother were at the time, Twain does not tell us. His biographer says that Jane Clemens had a weakness for this child, who had been born prematurely, was always sickly, and when well was forever getting into scrapes. Van Wyck Brooks thinks Sam was her favorite son, while Justin Kaplan believes it was not Sam but his younger brother, Henry, whom she preferred. What is possible, even likely, is that Jane's preferences shifted, as mothers' preferences often do. The angelic Henry would have been easier to love, but Sam, determined to be her favorite, did what he could in first one way and then another to get and hold her attention. That it took some doing is suggested by her having left him behind when she took her three older children and baby Henry to the farm, and by this quotation from Twain about how he was seen as a child:

> I was always told that I was a sickly and precarious and tiresome and uncertain child and lived mainly on allopathic medicines during the first seven years of my life. I asked my mother about this in her old age—she was in her eighty-eighth year—and said, "I suppose that during all that time you were uneasy about me."
>
> "Yes, the whole time."
>
> "Afraid I wouldn't live?"
>
> After a reflective pause, ostensibly to think out the facts, "No, afraid you would."

Further along he adds:

My mother had a good deal of trouble with me, but I think she enjoyed it. . . . Next to the unbroken monotony of Henry's goodness . . . I was a tonic to her.

"The secret source of humor," according to America's best-known humorist, "is not joy but sorrow." Son and mother (also a wit) were being humorous about a past that had caused both of them anguish.

Samuel Clemens, again like his character Huck, fought off being civilized during adolescence, and when he began life on his own lit out for the West, where his rackety existence, had his mother known the details of it, would have broken her heart. But as he began to be a successful writer, as his fame and fortune grew, and he became the financial and moral supporter of the family, the son who had been his mother's despair became, as Kaplan says, her joy (although she must have felt a pang or two at the fame being attached to a name that was not the one she and John Clemens had given him).

The writer with a new name (and what a name! He took it from his occupation as a pilot, where it was used as a measure of the depth of the water, but he could not have been unaware of "twain" as a signifier of separation, and permanent division) and a new persona sought to be educated in the ways of polite society as greedily as, during boyhood and adolescence, he had shunned being civilized, and eagerly accepted instruction from mother substitutes. In his marriage to Olivia Langdon (a lifelong civilizer on whose judgment he depended heavily), he was showered with the affection he craved, but so insatiable was his appetite for love and approval that it required the vast audiences he won through his best-sellers and his stage performances to appease it. At the height of his powers, he had won love the world over.

Twain's *Autobiography* is disappointingly unrevealing about his boyhood and adolescence. He began and broke off work on it repeatedly. According to Bernard De Voto, this was because he was unwilling to give it a coherent structure out of "dread" of examining his feelings about those early years. What he left out of the autobiography he had already written into fiction, free of inhibiting restraints. The pages of *Tom Sawyer* are infused with nostalgia for the happy days he and his band of friends had known in Hannibal. The original of Huck, he claimed, was one of the band, Tom Blankenship; and for the Huck of the earlier novel, whom we see only from the outside, this is true. But for the orphan hero of *Huckleberry Finn,* who, through the first-person narrator, reveals his innermost thoughts—what it feels like to be abandoned, to suffer the ache of loneliness, to be haunted by the dead—he drew from deep within himself to create what Leslie Fiedler called "the first existential hero" in literature.

Henry James's orphan heroines are neither poor nor little. What interested James was the crisis of a young woman living in a privileged society but unprotected by parents. Isabel Archer in *The Portrait of a Lady* (1881) lost her mother in childhood and the indulgent father who raised her just a year before the opening scene. She is taken up by a rich aunt, Mrs. Touchett, a visitor from England, who sees in this intelligent, attractive, and spirited girl possibilities for development that a period of living abroad would give her. Isabel, eager to have a broader view of life than the one offered by Albany, accepts the invitation, but draws back when Mrs. Touchett calls her a "candidate for adoption." With her high temper, bold wit, and strong will, Isabel's personality is already formed, and she feels no need of a protector. Rather, what she seeks is freedom to make her own choices. When Caspar Goodwood, who has been courting her unsuccessfully, warns her that an unmarried woman her age can't move about freely, she reminds him that, being an orphan, she "belongs quite to the independent class."

In England, Isabel is a great success. The Touchett men,

father and son, are so taken with her and her eagerness for new experiences that they agree that the elder Touchett should leave her an inheritance, which will permit her to fulfill her great expectations of life. What she chooses with the freedom that money gives her is marriage to the impecunious but intriguing Gilbert Osmond. It isn't long before she discovers that the duplicitous Madame Merle, who guided her toward him, has been Osmond's mistress and that Pansy Osmond is their illegitimate child. When word of Isabel's situation reaches Caspar Goodwood, he presses his suit again, and is again rejected. Renouncing this easy solution to her dilemma, she returns to Osmond and to her responsibilities toward his child.

While a thoroughly convincing character, Isabel Archer is not a convincing orphan. We feel that James freed her of parents because he needed a heroine whom society would permit to play the role he had cast for her. She bears none of the scars of orphanhood, and her strong personality makes us suspect that her father (assisted by a nurse) must successfully have played both parental roles until she was an adult. Perhaps if she'd had parents, she would not have been taken in by Madame Merle; or had she been, her parents would have rushed to her side to advise against the marriage. But when have high-spirited, adventurous American girls listened to their parents in affairs of the heart? Since the novel is a masterpiece, it matters not at all that Isabel is an orphan of convenience (except to the reader looking for insights into the orphan experience).

Milly Theale in *The Wings of the Dove* (1902) has more than her black garb to convince us that she is the real thing, an "isolated, un-mothered, unguarded" orphan. Her mother, father, brothers, and sisters having died by the time she was ten, she is freer than anyone would want to be, as "free as the wind in the desert." Despite her immense wealth, she is a grown-up waif who hasn't even a relative she can call on to act as chaperone, so she turns to a cultivated older woman from Boston, Mrs. Stringham (a half orphan in a novel almost as full of half and full orphans as *David Copper-field*), who agrees to accompany her on a trip abroad.

Mrs. Stringham, who has been rounding out the American heiress's education with visits to European museums and monuments (for, waiflike, Milly has had less education than someone with her background and fortune should have had), suggests a pause for a few days in Switzerland. Coming upon Milly, who has gone for a solitary walk, seated at "the dizzying edge" of a precipice, the older woman has a moment of alarm. She knows by now that the generous, tenderhearted, and proud young woman she's traveling with has a "sensibility too sharp" for her own comfort, and wonders if she also has a "horrible hidden obsession" that would make her contemplate suicide. What Milly was brooding about as she looked down "into the kingdoms of the world" was how much longer she would be part of it, for her joy in life is always shadowed by a presentiment of an early death.

The two women agree that what Milly needs is the company of people her own age. They go to London, where, with the Bostonian's connections and the New Yorker's money, they are launched in society and Milly is taken up by the novel's other heroine, Kate Croy. Clever, ambitious, beautiful Kate, a maternal orphan, is as poor as Milly is rich. She has family, all right, but since the recent loss of her mother, she has been left with the kind of relatives who drain rather than nourish one. Her shiftless father has just rejected her offer to make a home for the two of them, leaving Kate no choice but to accept the hospitality of a rich and menacing aunt. Her sister blandly counts on Kate to make a loveless marriage, although she knows that Kate is in love with the impecunious Merton Densher, so that she and her "portionless brood" will be looked after financially.

At the country house of Lord Mark, where the new acquaintances are assembled, the host takes the American "princess" to see a Bronzino portrait he owns of a woman he claims greatly resembles her. Milly, who this day has been feeling acutely both her excess of joy in life and her fear that she will have less than a full share of it, thinks as she studies her likeness: "She is dead, dead, dead." Soon afterward she asks Kate, whom she's come to think of as a close friend, to accompany her to an appointment with a famous medical specialist. Sir Luke gives Milly a diagnosis so subtly worded that the reader doesn't know what she's suffering from (tuberculosis seems most likely), and encourages her to live life to the fullest. Although many "hard things" have happened to her in the past, he urges her to remember that she has as much right as anyone to happiness.

Suspecting that the diagnosis is grave, suspecting also that Milly is in love with Densher, Kate urges him to court the heiress. Milly will have her moment of happiness, and at her death will leave Densher the money on which he and Kate can marry.* The plan works well until Lord Mark, whom Milly has rejected as a suitor in favor of Densher, smokes out Kate's deviousness and exposes it. With one stroke, Milly loses the two people who attach her to life— her new friend, and the man she thought loved her. Once again, she is bereft, alone, orphaned. The pull of her dead being stronger than any tie to the world of the living, she turns her face to the wall and dies. When Densher learns that she has left him her fortune, his remorse at having deceived her, and his admiration for her generosity, cause him to fall in love with her spirit. As the novel ends, he and Kate are, as R. P. Blackmur has said, forever separated and forever bound together by the dead girl.

* * *

*Kate's steadiness of purpose is in marked contrast to Lily Bart's vacillation in Edith Wharton's *The House of Mirth.* Lily, an equally beautiful young woman raised to live a life of luxury, finds herself on the death of her parents to be an orphan without means. She repeatedly sets herself to marry for money as the sensible solution to her predicament, but through irresoluteness and distaste for what she must do, she misses one opportunity after another. Her slide down the social scale ends in a dingy boardinghouse, where she dies of an overdose of chloral.

By contrast to writers like Dickens and Mark Twain, who were temporary orphans, Henry James had a family so powerful that in order to free himself from their sometimes overpowering attentions he had to become an expatriate. As a boy, calling on his cousin Minny Temple and her sisters, who, after the death of their mother and father, were being looked after by a relative in a "little orphanage nursery," he was struck by the contrast between their situation and his. To one who lived with a father, mother, and aunt, whose expectations for him he was constantly made aware of, Minny's orphanhood appeared to allow her an enviable freedom. As she grew into an intelligent, beautiful, and audacious young woman, he developed a deep affection for her, and was as much in love with her as he could allow himself to be with any woman. They maintained their closeness after he moved abroad through correspondence. After she developed "galloping consumption," her letters reported on the progress of her illness and her fight to stay alive. She told him, as many tuberculars were told in those days, and believed, that it "all depends on myself whether I get through or not." It didn't, of course, and having outlived her brothers and sisters, she died at age twenty-four. "Death at the end was dreadful to her," James wrote in *Notes of a Son and Brother,* ". . . she would have given anything to live." For him and his brother William, it was an immense loss. "We felt it together," he says, "as the end of our youth."

Henry James continued to feel it. Minny began to appear in his short stories and then in *The Portrait of a Lady,* where Isabel Archer lives out the life James imagined Minny might have had had she not been tubercular. In creating Isabel, he was still contrasting what he had seen as Minny Temple's high spirits and audaciousness, which he had connected with the freedom her orphanhood had given her, with his early indecisiveness, the result of a crushing need to satisfy his parents' ambitions for him. During the twenty-one years between *The Portrait* and *The Wings,* he came to understand these qualities as a façade, Minny's defense against her devastating early losses.

F. O. Matthiessen says of *The Wings*, "James' sense of loss at Minny's death, remaining at the source of his personal life and yet ramifying outward through long years . . . empowered him to create in Milly . . . the most resonant symbol for what he had to say about humanity." She is also one of the most convincing orphans in literature.

Thomas Mann's orphan hero of *The Magic Mountain* (1924), like Milly, has inherited money, an inherited susceptibility to illness, and few family ties. Also like Milly, and unlike the physically deprived and psychologically harassed Oliver, David, Jane, and Huck, he was looked after in childhood as well as children without parents can be. Not childhood but the beginning of adult life is his time of crisis.

If Milly's illness is kept off-stage so that there is no odor of the sickroom, no deathbed scene in *The Wings, The Magic Mountain* reeks of disease and death. They are so graphically described that more than one reader put the book down in fear of contracting tuberculosis through suggestion. My own reaction on reading it during my college days was so strong that I not only developed some of Hans's symptoms, but was so taken up with his illness, and the sanatorium atmosphere (which revived memories of my time at the Preventorium and what I'd heard about my mother's stay at Saranac), that I paid little attention to the theme of Hans Castorp's orphanhood.

Hans has lost mother, father, and the beloved grandfather in whose house he was raised after his parents' death. Feeling run down and in need of a rest after completing his studies to become an engineer, he decides to offer himself a little vacation before beginning his career, and goes to visit his cousin Joachim, one of his few remaining relatives, who is taking a cure at the International Sanatorium Berghof in Switzerland.

What was planned as a few weeks' absence from the

bourgeois society in which he was raised, where work, order, cleanliness, and conscientiousness are highly valued, turns, when he is discovered to have a marginal (and perhaps psychogenic) case of tuberculosis, into a seven-year sojourn in the rarefied air and magical world of the Berghof. With no strong ties to pull him back to Hamburg, and money from his estate being forwarded regularly by his lawyer, he devotes his new freedom to study and contemplation, to broadening the education for which there was no time during his professional training.

After an uncomfortable period of adjustment, Hans finds that sanitarium life suits him. He is fascinated by illness and death, which he saw so intimately when he was a child. ("Don't you like the sight of a coffin? I really do," he says to Joachim.) He knows how to get on with people who are "down cast." ("I even think that, on the whole, I get on better with sad people than the jolly ones. Goodness knows why. Perhaps it's because I'm an orphan.")

While at first he is repelled by the pervasive air of eroticism at the Berghof, in time the lax morals of the inmates allow him to explore a side of his nature previously repressed, the culmination of which is the night he spends with the object of his obsessive fantasies, the seductive Claudia Chauchat. Most important of all, the Berghof becomes a home to the homeless orphan, with a built-in family. There are doctors and nurses to give him the kind of attention he may have wished to have more of in childhood, and siblings who gather together for communal meals in the dining room, where they are overfed, like greedy children. For one who feels "an uneasy need" for "fatherly authority," there are the humanist, Settembrini (who calls Hans "life's delicate child"); the Jesuit, Naphta; the hedonist, Peeperkorn; Dr. Behrens, the director of Berghof; and the psychoanalyst, Dr. Krokowski—each of whom in one way or another adopts Hans and satisfies his need for a mentor and father.

Castorp's aloneness and flirtation with death reach a cli-

max when this unathletic young man and novice skier sets
out on a solitary and "unlawful escapade" (strenuous exer-
tion being forbidden to patients), to satisfy his desire to get
in "freer touch" with the mountains. He leaves home (as he
and the other inmates refer to the Berghof) insufficiently
clad, and provisioned only with some chocolate and a little
port. Seduced by the beautiful and silent world of snow,
which had recently been falling in "monstrous and im-
measurable" quantities, he gets caught in a blizzard, loses
his way, and muddles his already confused thinking by
drinking the port. Still, he is aware that he had deliberately
set out to lose his way, to set himself a challenge for which
he was ill prepared. Coming upon a shack, he succumbs to
the desire for rest, falls to dreaming, and through his
dreams takes stock of his life:

> I will keep faith with death in my heart, yet well remember
> that faith with death and the dead is evil, is hostile to human-
> kind, so soon as we give it power over thought and action.
> *For the sake of goodness and love, man shall let death have no
> sovereignty over his thoughts* [Mann's italics].

He tears himself out of sleep, knowing how dangerous it is
to his "young life."

Starting up in "horror" and "rapture" at the narrow
escape which showed him that "life meant well by her lone-
wandering delicate child," he returns to the village. He is
scolded and fed by Settembrini, who is horrified to hear of
his student-son's brush with death; then returns home to be
"caressed" by the "highly civilized atmosphere" of the
Berghof.

Castorp continues to live what Mann called his hero's
"seven fairy-tale years of his enchanted stay," until the eve
of World War I, when, throwing off the residue of his illness, he goes down to the flatlands to take his place on the
front line in the defense of his country. The orphan leaves
one family, the sanitarium, for another, the army, which will

provide him with other father surrogates, other siblings. Whereas Milly's crisis is resolved by a succumbing to death, Hans's, like Jane Eyre's, is a victory for life. (As the novel ends, the reader feels that Hans has as good, or as poor, a chance of surviving the war as any other soldier.)

Thomas Mann found on a visit to his wife, Katya, at Davos, where she was being treated for tuberculosis, that the high altitude robbed him, as it does Hans, of the pleasure he ordinarily took in his very special cigars. Also like Hans, he developed respiratory symptoms sufficiently troublesome to warrant an examination. But when the Davos specialist told him that he was potentially tubercular, and recommended that he prolong his visit, the novelist, unlike his hero, packed his bags and fled. The germ he carried down to the flatlands was the germ of his opening chapter.

What Mann originally planned to write was a sardonic novella, one that would be "easy and amusing and did not take up much space," a reworking of an early story, "Tristan." But as so often happens with works of art, the book that was to take up little space took as long to write as its hero spent in sequestration. Its two-volume bulk, the author feared, would make the novel unsalable. When it became instead an instant success, Mann, looking for an explanation, decided that the German reader recognized himself in "the simple-minded but shrewd" protagonist. When its postwar audience, which had lived through the near death and rebirth of Europe, pushed sales in four years to the one hundredth printing, he came to feel that its success was based on a "community of suffering." What explanation would he have given, one wonders, if he had lived to see it become the novel on which his international reputation today depends?

In a novel crowded with themes, it is not surprising that Castorp's orphanhood has attracted little attention from critics and readers alike. Yet Hans is thoroughly orphaned, and his creator made him so by design and not for convenience. In Mann's early years, he was as rich in family connections as Castorp was poor. After what he describes as a "happy and sheltered childhood" in a household with parents, four siblings, and a large staff, his life changed radically when his upright, intimidating, and powerful father (who had been gravely disappointed to see first his oldest son Heinrich and then Thomas reject commerce in favor of art) died, his mother moved to another city, and the adolescent student was left to board in a professor's family while he completed his education. Of this period, Mann had "the most jovial memories." While Heinrich collapsed with tuberculosis and had to be sent away for treatment soon after their father's death, Thomas seems to have grieved little. For him, it was a fortunate loss, coming at just the right time. It freed him from school, which he loathed, freed him from the pressure to take up a career, freed him to develop his own interests. If he can be said to have had a magic mountain period, it was when he joined Heinrich (as Hans joined Joachim) in Italy. With checks arriving regularly from home, he was at liberty to loaf, educate himself, and get down to the real business of his life: writing.

In marked contrast to leisurely nineteenth- and twentieth-century novels, with many interwoven themes, is Stevie Smith's naked treatment of orphanhood in her poem "The Orphan Reformed," from *Harold's Leap* (1950), in which she presents the situation of the parentless child in nineteen lines as sharp and stinging as raps on the knuckles:

> The orphan is looking for parents
> She roams the world over
> Looking for parents and cover.
> She looks at this pair and that.
> Cries, Father, Mother,

Likes these, does not like those,
Stays for a time; goes,
Crying, Oh hearts of stone.
But really she is better alone.
Orphan, the people who will not be your parents
     are not evil,
Not the devil.
But still she cries, Father, Mother
Must I be alone for ever?
Yes you must. Oh wicked orphan, oh
     rebellion,
Must an orphan not be alone is that your
     opinion?
At last the orphan is reformed. Now quite
Alone she goes; now she is right
Now when she cries, Father, Mother, it is only
     to please.
Now the people do not mind, now they say she is
     a mild tease.

Stevie Smith's biographers, Jack Barbera and William McBrien, say that "The Orphan Reformed" is probably self-admonitory, for the poet was effectively an orphan. Her wandering father, absent at the time of her birth, abdicated the parental role when she was three, and appeared infrequently thereafter. From her fragile and then invalided mother, Stevie was separated at age five, when she was sent away for treatment of tubercular peritonitis. Her three-year exile from home was so painful that by the time she was eight, she had already contemplated suicide; she made a serious attempt as an adult, and continued "a soft sighing after shadowy death" throughout her life. Despite the devotion of the aunt who kept house for her and did what she could to replace her mother, who died when Stevie was sixteen, Stevie, like the orphan in the poem, continued to hunger for parents as an adult, and sought to attach herself to the families of her closest friends. Institutional life, an absent father, and a sickly mother had left her with a need to be cosseted. Once, when her aunt was away for a few days, she asked to stay with a friend. Her hostess, returning home from a dinner party at 2:00 A.M., found her guest sitting forlornly in the kitchen. This conversation followed:

> "What's the matter, Stevie?" I asked. "Why haven't you gone to bed?"
> "There was nobody to warm my milk," she said plaintively.
> I was amazed. "But couldn't you do that for yourself?"
> "No." She shook her head. "Aunt always does it for me."

Others corroborated her need for "feeding" ("You have weaned me too soon, you must nurse me again," she wrote). Orphanlike, she was apprehensive about getting her share of food—not greedy (she was small and thin), just nervously checking. Her craving for affection and attention was so strong that, as her friends remarked, she was competitive with their children. During a holiday with one family who had warned her that they would have their son with them and would have to devote their time to him, Stevie became rivalrous with the boy, and in the concluding stanza of *The Holiday* wrote of that time:

> Say goodbye to the holiday, then,
> To the peace you did not know,
> And to the friends who had power over you,
> Say goodbye and go.

Throughout her adult life, Stevie behaved like an orphan who needed reforming.

There is no starker artistic projection of the essence of orphanhood than Samuel Beckett's fifteen-minute play *Not I*. When it was first performed in London and New York in

1972–73, reviewers no less than audiences were baffled by what to many was an incomprehensible yet shattering theatrical experience. On a darkened stage are two characters, Mouth, a seventy-year-old Irish crone, of whom we see only red lips, pale skin, white teeth; and Auditor, a tall figure of undetermined sex enveloped in a hooded black djellaba. After some moments of babbling to herself, Mouth, addressing Auditor, pours out a torrent of phrases, uninterrupted for the length of the play, in which she tells us her pitiable history.

Born prematurely, abandoned immediately after conception by her father and eight months later by her mother, she has received:

> no love . . . spared that . . . no love such as normally vented on the . . . speechless infant . . .

Nor was there any love in the years that followed. There was a period in an orphanage where she was raised with other waifs and taught to believe in:

> a merciful . . . (brief laugh) . . . God

So little was she convinced of His mercy that she has lived her life under a crushing sense of guilt, for what offense she doesn't know, having passed her days alone, drifting around, walking, stopping, staring: a life with little incident. There was a brush with the law (for vagrancy?), an occasion when she was expected to feel pleasure but felt none (sexual?), and the time when, "already an old hag," she wept, perhaps for the first time since the birth cry:

> Sitting staring at her hand . . . there in her lap . . . palm upward . . . suddenly saw it wet . . . the palm . . . tears presumably . . . hers presumably . . . no one else for miles

. . . no sound . . . just the tears . . . sat and watched them
dry . . . all over in a second . . .

Then, on this day in her seventieth year, there is a well-
ing-up inside her and the words come flying out at break-
neck speed despite her efforts to control them: "begging
the brain . . . begging the mouth to stop."

Four times this "mouth on fire" repeats the story of her
life, punctuating its anguished soliloquy with screams,
while Auditor, who says not a word, four times makes a
gesture of "helpless compassion."

Trying to understand the reason for this blizzard of
words, Mouth wonders what unleashed them. Was it

perhaps something she had to . . . had to . . . tell . . . could
that be it? . . . something she had to tell. . . . how it had
been . . .

Yes, she is overwhelmed by a compulsion to say what it
was like to have been abandoned as an infant, to have
grown up without parents, to have lived in an orphanage,
to have been a wanderer. She protests, she screams, then
she goes off to continue her solitary, loveless existence
until the end—which one feels is not far off.

If, as has been said, *Waiting for Godot* is a play in which
nothing happens twice, it could also be said that in *Not I*
nothing happens four times. In place of the richly textured
and crowded canvases of a writer such as Dickens, Beckett's
play is an abstract painting: all black with a gash of red. He
stripped his subject down to the barest essentials, and with
dazzling economy tells us everything we need to know to
understand Mouth. Talking about his inspiration for this
character, the playwright told his biographer, Dierdre Bair,
that he had seen many crones like Mouth wandering
around Ireland.

Unlike Mouth, Samuel Beckett had what, on the surface,

was a privileged childhood. Born and raised in an affluent suburb of Dublin, he lived with his parents, a brother, and three cousins. Of his early years, he said:

> You might say that I had a happy childhood . . . although I had little talent for happiness. My parents did everything they could to make a child happy. But I was often lonely. We were brought up like Quakers. My father did not beat me, nor did my mother run away from home.

In *Samuel Beckett,* Bair says that if the last statement were reversed, it would come close to the truth. Bill Beckett, an athletic, gregarious businessman, whom Sam loved and admired as a boy, absented himself from home more and more as life with his unstable and tyrannical wife became increasingly uncomfortable.

Between May Beckett and her younger son there was a clash of wills that began when the boy was three and continued until her death. During Beckett's early years, it was May who administered beatings when he misbehaved. It was she who with formidable energy prodded him to fight indolence and sloth during his university years, prodded him as an adult to decide on a career and find work. He seems to have used an equal amount of energy to resist her. Instead of finding work, he stayed at home, where he was crippled with debilitating physical and mental symptoms, and spent periods in bed, curled in the fetal position.

Over and over again, Beckett tried to separate himself from his mother by going abroad, but he was unable to stay away. At age twenty-eight, he decided to undergo psychoanalysis, and was treated for two years by a Jungian analyst. At a moment when the patient was deciding that it was time to terminate therapy, his analyst took him to hear a lecture given by Carl Jung. A remark Jung made about a ten-year-old girl who felt she had "never been born entirely" struck Beckett forcibly: this was the core of his own neurosis! His inability to get out of bed as well as his failure to separate himself from his mother were "aspects of an improper birth."

When Beckett finally did make the break with home, he went to live in Paris. While he did not, like Samuel Clemens, change his name, he could count on hearing it deformed by the French pronunciation, and to the degree that he was able, he transformed himself from an Irishman into a Frenchman. During the war, he was a member of the Resistance and was decorated with the *Croix de Guerre* for heroism. He used the language of his adopted country not only for speaking but, what is more astonishing in an author, also for writing.

Beckett, who had had love "vented" upon him as a child, and referred to Ireland as "the country of my failed abortion," created in *Not I* a character whose air-splitting scream is the motherless infant's way of expressing the terror of its helplessness. Mouth's howl of protest at life is the protest of all who have been improperly born, or who, with or without parents, feel orphaned.

CHAPTER 13

The Changing Aspects of Orphanhood

CHARLIE CHAPLIN, HAD he known the expression, might well have called himself a psychic orphan, for, from the evidence in his autobiography, he clearly was one. Although we think of him as very much a man of the twentieth century —modern times—he had a nineteenth-century Dickensian boyhood in the slums of London.

Chaplin's father, an improvident and alcoholic vaudevillian, absented himself from the household so frequently that Hannah Chaplin left him soon after their son was born. Thereafter, she tried valiantly to support herself and her children, first as a soubrette and, after she lost her voice, as a dressmaker. When Charlie was seven and his half brother Sydney eleven, she had to admit defeat, for she could no longer afford to buy food and pay the rent. All three entered a workhouse, from which the boys were later sent to an orphanage.

To her sons, Hannah appeared an attentive mother, endearing and courageous. She did what she could to reestablish a home for them but, after a brief respite, once again had to send them to an orphanage. While they were there, she had a breakdown and was admitted to an insane asylum.

Technically Chaplin was not an orphan, since both his parents were alive. Psychically he was one. The separations, institutional life, and the hand-to-mouth existence during these years made him feel "sad" and "forlorn." An even more harrowing period lay ahead. After Sydney left home for a job, and Charlie and Hannah were living together, the boy, now thirteen, felt his mother drifting away from him into silence and indifference. She could not look after herself, much less a child. She was there, so he had to worry about her; yet she was no longer there as a mother. In resentment, he attacked her for behavior he found incomprehensible—"All you do is sit around this filthy room and look awful." Forced to witness her deterioration in such close quarters, he felt even more keenly what he had felt at the time of her first breakdown—that she had "deliberately escaped from her mind and deserted" him. Helplessly he watched as she slid from depression into psychosis. When it came time for her to be committed again, it was he who took her to the doctor:

> As I walked away from the hospital, I could feel only numbing sadness, but I was relieved for I knew mother would be better off in the hospital than sitting alone in that dark room with nothing to eat. . . . Emotionally exhausted I slept soundly that night. In the morning I woke to a haunting emptiness in the room.

Until Sydney returned and rescued him, Charlie lived furtively (afraid he'd again be sent to an orphanage), a child of the streets.

Emotional damage is never easy to measure, but mothers

who are alive but psychically absent impose filial burdens which knot their children's feelings in a way biologic orphans are spared. Chaplin continued to be caught and bound by the twisted skeins of love, admiration, fear, resentment, and guilt toward Hannah throughout his life. She was always a reminder of the anguish each had suffered, and that he was never able to forget.

Psychic, emotional, or spiritual orphanhood, as it is variously called, is not difficult to see in children who are as deprived as Chaplin. But recently—at about the time the orphan population dropped precipitously—the concept began to be used in conversation by those who felt that as a result of a fracturing of the protective family shield (caused by divorce, the remarriage of one or both parents, or the unsuitability of either for the role), they had suffered sufficiently in childhood to say of that time, "I felt like an orphan." Talking about his childhood to an interviewer not long before his death, Truman Capote said that when he was very young, he became aware that his mother couldn't bear the sight of him (because he resembled his father). She locked him in a room for long periods of time, and sent him away to live with relatives. "I felt like a spiritual orphan," Capote said, "like a turtle on its back."

Psychic orphanhood is not new (any more than real orphanhood was in Coleridge's day). What is new is putting a name to the feeling, articulating it as a concept. The popularization of psychoanalysis, together with an intensifying of an introspective point of view, was partly responsible for this change in the way people began to describe their early years. But equally important was a demographic factor. For hundreds of years, the word "orphan" had been vividly associated with massive asylums and the pale, undersized inmates in institutional garb incarcerated within their walls. It was necessary for these associations to fade, as fade they did with the sharp decline in the number of orphans, before the word could be used as a simile: I felt *like* an orphan.

With increasing frequency one also sees the concept used in a metaphoric sense. To take two examples: Michiko Kakutani, reviewing a collection of short stories by Mavis Gallant, says that Gallant's characters "are all spiritual orphans, those people—parentless children, refugees, expatriate—or simply displaced individuals who've shucked off their pasts in search of some vague idea of 'freedom,' or 'liberation,' or escape.' " John Russell, in accounting for the advent of modernism in painting and sculpture, says in *The Meaning of Modern Art* that by the nineteenth century, as a result of political revolutions and the Church's loss of authority, "whole sections of humanity felt themselves orphaned."*

Nowhere had this feeling been more prevalent, or of longer standing (it predates the European manifestations Russell writes about by two centuries), than in this country. The United States, which has been called the home of the persecuted and the dispossessed, has been since its founding an asylum for emotional orphans. For over three hundred years, refugees from political oppression, religious persecution, famine, poverty, and a rigid class system which limited educational and economic opportunities have been leaving their native villages and cities and coming to the United States in search of freedom and a better life.

The opening pages of William Bradford's *History of Plymouth Plantation* (mid-seventeenth century), in which he recounts the settling of the Pilgrims in the New World, read like a fairy tale about the ordeal of children without parents in search of a home. Bradford, who was orphaned early and like so many who followed him had only weak ties in the Old World, writes that after a two-month voyage on "the vast and furious sea," the *Mayflower*'s passengers disem-

---

*Inanimate objects are also increasingly said to be orphans. An "orphan" drug, an "orphan" computer, an "orphan" book—whatever has lost its sponsor, is unsupported, or has to make it on its own.

barked on "a hideous and desolate wilderness, full of wild beasts and wild men." In the "sharp and violent winter" of 1620–21, they suffered so cruelly from hunger, cold, illness, and fright that their numbers were reduced by more than half. What sustained the survivors was the intensity of their religious convictions (they lifted up "their eyes to Heaven, their dearest country"—as so many biologic orphans before and since have been urged to do), as well as the strong bonds forged among them through the communal life of the plantation, which helped to replace families left at home and diminished the Pilgrims' sense of orphanhood.

For a century and a half, the growing colonies had the support of their tie with the mother country, however distant and neglectful she may at times have seemed to be. But as they grew in size and strength, they became more independent, even rebellious—"sniffing," Edmund Burke said, "the approach of tyranny in every tainted breeze." As the revolutionary fever rose in New York, Boston, and Philadelphia, sensible men, trying to calm the hotheads, counseled their leaders to adopt a judicious tone in communicating with the Crown. In one of the so-called "Farmer's Letters," which began to appear in colonial newspapers, John Dickinson wrote:

> Let us behave like dutiful children, who have received unmerited blows from a beloved parent. Let us complain to our parent; but let our complaints speak at the same time the language of veneration.

With the imposition of the Townshend Acts, the "children" in Boston, feeling that their complaints about excessive taxation were not being heard across the sea, responded with the Tea Party. The angry parent's retaliatory punishment was to close their port. The War of Independence was declared.

If one accepts the family metaphor—England, the

mother country; George III, the authoritarian father; the colonies, the children—it is a small step to the formulation that in throwing off the parental yoke, the children, who had grown to adolescence and were protesting that they were too old to be disciplined and governed in a high-handed manner, had orphaned themselves.

In the mid-nineteenth and twentieth centuries, the wave upon wave of immigrants that broke on these shores (thirty-five million between 1850 and 1930) often had crossings—jammed together as they were in steerage class, with foul air, poor food, and primitive hygiene—only less harrowing than the Pilgrims'. If the cities where they disembarked were by now rich in amenities, they were not so for impoverished greenhorns. No, the streets were not paved with gold, as they had imagined. If they hoped to support themselves, they would have to work long hours for little pay. And while the wild beasts had vanished, men, no less dangerous than the Indians of old, but disguised as friends, were waiting on the dock with work contracts for them to sign that turned out to be a new kind of servitude.

Those who had left behind spouse, children, parents, relatives, friends, and native language felt as alone and defenseless as orphans. Small wonder so many died of the trauma, leaving their orphaned children to be raised in asylums. Those who survived learned that they would be expected to conform, as quickly as possible, to patterns of behavior established by the earlier settlers. As the children began to be educated, parents learned also that their authority would be undermined by the school. In the New World, it was teachers rather than parents who knew best. They also felt menaced, Irving Howe says in *The World of Our Fathers,* by the street, for it was to street life that Americanized children ran to escape from their Old World households.

To further complicate the relationship between immigrants and their children, it fell to English-speaking sons and daughters of Italians, Jews, Swedes, and Germans to act as scribes for their parents, fill out forms for them, accompany them to social agencies, speak up in their place —the way the larky protagonist of Saul Bellow's novel *The Adventures of Augie March* does for his mother. This reversal of roles—the child becoming parent to the parent—took its toll on both generations. So, too, did the children's daily swing from one culture to another. In *The Time That Was Then* (1971), Harry Roskolenko says that those growing up with him on the Lower East Side in New York, who spent six hours a day in an environment alien to the one at home, "were all like orphans in some strange way."

Others wished they were orphans. In *New York Jew* (1978), Alfred Kazin writes:

> Thinking about the mystery of my father's powerlessness, my unfatherly father's frequent references to the shock of his father's death and his long absence from his mother, I used to think of him as "the orphan"—something I certainly was not. I felt myself engulfed in my parents' marriage; trapped in their loneliness with each other . . . I could not imagine a life in which they had no place. To be free of so much belonging! To have had, as my father said, "no family"! But he was an orphan, and I was not. . . .

Among the members of Kazin's generation were many whose longing to be orphaned was so intense that they changed their names, sometimes even their physiognomies, in an effort to cut themselves off from their families. Many who separated themselves in this way paid a heavy price. They felt guilt-ridden at having rejected parents who had been able to tolerate an intolerable existence only by believing that their self-denial ("savage" self-denial Howe calls it) would guarantee a better life for their offspring. And *their* children often knew as little about their forebears as do many biologic orphans. When Mayor Koch of New York City was asked by a reporter, "How far back can you trace your lineage?," he responded, "Well, I think the best

I could do is go back to Ellis Island." Koch, bristling at the snobbishness he heard in the word "lineage" was pulling the reporter's leg. Nevertheless, he was speaking for a generation that couldn't go further back than Ellis Island in tracing its genealogy. Or didn't want to.

The price paid for assimilation is the subject of *An Orphan in History* (1982), Paul Cowan's story of a search for his cultural and religious roots. His father, who changed his name from Cohen to Cowan, was

> so guarded about his youth that he never let my brother or sisters or me meet any of his father's relatives . . . I always thought of myself as a Cowan . . . the Welsh word for stone-cutter—not a Cohen—a member of the Jewish priestly caste.

The name-changers and others of his generation have no way of estimating the price of their spiritual loss, didn't even imagine there would be one. Cowan claims that his sense of orphanhood is shared by millions of Americans, whether they be

> Frankie Ruggio, whose grandfather spoke Italian and was named Dante; or . . . a midwestern computer technician named Peter Holmes, whose Scandinavian-born grandfather was a fisherman named Per Hansa; or . . . Joe Martin, whose father, Jose Martinez, was a highly skilled cigar maker from Havana.

One might imagine that the Irish would have had an easier time of it, for they spoke the language, had pronounceable names, and didn't look "foreign." Yet no immigrant group suffered more cruelly its separation from the country it loved so passionately. According to Kerby Miller's *Emigrants and Exiles* (1985), the majority who came to the United States were "superfluous" sons and daughters of parents so poor they could not give their children a dowry or a bit of land. If these exiles "set adrift in an alien world" felt like Hansels and Gretels, it was not their parents they blamed for their aching homesickness, but their wicked stepmother, England, whose colonial policy had impoverished Ireland.

On the eve of departure for the United States, it was the custom to hold an "American wake" at which those who were leaving, and those who stayed behind, recognized that the rupture from family and clan was a symbolic death: parents would no longer have their child, the departing children would no longer have parents. The new arrivals in Boston and New York found that though they spoke the language, their brogue did not fall sweetly on the ears of their new compatriots. And when they went hunting for jobs, the signs "Irish need not apply" made it clear that they were no less repellent as a group than Jews from Russia or Italians from southern Italy. Even during the years of the great famine, those who had the luck to get away were so "beset with insecurity," according to Miller, that "a significant minority . . . drifted into the relative haven of insanity."

What the Pilgrims suffered we know because William Bradford was a remarkable writer. The immigrants who came to this country a century and more later, who often had had little education and spoke another language, suffered their sense of loss mutely, the way children too young to express grief do. Husbands and wives were trapped in their loneliness, as Kazin says. Their children, trapped with them, dreamed of getting away. When they did, they felt less liberated than they had imagined they would. Filial ties pulled them back to the old couple, the old neighborhood. From these visits they reeled away with the same feelings of dislocation, confusion, and guilt they had experienced as children in the daily swing between home and school.

It had come to be accepted in America that young people who wanted to leave home were free to do so if the community offered limited possibilities for employment, or, in the middle class, after they had finished their education and were able to support themselves. Beginning in the fifties, adolescents began to leave home prematurely, often stealthily. Instead of moving away, they ran away. Such a one was the hero of J. D. Salinger's novel *The Catcher in the Rye* (1951). Holden Caulfield, son of upper-middle-class parents living in New York City, has been kicked out of four private schools and is about to flunk out of another when he runs away. In rebellion against the "phoniness" of adult society, he suffers from *la nostalgie de l'enfance*—a time when life had been simpler for one as hypersensitive and peace-loving as he. Waiflike, he bums around Manhattan in a state of spiritual nausea, comforted only by his kid sister and the memories of his idealized dead brother. When he finally goes home, he "gets sick," and is sent to a private psychiatric clinic. His parents and psychiatrist hope that at the end of treatment he will enter yet another school and this time "apply himself." Holden makes no promises.

Adolescence, which evolved as a stage of life comparatively recently (it didn't exist in mid-nineteenth-century America, according to Tocqueville), had gradually been spreading downward into childhood and upward into maturity. As its population increased, because of both this spread and the post–World War II baby boom, it became more conscious of itself as a group, more critical of its elders, more restless and dissatisfied. The immense success of *The Catcher in the Rye* can be explained, at least in part, by Salinger's dramatization of these feelings.

In 1950, David Riesman, analyzing the growing desire of the young to orphan themselves (although he nowhere used the word "orphan") wrote in *The Lonely Crowd:*

As the size and living space of the family diminishes and as the pattern of living with older relatives declines, the child must directly face the emotional tension of his parents. . . . With no buffer to protect them, the young, unable to

tolerate this intimacy, seek a new family . . . which will offer
them greater freedom than their parental families.

At the same time, parents, questioning their own values,
were by no means sure that they were wiser than their
children. What greenhorns had felt vis-à-vis their Ameri-
can-born offspring, a generation of parents now felt. (As
Margaret Mead put it, "Parents feel like immigrants in the
country of the young.") The young responded to this loss
of adult legitimacy with confusion, anxiety, and rebellion.
Increasingly they turned toward their contemporaries and
the media for guidance.

In the late fifties, a more buoyant model than Holden
Caulfield for those who were impatient to leave home was
Jack Kerouac's orphan hero, Sal Paradise, in *On the Road*
(1957). One of Kerouac's followers, Joyce Johnson, describes in *Minor Characters* (1983) the Beat scene in the East
Village and the lives she and her friends lived there. The
only child of middle-class parents, Johnson said she "deliberately orphaned" herself in search of sexual freedom and
intellectual excitement. On a deeper level, what she was
seeking among those who hung out at the Cedar Tavern
was escape from a claustrophobic household, and adoption
by a large and loosely organized intellectual and artistic
family. The older men, like the painter Franz Kline, were
kindly father surrogates, and among her contemporaries
were any number of brothers and sisters an only child could
choose from.

It is a giant step from Chaplin's psychic orphanhood to
the situation of Salinger's waif, yet literary critics have seen
Caulfield as an orphan. Holden suffered no physical deprivation in childhood, and has parents who, if they are preoccupied with work (father), and are "nervous as hell"
(mother), have not in any obvious way abdicated their role.
What seems to be to blame for the boy's crisis is nothing
so simple as neglect. It is the state of the world in which he

lives. Johnson's need to orphan herself is less a rebellion against her parents than against the nuclear family.

What of adolescents, younger than Johnson and her friends, who followed college activists in the antiwar, counterculture movement to the East Village and the Haight-Ashbury district in San Francisco? When I returned to New York in 1966 after a four-year absence in Europe, I was struck by how much they looked like the orphans I'd seen in turn-of-the-century photographs of slum children living on city streets. My impression was echoed by parents who said bitterly that the children they had raised with every advantage were choosing to live and dress like "poor orphans."

Unlike the activists, who were able to look after themselves, these disaffected high school dropouts were fleeing failure in school and discord at home. They wandered the streets where they found one another and huddled together, as Joan Didion wrote in *Slouching Towards Bethlehem* (1968),

> in a desperate attempt of . . . pathetically unequipped children to create a community in a social vacuum.

A floating population of them drifted in and out of empty lofts and warehouses that they claimed for living space. The older looked after the younger, the stronger after the weaker. When they could no longer manage on their own, they turned to the idealistic doctors, clergymen, and students of sociology who offered them medical care, guidance, and shelter.

Of the estimated 75,000 who passed through Haight-Ashbury between 1965 and 1967, it is difficult to find statistics on how many belonged to the group who were activists, and how many the disaffected. Stephen Pittel, a sociologist who directed the Haight-Ashbury Research Project, sampled 250 participants in the 1967 "Summer of Love" in San

Francisco. Of them, an estimated 40 percent were idealists who believed in the mystique of the district, and had gone to San Francisco because they saw it as a model for the rest of the world. For the most part, they came from "supportive" families with whom they never completely broke contact. When they left California, it was relatively easy for them to return home and continue their education, or choose a career.

It was the others, who did not want to go home when Haight-Ashbury fell into a decline, who orphaned themselves. Some, looking for new and exotic scenes, went to Nepal and India. Others joined what Bryan Pfaffenberger called the "20th century communitarian renaissance." At its height, there were 750,000 living in over fifty thousand communes. Among those most frequently reported in the media are the Moonies and Hare Krishna disciples. Stephen Gaskin's "The Farm" is one of the most successful communes. Today it has twelve hundred living in a "family" monastery in rural Tennessee, and another fourteen hundred in ten branches around the country.

Perhaps what is happening at "The Farm," and communes like it, has more to do with the history of the family than with orphanhood, but it is interesting to see what those who changed their names, their parents, and their siblings were looking for. From the freewheeling days of sexual liberation in the sixties, the communards at "The Farm" have gradually returned by a circuitous route to what looks like old-fashioned morality: premarital chastity, a serious commitment to marriage, opposition to artificial birth control and abortion. Equally surprising is the insistence on conventional gender roles, the men working on the farm, or as carpenters and builders, the women devoting themselves to domestic duties and the care of the children. The children, who are not raised permissively, are famously well behaved, and Gaskin is eager to take in others, those unwanted by their parents as well as orphans. When asked what "The Farm" hoped to accomplish with the children, one of Gaskin's followers replied:

> We are taking seriously what our parents *said* as opposed to what they *did*. We want to produce moral children who believe in marriage, telling the truth, working hard and helping their neighbors.

Parents of the communards who have kept in touch with them, unable to reconcile themselves to the loss not only of their children but their grandchildren as well, have lived with the hope that when the next generation reaches adolescence, as it is currently doing, it, in turn, will rebel, and, rejecting communal life, will return to the family fold and take back the family name.

If few sociologists predicted the size and strength of the counterculture movement, fewer still predicted a new wave of real orphans. As the consensus among those who looked after children without parents grew, that for their future mental health these children needed more than custodial care, an effort was made to mimic family life by housing them in cottages run by couples. With greater attention paid to the children's emotional needs, with a relaxation of discipline, and an enriched diet, the cottage plan was a great improvement over the asylum.

As a result of the marked decline in adult mortality due to infectious diseases (especially tuberculosis), the slowing down of immigration, the reduction of the size of the family made possible by birth control, and welfare programs that allowed widows to keep paternal orphans at home, the number of children without parents requiring institutionalization dropped sharply. While there had been 750,000 full orphans in 1920, there were only 66,000 in 1953. Since there was every reason to believe that this trend would continue, orphanages and cottage-plan institutions were phased out. The ever-diminishing number of orphans could be looked after by what many social workers thought would be the ideal way of replacing parents: foster home care.

Before long, however, it became clear that foster care was as problematical as institutional care had been. A successful match between child and surrogate parents was not easy to arrange, especially since many foster families were more interested in augmenting their income than in looking after someone else's child. Few of the children were adopted by their families, and far too many were shunted from one household to another, with predictable results.

Then, in the early seventies, there was a demand for foster homes that could not be satisfied. The new orphans requiring care were not called orphans. They were, and are, "the homeless," of whom, in the chilling new vocabulary used to describe them, some are "push-outs" and "throw-aways"—meaning that the adults they lived with urged them to leave, knowing they had no place to go. Statistical tables show that there have always been more paternal than maternal orphans, but today this is dramatically the case. These children have not lost their fathers in a war (as have the orphans in Cambodia, Vietnam, Lebanon, and Northern Ireland). They have lost them as a result of the breakdown of the family and the epidemic of teenage pregnancies.

At the height of the asylum era, the most vulnerable strata of society—the poor, new immigrants, the unemployed, widows and widowers, deserted spouses—had the possibility of placing children they couldn't look after in orphanages, sometimes only until they got through a bad period, sometimes permanently. Today's vulnerable families do not have this choice.

With the increase in the number of single girls and women with children living below the poverty line, welfare agencies have been so inundated with demands for placements that children have had to sleep on tables and desks in agency offices. One irate social worker was quoted as having said, "Newborn babies are here night after night after night. The whole system is in chaos."

Other children go with their homeless mothers to shelters; still others to welfare hotels. In place of dormitories with long rows of beds covered with white sheets, what one sees in welfare hotels is overcrowded rooms with unmade beds. Instead of a subsistence diet and clockwork discipline, there is junk food on demand, little supervision, and close proximity to adults who are alcoholics, drug addicts, and prematurely discharged psychotics. Were conditions so much more shocking in the workhouse where Oliver Twist was born?

The system is indeed in chaos. Foster homes, shelters, and welfare hotels are grossly inadequate to the need. With hindsight, one can see that cottage-plan institutions were phased out too soon. Some modification of them may be needed, with nurseries for infants of girls and women who are incapable of giving maternal care. Religious groups, which had thought that there was no longer any need for them to offer asylum to orphans and foundlings (in war-torn and Third World countries of course, but in affluent America?), are today once more directing their attention to unwanted and homeless minors.

The number of children who lose one or both parents prematurely rises and falls with the times, and the nomenclature by which they are called changes, but as long as there are wars, earthquakes, epidemics, economic upheavals, or social revolutions, there will be orphans.

CHAPTER 14

A Mythic Orphan

A POOR LITTLE orphan girl who made her appearance on the American scene a century ago has lived on to become a mythic figure in this country's folk culture. After making her debut in a poem, she became the heroine of one of the longest-running and most popular comic strips, of a radio serial that kept children glued to their sets at 5:45 P.M. for ten years, of a smash-hit Broadway musical, and of no less than four movies. (Although she remained poor, she was a gold mine for her creators.) Homeless and without a relative in the world, she was adopted by millions of families who took her into their hearts and their households. The price she paid for her eternal youth and astonishing longevity was to remain a wanderer, an outsider, an orphan.

James Whitcomb Riley's poem "Little Orphant Annie" (1885) was published at the time the orphan trains were taking waifs from noisome city streets westward. The Hoosier poet's Annie, said to have been modeled on the orphan taken in by his family, works all day, according to the poem, washing, cooking, cleaning to "earn her board 'an keep." After her housework is done, she looks after the children, entertaining them with "witch-tales" until bedtime.

At Riley's public readings, which made the poem famous, and in school recitations, what children loved was the taunting refrain—

An' the Gobble-uns 'alt gits you
Ef you
Don't
Watch
Out!

—which the narrator of the poem aims at them, and which they, with squeals of scary delight, lob at one another. (The goblins will get not me but *you*.) Children also took pleasure in the idea of having an orphan girl to do the chores that, but for her, they would have been expected to do, one who worked like a slave good-humoredly (as the rhythm of the lines told them she did), with energy left over at the end of the day to amuse them.

Riley's poem continued to be so popular it was frequently reprinted in the *Chicago Tribune*. It was, or was not, depending on what account of the creation of the myth you read, the inspiration for the comic strip Joseph Patterson was looking for in the early twenties to boost sales of his fledgling tabloid, the *Daily News*. Harold Gray, then a young and ambitious cartoonist, submitted many sketches, all of which were rejected, until one called "Little Orphan Ottor" caught Patterson's eye. He liked the idea of the orphan, but said, according to many reports, that Ottor "looked like a pansy. Put a skirt on him and we'll call it 'Little Orphan Annie.' "

When we first meet Gray's Annie, she is an inmate in an

orphanage run by a dried prune of a director, Miss Asthma. As the children jump with joy at the news that they are going to have ice cream (doled out to them once a year) for dessert, Miss Asthma reminds Annie that because she neglected to make her bed, she will be given a bowl of milk and mush instead. When the other kids tease Annie about her punishment, she loses her temper. The bowl of mush in her hand, she spins around like a discus thrower, lets fly with the bowl, misses the children, hits Miss Asthma . . . and we're off!

A few days later, Miss Asthma tells Annie that though she doesn't deserve it, she may be adopted by a rich woman, and reminds her that she should be grateful for the charity she has received at the asylum. Annie, who is scrubbing floors, confides to the reader that she hates being reminded that she is an orphan, hates the home, and hates herself for being so poor. She wishes some "nice folks would adopt" her. "Then I could have a real papa and mama like other kids." Should this not be enough to wring the reader's heart, she gets down on her knees to pray to God for parents and "if it's not too much trouble, I'd like a dolly too."

Instead of nice folks, the rich and stuck-up Mrs. Warbucks comes to take Annie home—on trial. The trial goes poorly, for this orphan is insufficiently docile and, with her tomboyish ways, is forever getting into scrapes in the mansion. Mr. Warbucks, a bald-headed giant of a man, returns from a business trip and, spying the child for the first time, says:

> "Say, whose kid are you?"
> "I'm nobody's kid," Annie replies, "I'm just an orphan Mrs. Warbucks took home on trial."
> "WHAT? On trial eh?" says Mr. Warbucks [for whom it's love at first sight]. "Don't you ever dare to call me Mr. Warbucks again. You call me DADDY, see?"

So Annie's prayer is partly answered. She has a daddy and before long a companion more satisfying than a doll, a dog. She would be on her way to having a homelife as well if Warbucks didn't go off on the first of his many mysterious business trips, leaving Annie at the mercy of his wife, who, seeing the nine-year-old child as a rival, sends her back to the orphanage.

For forty-four years, from 1924 until Gray's death in 1968, Annie's life was full of perils, reversals of fortune, separations, and losses. Daddy Warbucks, who is sometimes the richest man in the world, sometimes dead broke, is hopelessly irresponsible as a guardian. As a result of his frequent disappearances, Annie is sent to asylums, or placed in households where she is mistreated, or, fleeing them, becomes a vagrant. When, from time to time, she has the good fortune to find kindly surrogates, like the Silos, a farm couple, Daddy reappears and takes her away. Often he is the child, and Annie the adult, as he confides in her about his marital and financial difficulties. Not infrequently, it is she who comforts and looks after him, she who is the breadwinner.

Warbucks's absences, often after a period of such stirring adventures that the reader has forgotten the precariousness of his ward's existence, provide the occasion for restating her situation. Nine days before Christmas, for example, we find her out on the street, cold, hungry, and alone. In a typical sequence of self-pity, denial of self-pity, and heart-rending yearning, Annie reminds herself that there are millions worse off than she is, but seeing a lighted window, she cannot suppress a cry of envy:

Gee! Those lucky, lucky kids! Brothers and sisters and folks.
Real folks 'o their own!

Gray, a shrewd judge of how much sentimentality his readers could take (heavy doses), reassures them after such a sequence that Annie is a feisty kid who may be down but is certainly not out.

At the height of its popularity, "Little Orphan Annie" appeared in five hundred newspapers and had an estimated sixteen million readers (of whom there were more adults than children). The strip's fans were so passionate that on many occasions they flooded the newspaper with letters advising, protesting, applauding what was going on in Annie's life. When Patterson, feeling that Gray was putting the orphan in an environment that might be considered too ritzy by the readers, killed the strip, there was such an uproar that it was immediately reinstated, and Patterson wrote a front-page apology, promising it would never happen again. Another time, when Annie's dog was lost for what many felt was an unbearably long time, in the mountain of mail the *Tribune* received was a telegram from Dearborn, Michigan, which said, "Please do all you can to help Annie find Sandy," and was signed "Henry Ford."

There were those, with hearts of stone, who hated Annie. For the most part, they were politically liberal adults repelled by Warbucks the big-time capitalist, profiteer, and virulent anti–New Dealer who was not averse to taking the law into his own hands. Even after Gray was ordered to stop editorializing, the *Nation*, not mollified, suggested that "the Society for the Prevention of Cruelty to Children should take her [Annie] under their control until her syndicators, Hearst and the Chicago *Tribune*, can demonstrate their moral fitness to be guardians of a child as impressionable and dull as Annie."

It would have comforted me to know that I was not alone in hating Orphan Annie. Why my school friends were so crazy about her was a mystery to me. More mysterious, I see now, was why I disliked the comic so intensely. I thought it was because the garish color of Annie's hair caricatured mine, and because her smile was fake (the kind of smile you

put on when you're afraid you'll cry).* Also, there was
something menacing about her guardian. He looked like a
bully to me, and the massive diamond he wore in his tuxedo
shirt front reminded me of the light doctors were always
shining in my eyes when they told me to say, "Ahhh." I
certainly wouldn't have wanted him to be *my* daddy.

It wasn't until I was in high school that I found the
literary orphan I was willing to identify with, and the daddy
I would have been happy to have, in Jean Webster's *Daddy-
Long-Legs* (1912). Judy Abbott, after years of living in an
orphanage, where she works as hard as Riley's Annie looking after the younger children in the asylum, is rescued by
an anonymous benefactor who pays for her to go away to
college. His one request is that she write to him. She fills
her letters with accounts of her academic progress, and
undergraduate activities (oh so innocent and girlish in the
fictionalized Vassar of those days). She can't thank him
enough for the allowance he sends, nor for the wardrobe
which helps to erase the bitterness of having had for so
many years to wear hand-me-downs.

What attracted me to the novel was that Judy's years in
the asylum are passed over with merciful rapidity. (We are
given only enough detail to highlight the contrast between
the old life and the new.) She goes *away* to college (which
I had little hope of doing). Daddy is as generous as I could
have wished a daddy to be. And, best of all, there was the
developing romance between guardian and ward.

My affection for the novel was shared by many other
girls. It was immensely popular and was translated into
sixteen languages. (What nonorphans found attractive
about it, I think, was the facile resolution of the Oedipal
conflict. There was no mother to be rivalrous with, and

*America's richest and best-known paternal orphan, Gloria Vanderbilt, did
not share my feelings. In an interview, she said, "Annie inspired survival and
showed you how to go on when grown-ups let you down. She once said, 'You're
never fully dressed without a smile.' Her words have gotten me over a lot of rough
spots."

since Daddy-Long-Legs is not the heroine's real daddy, they can become lovers without guilt.) It was filmed twice. The version I saw when I was an adult starred Leslie Caron and the man who in my high school years had been my cinematic father after I saw him dance in *The Gay Divorcee,* Fred Astaire.

Rereading "Little Orphan Annie" recently to discover why I found it so unappealing, I saw that it was not only the terrible separations that put me off (in one strip Warbucks even dies but, being Warbucks, he comes to life again). It was also that Annie's orphanhood is unending. There is no promise of a better future, no time when, being grown up, she will no longer be at the mercy of adults. Small wonder I wasn't tempted to read this funny, nor to listen to "Adventure Time with Little Orphan Annie," the radio serial that pursued me for years.

The program, which I could not escape hearing in friends' houses, opened and closed with a signature song which described Annie as a cute little chatterbox with a sunny smile, auburn locks, and rosy cheeks. This image of well-nourished cheerfulness, the lyrics suggested, was someone to envy:

> Now, wouldn't it be worth your while
> If you could be
> Like Little Orphan Annie?

Richard Gehman, writing in the *Saturday Review,* said of the serial's popularity during the thirties and forties: *"All* people during that period—budding delinquents, safecrackers, stock market manipulators, or whatever . . . listened to 'Little Orphan Annie'!"

Not me! Except under duress. My favorite serial, "Mert and Marge," was about two independent young women, living on their own. Marie was Mert, I was Marge. We were having the time of our lives going dancing with a round of attractive escorts, all of whom looked and danced, in my imagination, like Astaire.

Annie, in the meantime, was having no easier time of it on the radio than she had in the newspapers. Again the constant threat of danger, again the frequent separations during her interminable childhood. Ovaltine, the show's sponsor, offered premiums—ceramic mugs, pictures of Annie, watches—that were collected greedily by fans. A poll taken in 1937 showed that Annie rated number one for children between the ages of five and eight, and ran a close second to "The Lone Ranger" for nine- to fourteen-year-olds, with an estimated audience of six million.

Despite the vast popularity of the strip and the serial, Martin Charnin, Thomas Meehan, and Charlie Strouse, who fashioned *Little Orphan Annie* into a musical, found that Annie was not a natural for the Broadway stage. Thomas Meehan's Annie is a foundling, and her story became, as he said in an interview, "a child's *Odyssey*-like quest for her missing mother and father." While Gray's Annie showed no curiosity about her parents, Annie of the musical yearns to be reunited with hers.

Even with the simplified title, *Annie*, and the switch from orphan to foundling, the audience had no difficulty supplying the "little" and "orphan" to this girl who is dressed like an orphan and lives in an orphanage. Behind the sassy kid who runs away from Miss Hannigan's tyranny (Miss Hannigan replacing Miss Asthma), there is, as Meehan said, "the lost, wandering child, brave, indomitable." Charnin, who with Strouse wrote the score, is even more explicit about the orphan theme: "We wanted to make it a love story between two orphans. Warbucks is as much an orphan in this musical as Annie. He doesn't find his parents, he finds his child."

Opening to rave reviews (although with some muted protest about yanked heartstrings: "To dislike the new musical *Annie,*" Clive Barnes wrote, "would be tantamount to disliking motherhood, peanut butter, friendly mongrel dogs, and nostalgia"), the musical ran for 2,377 performances. By the time it closed in 1983, it had won twenty-two prizes and grossed $225 million.

Hollywood paid $9.5 million for the rights and spent between $40 million and $50 million to produce a big, brassy screen version of the musical. Annie is again an orphan, not a foundling. She comforts herself with the daydream that her parents are alive and will return to get her. Little time is allowed for sad reflections. Though the children sing that in the orphanage "It's A Hard Knocks Life," they do so with such manic energy one wonders what happened to the lethargy and malaise that should have come from the poor nourishment and lack of attention built into asylum life. Miss Hannigan is so comically lascivious, and broadly drawn ("Why any kid would want to be an orphan is beyond me," she says, reeling from bathtub gin), that it is impossible to take her seriously as a villain. And Warbucks has been reformed so that Gray wouldn't recognize him. A conscientious guardian, rich and powerful enough to call on the President of the United States for assistance in finding Annie after she has been kidnapped, Daddy puts all his resources at Annie's disposal so that she can trace her lost parents. With such a perfect surrogate father, one wonders at her need for real parents. Fortunately hers turn up dead, leaving Warbucks free to adopt her. If we didn't know her history better, we might be fooled into believing that Annie would live happily ever after.

"Indecent" success, as Bob Abel called it, such as "Little Orphan Annie" has had, calls for explanations, and they have not been lacking. Some said Dickens with little text and spirited drawings accounted for the comic's popularity. Others, that its Calvinist morality and conservative politics reflected American middle-class values. Certainly Gray's strip was not read for humor. As he himself admitted, it was a very unfunny funny. "Life to Annie was deadly serious.

She had to be hard to survive and she meant to survive."
Maurice Horn saw Annie's story as "a parable of Good and
Evil, a brooding metaphor of life, in which all the situations
became permeated with a haunting sense of betrayal and
doom." For Ignatius Mattingly, like Meehan, Annie's quest
for Daddy Warbucks was a modern-day version of Telema-
chus's search for Odysseus. Coulton Waugh's explanation
is less high-flown. "Annie gathers the heart strings into
both hands," he said, "and then yanks."

All true, perhaps, but the orphan's subliminal appeal
from the time of Riley's poem to the movie was to the
middle-class family. Annie's losses, her homelessness, were
the family's gain. She reminded children that they were
fortunate to have mothers and fathers, reminded mothers
that but for them their offspring would be at the mercy of
the Miss Asthmas, Mrs. Warbuckses, and Mrs. Bleating-
Harts of this world; reminded fathers that but for them
their daughters would be endlessly looking for a surrogate.

Children who wished they were orphans—and what child
does not at one time or another?—were able to imagine
themselves as Annie for the length of the strip, or the
duration of the daydreams the strip engendered, and yet be
free to return to the shelter, if not joy, of home and family
when it was over. Those who suspected they were orphans
(because of the way their parents treated them) could separate themselves from the adults they had to live with, and
lead a happier or more adventurous life on their own.

Annie outside made those inside feel cozier than they
would have without her to reflect their good fortune. As her
readers sat at the kitchen table, or sprawled on the living
room rug, Annie, out in the world, acted out their wishes
and fears. Her pluck, energy, and resourcefulness gave her
fans the comforting reassurance that though she was touching, she was also tough. They knew that no matter what
peril she underwent, what pain she suffered, she would
triumph. An indestructible little scapegoat, Annie was an
orphan *for* them. Small wonder she was so well loved.

Postscript

IT WAS NOT research into the past but hunger that led me back to the Convent of the Sacred Heart for the first time since the day I left it with the picture of the Little Flower pinned under my middy blouse. One Columbus Day, long before I thought of writing about orphans, Bob and I were on our way up the Hudson for the weekend, and had for some time been looking for a place to lunch when, approaching Dobbs Ferry, I saw a billboard that said: "Dixie Inn—two miles ahead." The raffish roadhouse had been converted into a family restaurant, the kind with plastic flowers on the table and a high chair in the corner for a family with a baby. The waitress gave us a table facing the river. Through the windows, one could see beyond the almost denuded trees to the river glistening in the autumnal midday sun. The seat I chose faced the Convent's ground-floor veranda and, above it, the window of Saint Roch's room. This accidental stumble back into childhood flooded me with memories. As we were having coffee, Bob said, "Why not take a look at the interior? There's plenty of time, and who knows when you'll have another chance?" He would entertain himself exploring the town of Dobbs Ferry and would return for me in an hour.

Under the porte cochere, to the right of the door, I found the bell handle and pulled it. Its sound echoed down the entrance hall. After a long silence, and another ring, I was about to turn away when the door was opened just wide enough to let a strong odor of floor wax escape. To a hidden figure I said why I was there. A hand tugged the sleeve of my coat, as if it were a child's, pulling me into the somber vestibule. In heavily accented English, the short and round Mother Josefina, the Convent cook she said she was, told me that, it being a holiday, the nuns and children had gone up the Hudson on an outing. Out of politeness perhaps rather than conviction, she claimed to remember Marie and me (she had been at the Convent in our day). As we walked past the photographs of the Colosseum, St. Peter's and the Leaning Tower of Pisa, I asked about the nuns I had known. Our Mother Superior had died, the unstable Mother Gaetana had been transferred, Mother Giovanna had been sent back to Italy after she became infirm.

We went up to the dormitory to take an evil-smelling concoction to a pale-faced, skinny little girl with a runny nose who had been left behind because she was sick. The girl (who in my day would have been me) got out of bed and trailed around after us in her nightgown. At the door of Saint Roch's room, my eyes were struck by a burst of color. The white pillow shams and bedspreads had been replaced by others in hot pink. The room across the way had been done in purple: the colors of the eggs in the Italian Easter bread. In the dormitory, there were dolls and stuffed animals on the beds. These startling changes made me ask if the girls still wore uniforms. Mother Josefina rotated her hand in a yes-and-no gesture, which I took to mean that the uniforms were no longer as uniform as they had been.

My guide was impatient to show me the latest improvement, the new stall showers in the bathrooms. What did I think of *that?* she asked turning on the water and clapping her hands with excitement. I thought it probably meant that the bathing garments had long since been cut up for polishing cloths. What was it like living here now, I would like to have asked a student, one a little less timid than the runny-nosed girl who ducked behind the voluminous folds of the nun's habit whenever I addressed her.

Downstairs we "paid a visit," as we used to say, to the chapel, which was unchanged and as pretty as I remembered it. The cook, who had lost interest in our tour after we'd seen the showers, said she had to get back to the kitchen. I asked if I might take a minute to look at the reception room. Here, as in the chapel, and the nun's habit, there was no sign of modernization. The brown velvet draperies, the furniture, the antimacassars, even the giant rubber plant were the same, or had been replaced by exact replicas of the originals. It was comforting to think that while the outside world spun around dizzily, here all was stable and orderly.

My second return to the past was premeditated. After I'd written the Preventorium chapter, a yearning to see and smell the pine forest again sent me to Farmingdale one Sunday in late spring. A sign on the highway pointed the way to the Arthur Brisbane Treatment Center, which I took to be a new and more discreet name, but as I approached I saw a forbidding-looking building with windows high off the ground. This, the receptionist told me, was not the "Old Prevent." It was a school for disturbed children. The place I was looking for was a mile or so down the road. It had recently been bought by a developer who was going to turn it into a golf course. The bulldozers were already at work, or would begin any day. If I wanted to see what was left, I'd better hurry over.

As luck would have it, the developer's wrecking crew

were to begin their work the following morning. Nevertheless, the property was already barely recognizable. Where there had been a pine forest and an apple orchard, there was now a colony of bungalows each with a picture window. A highway cut close to the Preventorium compound, exposing the cabins where we had slept. They stood on a treeless hill looking as fragile and gawky as we pretubercular children must have looked.

The arrangement of the cabins and their floor plan was just as I had remembered them, but the outdoor sleeping porches and schoolrooms had been enclosed, and radiators installed. A primitive attempt had also been made to insulate the exteriors by plastering the wood with grayish-pink stucco. From the look of things, the Preventorium had been closed for some time. The interiors had been stripped bare of movable objects by people living nearby, and the walls were covered with graffiti. While I was there, a young couple were giving the place a final going-over, the wife digging up clumps of sweet william from outside the director's office and putting them in the back of their station wagon, while the husband rooted around the kitchen for the odd piece of cooking equipment that might have been overlooked.

In Cottage B, the only sign of the former occupants was a broken-down metal cot, a leather mitten, and a pair of torn underpants. A pigeon nesting in the cubbyhole I remembered as having been mine flew out irritably when I opened the door to inspect it. The Lower House, the former hunting lodge of the old estate, which must have been sold separately, was intact and inhabited by a family with many children, some of whom were playing in the yard.

After wandering over what had been wooded paths, covered now with violets and trillium, I sat on the steps of the administration building for a few minutes before leaving. Comparing the "Old Prevent" with the newer institution a mile away, I was reminded of a recent visit to the Smithsonian Institution. In the Hall of Aviation, *The Spirit of St. Louis* is displayed side by side with the space ship that took the first astronauts to the moon. What struck me was not the fragility of the plane in which Lindbergh crossed the ocean (and landed on his return not far away, in Lakehurst), but the wiry resiliency which had enabled it to withstand the elements. So the Preventorium's flimsy cabins, with surprisingly little reinforcement, had sheltered generations of youthful patients.

The sign of changing times I'd found at Farmingdale made me hurry back to the Convent, where I wanted to check my memory about a detail or two. (Where, exactly, was the infirmary? Was there more than one bed in it, or had I, as I remembered it, been the only patient in a small back room?) As I approached the town of Dobbs Ferry, I began to look for the Villa. I drove the stretch of familiar road twice and couldn't find it. Seeing a gardener clipping a hedge, I stopped to ask directions: How could I have missed it? The gardener said, "Easy. It's gone. They tore it down last year to put up a nursing home for old folks."

Gone. The glass house with the statue of the Sacred Heart, its door open and swinging in the wind, was all that remained. I closed the door and walked up to the ugly but functional new building that stood in its place. While I waited to talk to the switchboard operator, I saw a solarium on the riverside where patients in wheelchairs were faced toward the view.

Where had the children gone? "There are no more orphans," the switchboard operator said. And, as if in response to my bewildered expression, she added, "Parents don't die young anymore."

What I had seen as a symbol of stability and order—the Convent's reception room—had been nothing but an assemblage of well-cared-for furniture. The Missionary Sisters of the Sacred Heart had moved with the times. Because of what an official at the Children's Bureau called "the vanishing orphan phenomenon" (and because the homeless had not yet become a grave concern), the Order had turned its attention to a new population in need of care, the elderly.

On the drive home from Dobbs Ferry, I felt sorely frustrated. It was not only because of the erasure from the landscape of a handsome villa I had imagined would always be there. It was also that I was left with an unanswered and troubling question I had planned to put to the current mother superior. While reading a biography of Mother Cabrini, I had come upon an electrifying sentence in which the author referred to the Convent I had gone to as "the Dobbs Ferry orphanage." A careless error, I thought, ticking it off. He had confused the Villa with the institution at West Park. I continued to read, but distractedly, my thoughts returning to that sentence. A few pages further on, there it was again: ". . . the Sacred Heart Villa Orphanage . . ."

The elegant Villa an orphanage? Surely not. It didn't look like an orphanage. (But, then, I didn't look like an orphan.) It was true that most of the girls had been orphans. Was it possibly *not* an error? As I continued to move the pieces of the puzzle around, trying to get them to fit, I realized that it was also true that if it was an orphanage, our relatives would have been capable of keeping this from us. As I thought about it, I realized that for this deception I would have been grateful to them. The truth would have been a heavy burden to me as a child. As an adult, it would have interfered with my view of myself as having been lucky. An orphan who goes to an orphanage is far more orphaned than one who goes to a convent boarding school.

Today I tell myself that it no longer matters. And yet . . . when I got over my frustration at not being able to talk to the mother superior, I found I was not sorry to leave her answer in doubt.

Acknowledgments

I would like to express my gratitude to the John Simon Guggenheim Foundation for a fellowship in 1984; to the Rockefeller Foundation for a residency at the Villa Serbelloni at Bellagio, Italy; to the Corporation of Yaddo, the MacDowell Colony, and the Virginia Center for the Creative Arts; and to my hostess and host at the Casa Nuova for their generous hospitality.

251

Bibliography

CHAPTER 1

Bettelheim, Bruno. *The Uses of Enchantment.* New York: Alfred A. Knopf, 1976.

Bowlby, John. *Attachment.* New York: Basic Books, 1969.

———. *Separation.* New York: Basic Books, 1973.

———. *Loss.* New York: Basic Books, 1982.

Troyat, Henri. *Tolstoy.* New York: Doubleday & Co., 1967.

CHAPTER 10

Ariès, Philippe. *Centuries of Childhood.* New York: Vintage Paperback, 1962.

Banks, Jules. "A Study of One Hundred Eight Boys Discharged from the Brooklyn Jewish Orphanage." *Graduate School for Jewish Social Work Studies,* ser. 4, monograph 2 (1936).

Barnes, Marian. "Reactions to the Death of a Mother." In *Psychoanalytic Study of the Child* 19. New York: International University Press, Inc. (1964).

Brace, Charles Loring. *The Dangerous Classes of New York.* New York: Whykoop and Hallenbeck, 1872.

Bremner, Robert. *Children and Youth in America.* Vol. 1. Cambridge: Harvard University Press, 1970.

Buchwald, Art. "Reminiscences." In Jacqueline Bernard, *The Children You Gave Us.* New York: Jewish Child Care Association of New York, 1973.

Buckingham, Clyde. "Early American Orphanages: Ebenezer and Bethesda." *Social Forces* 26 (March 1948).

Burlingham, D., and A. Freud. *Infants Without Families.* New York: International University Press, 1944.

"A Campaign of Calumny." *The New York Charities Investigation.* Pamphlet. New York: The American Press. Undated.

Davis, Robert A. *Mentality of Orphans.* Boston: Gorham Press, 1930.

de Mause, Lloyd, ed. *The History of Childhood.* New York: The Psychohistory Press, 1974.

Ehrenpreis, Irwin. *Swift: The Man, His Work, and The Age.* Vol. 1. Cambridge: Harvard University Press, 1962.

Folks, Homer. *The Care of Destitute, Neglected and Ailing Children.* New York: The Macmillan Co., 1902.

Freud, A., and S. Dann. "An Experiment in Group Living." In *Psychoanalytic Study of the Child* 6 (1951).

Holmes, G. W. *The Likes of Us.* London: Frederick Miller, 1948.

Johnson, R. Brimley, ed. *Christ's College: Recollections of Lamb, Coleridge and Leigh Hunt.* London: C. Allen, 1896.

Moskovitz, Sarah. *Love Despite Hate.* New York: Schocken Books, 1983.

Rothman, David. *The Discovery of the Asylum.* Boston: Little, Brown & Co., 1971.

Sharlitt, Michael. *As I Remember.* Privately printed, 1959.

Stone, Lawrence. *The Family, Sex and Marriage: 1500–1800.* New York: Harper Colophon Books, 1977.

Thurston, Henry W. *The Independent Child.* New York: Columbia University Press, 1930.

Vogt, Martha, and Christia Nelson. *Searching for Home.* Grand Rapids, privately printed, 1979.

CHAPTER 11

McCarthy

McCarthy, Mary. *Memories of a Catholic Girlhood.* New York: Harvest/Harcourt Brace Jovanovich, 1962.

Rousseau

Guehenno, Jean. *Jean-Jacques Rousseau,* Vols. 1 and 2. New York: Columbia University Press, 1966.

Rousseau, Jean-Jacques. *Émile.* Trans. Barbara Foxley. London: Dent, 1911.

————. *Confessions.* London: Penguin, 1953.

Russell

Clark, Ronald W. *The Life of Bertrand Russell.* New York: Alfred A. Knopf, 1976.

Russell, Bertrand. *The Autobiography of Bertrand Russell,* Vols. 1 and 2. Boston: Little, Brown and Co., 1951.

Scharfstein, Ben-Ami. *The Philosophers.* New York: Oxford University Press, 1980.

Sartre

Sartre, Jean-Paul. *The Words.* New York: Braziller, 1964.

Tolstoy

Pritchett, V. S. "Two Bears in a Den." *New Yorker,* August 21, 1978.

Tolstoy, Leo. *Childhood, Boyhood, Youth.* Trans. Rosamond Edmunds. London: Penguin, 1964.

Troyat, Henri. *Tolstoy.* New York: Doubleday & Co., 1965.

CHAPTER 12

Beckett

Bair, Deirdre. *Samuel Beckett.* New York: Harcourt Brace Jovanovich, 1978.

Beckett, Samuel. *Not I.* In *First Love and Other Shorts.* New York: Grove Press, 1974.

Brontë

Brontë, Charlotte. *Jane Eyre.* New York: Penguin Books, 1966.
Langbridge, Rosamond. *Charlotte Brontë.* New York: Doubleday, Doran, 1929.

Dickens

Dickens, Charles. *David Copperfield.* Cambridge: Riverside Press, 1958.
———. *Oliver Twist.* New York: The American Library, 1961.
Johnson, Edgar. *Charles Dickens: His Tragedy and Triumph.* New York: Penguin Books, 1977.
Malot, Hector Henri. *Sans Famille.* In English, *Nobody's Boy.* New York: Platt & Munk, 1962.
Wilson, Edmund. "Dickens: The Two Scrooges." In *The Wound and the Bow.* Boston: Houghton Mifflin, 1941.

James

Edel, Leon. *Henry James: The Untried Years.* London: Rupert Hart-Davis, 1953.
———. *The Middle Years.* Philadelphia: J. B. Lippincott, 1962.
———. *The Master.* Philadelphia: J. B. Lippincott, 1972.
James, Henry. *Notes of a Son and Brother.* New York: Charles Scribner's Sons, 1914.
———. *The Portrait of a Lady.* New York: Random House, 1950.
———. *The Wings of the Dove.* J. D. Crowley and R. A. Hocks, eds. New York: Norton Critical Edition, 1978.

Kipling

Carrington, Charles Edmund. *The Life of Rudyard Kipling.* Garden City, New York: Doubleday, Doran & Co., 1955.
Kipling, Rudyard. "Baa Baa, Black Sheep." In *Under the Deodars.* New York: Macmillan, 1897.
———. *Something of Myself.* Garden City, New York: Doubleday, Doran & Co., 1937.
———. *Kim.* New York: Bantam Books, 1983.

Mann

Mann, Thomas. *A Sketch of My Life.* New York: Alfred A. Knopf, 1960.

———. *The Magic Mountain.* Trans. H. T. Lowe-Porter. New York: Vintage Books, 1969.

Weigand, Hermann J. *The Magic Mountain.* Chapel Hill: University of North Carolina Press, 1964.

Winston, Richard. *Mann: The Making of an Artist.* New York: Alfred A. Knopf, 1981.

SMITH

Barbera, Jack, and William McBrien. *Stevie.* London: Heinemann, 1985.

Smith, Stevie. "The Orphan Reformed." In *Collected Poems of Stevie Smith.* New York: New Directions, 1972.

———. "The Holiday." In *Me Again.* London: Virago Press, 1981.

TWAIN

Brooks, Van Wyck. *The Ordeal of Mark Twain.* London: Heinemann, 1922.

Clemens, Samuel. *The Autobiography of Mark Twain.* New York: Harper, 1959.

De Voto, Bernard. *Mark Twain at Work.* Cambridge: Harvard University Press, 1942.

Kaplan, Justin. *Samuel Clemens and Mark Twain.* New York: Simon and Schuster, 1966.

Paine, Albert Bigelow. *Mark Twain.* New York: Harper & Bros., 1912.

Twain, Mark. *The Adventures of Tom Sawyer.* New York: Harper & Bros., 1923.

———. *The Adventures of Huckleberry Finn.* Cambridge: The Riverside Press, 1958.

WHARTON

Wharton, Edith. *The House of Mirth.* New York: Berkley Books, 1981.

CHAPTER 13

Amster, Lynda. "Orphanages Vanishing for a Lack of Orphans." *New York Times,* December 26, 1974.

Bellow, Saul. *The Adventures of Augie March.* New York: Viking Press, 1953.

Bradford, William. *History of Plymouth Plantation, 1620–1647.* Notes and introduction by Samuel Eliot Morison. New York: Alfred A. Knopf, 1952.

Chaplin, Charles. *My Autobiography.* New York: Simon and Schuster, 1964.

Commager, Henry Steele. *The American Mind.* New Haven: Yale University Press, 1950.

Cowan, Paul. *An Orphan in History.* New York: Doubleday and Co., 1982.

Didion, Joan. "Life Style in the Golden Land." In *Slouching Towards Bethlehem.* New York: Farrar, Straus & Giroux, 1968.

Handlin, Oscar. *The Uprooted.* Boston: Little, Brown & Co., 1951.

Howe, Irving. *The World of Our Fathers.* New York: Harcourt Brace Jovanovich, 1976.

Johnson, Joyce. *Minor Characters.* New York: Houghton Mifflin, 1983.

Kakutani, Michiko. Review of *Home Truths* by Mavis Gallant. *New York Times,* April 20, 1985.

Kazin, Alfred. *New York Jew.* New York: Alfred A. Knopf, 1978.

Kerouac, Jack. *On the Road.* New York: Viking Press, 1957.

Koch, Edward. *Mayor.* New York: Warner Books, 1984.

Krebs, Albin. "Truman Capote Is Dead at 59." *New York Times,* April 26, 1984.

Miller, Kerby. *Emigrants and Exiles.* New York: Oxford University Press, 1985.

Morison, Samuel Eliot, Henry Steele Commager, and William E. Leuchtenberg. *The Growth of the American Republic.* London: Oxford University Press, 1969.

O'Neill, William. *Coming Apart: An Informal History of America in the 1960's.* New York: Times Books, 1971.

Perry, Charles. *The Haight-Ashbury: A History.* New York: Random House, 1984.

Pfaffenberger, Bryan. "The World of Husbands and Fathers." In *Sex Roles in Continuing American Communes.* John Wagner, ed. Bloomington: Indiana University Press, 1982.

Riesman, David, with Reuel Denney and Nathan Glazer. *The Lonely Crowd.* New Haven: Yale University Press, 1969.

Robinson, David. *Chaplin.* New York: McGraw-Hill Books, 1985.

Roskolenko, Harry. *The Time That Was Then: The Lower East Side, 1900–1941,* New York: Dial Press, 1971.

Rothchild, John, and Susan Wolf. *The Children of the Counterculture.* New York: Doubleday & Co., 1975.

Russell, John. *The Meaning of Modern Art.* New York: Harper & Row, 1974.

Salinger, J. D. *The Catcher in the Rye.* Boston: Little, Brown & Co., 1951.

Scharfstein, Ben-Ami. *The Philosophers.* New York: Oxford University Press, 1980.

Shudde, Louis O. *Orphanhood—A Diminishing Problem.* U.S. Department of Health, Education, and Welfare Research and Statistics, note 33, 1954.

Spitz, René. "Hospitalism." In *Psychoanalytic Study of the Child* 1 (1945).

Tocqueville, Alexis de. *Democracy in America.* New York: Anchor Paperback, 1969.

CHAPTER 14

Abel, Bob. "Leapin' Lizards! Has Annie Gone Pinko?" *New York,* April 25, 1977.

Bender, Loretta. "The Effect of Comic Books on the Ideology of Children." *American Journal of Orthopsychiatry* 11 (June 1941).

———. "The Psychology of Children's Reading and the Comics." *Journal of Educational Sociology* 18 (December 1944).

Riley, James Whitcomb. "Little Orphan Annie." In *The Complete Works of James Whitcomb Riley.* Collected and edited by Henry Ectel. Indianapolis: Bobbs-Merrill Co., 1913.

Ryan, Stephen. "Orphan Annie Must Go." *America,* December 8, 1956.

Smith, Bruce. *The History of Orphan Annie.* New York: Ballantine Books, 1982.

Waugh, Coulton. *The Comics.* New York: Macmillan, 1947.

Webster, Jean. *Daddy-Long-Legs.* New York: Grosset & Dunlap, 1964.

White, David Manning, and Robert H. Abel, eds. *The Funnies.* New York: The Free Press of Glencoe, 1963.

ABOUT THE AUTHOR

EILEEN SIMPSON'S SHORT stories have appeared in the *Southern Review*, *Transatlantic Review*, and the *Denver Quarterly*. Her novel, *The Maze*, was published in 1975; a book about dyslexia, *Reversals*, in 1979; and *Poets in Their Youth* in 1982. She lives in New York City, where she practices as a psychotherapist.